TWO BUDDHAS
Seated Side by Side

Nichiren's calligraphic maṇḍala depicting the assembly of the *Lotus Sūtra,* with Namu Myōhō-renge-kyō written vertically down the center. Courtesy of Hikigayatsu Myōhonji, Kamakura.

Two Buddhas
Seated Side by Side

A GUIDE TO THE *LOTUS SŪTRA*

Donald S. Lopez Jr. and
Jacqueline I. Stone

Princeton University Press
Princeton & Oxford

Published by Princeton University Press
41 William Street, Princeton, New Jersey 08540
6 Oxford Street, Woodstock, Oxfordshire OX20 1TR

press.princeton.edu

Library of Congress Control Number: 2019942250
ISBN 978-0-691-17420-4
ISBN (e-book) 978-0-691-18980-2

British Library Cataloging-in-Publication Data is available

Editorial: Fred Appel, Thalia Leaf, and Jenny Tan
Production Editorial: Kathleen Cioffi
Text and Jacket Design: Leslie Flis
Production: Erin Suydam
Publicity: Tayler Lord and Kathryn Stevens

Jacket image: The Buddhas Prabhutaratna and Sakyamuni seated side by side.
Courtesy of the Freer|Sackler, Smithsonian

This book has been composed in Arno Pro with Gotham display

Printed on acid-free paper. ∞

Printed in the United States of America

1 3 5 7 9 10 8 6 4 2

Contents

Acknowledgments

No book is completed without the support of many people. We would like first to thank our two manuscript readers and others for their valuable suggestions and criticisms. Advice from Daniel B. Stevenson in particular substantially improved the book. Any errors are, of course, our own. We thank Fred Appel, our executive editor at Princeton University Press, as well as others at the press who helped in the production process, including our editorial assistant, Thalia Leaf, and our production editor, Kathleen Cioffi. We would also like to acknowledge our copy editor, Susan Rescigno. Special thanks are due to the temple Myōhonji in Kamakura, for permission to reproduce the photo of Nichiren's maṇḍala that appears as the frontispiece to the print editions of this volume. Our appreciation also goes to Mary Mortensen, who compiled the index. Both of us, the authors, teach the *Lotus Sūtra* in our classes on Buddhism. Our final thanks go to our students, whose questions and responses to the *Lotus* have stimulated our thinking about the sūtra and helped inspire this volume.

A Note on Sources

All quotations from the *Lotus Sūtra* are taken from the translation done by Tsugunari Kubo and Akira Yuyama. See *The Lotus Sūtra*, rev. 2nd ed., trans. by Tsugunari Kubo and Akira Yuyama, BDK English Tripiṭaka Series (Berkeley: Numata Center for Buddhist Translation and Research, 2007). For the reader's convenience, we have provided in-text page references to this translation after each quotation. Please note that the pagination of the printed version of the text (used here) differs from the pagination of the version presently available online.

Kubo and Yuyama based their translation on the celebrated Chinese version of the sūtra produced by the Central Asian scholar-monk Kumārajīva in 406. In several places, however, they chose not to follow traditional Sino-Japanese interpretation but have instead consulted the Sanskrit and, in a few instances, the Tibetan versions of the *Lotus* (see their "Translators' Introduction," xiv). One way in which their English version departs from Kumārajīva's Chinese lies in the handling of proper names. Where Kumārajīva translated many names of figures appearing in the *Lotus Sūtra*, Kubo and Yuyama give them in the original Sanskrit. We have followed suit, not to give primacy to the Sanskrit text, but for consistency with the Kubo-Yuyama translation. However, some of the longer Sanskrit names can prove daunting to readers unfamiliar with that language. We have accordingly provided in parentheses with the first occurrence of such names the English rendering given by Leon Hurvitz in his translation of the *Lotus Sūtra*: *Scripture of the Lotus Blossom of the Fine Dharma (the Lotus Sūtra)*, published by Columbia University Press (1976; rev. 2009), or a translation of our own.

We have rendered the *daimoku*, the invocation of the *Lotus Sūtra*'s title taught by Nichiren, as Namu Myōhō-renge-kyō, which represents the proper romanization for scholarly writing. However, actual pronunciation may vary slightly according to the practice community; some groups collapse the second and third syllables, giving Nam Myōhō-renge-kyō (sometimes written without diacritics in their publications). The difference is not one of correct versus incorrect but simply reflects variations among the traditions of individual Nichiren Buddhist lineages.

Two extensive collections of Nichiren's writings have appeared in English translation, both intended for practitioners. One, supervised by Kyōtsū Hori with the assistance of other translators and editors, is *Writings of Nichiren Shōnin* (2003–2015), now numbering seven volumes, published by the Nichirenshū Overseas Propagation Promotion Association (NOPPA). At the time of this writing, limited previews of two of these volumes are available at Google Books. A second collection of Nichiren's works in English is the two-volume *Writings of Nichiren Daishonin*, translated by the Gosho Translation Committee and published by Sōka Gakkai. The entirety of this translated collection is available online as a searchable database (http://www.sgilibrary.org/writings.php). During much of the translation process, Sōka Gakkai had the assistance of the late Burton Watson, professor emeritus of Columbia University and an accomplished translator of Chinese and Japanese literature. Two volumes of these translations, edited by Watson's colleague, the late Philip Yampolsky, have also been published by Columbia University Press. In translating passages from Nichiren's writings for this volume, we have referred to existing translations and sometimes followed them quite closely. Often, however, we have modified them either to meet the demands of the present study (for example, to bring terminology in line with the Kubo and Yuyama *Lotus Sūtra* translation that we are using) or to reflect our wording preferences. In still other cases we have produced our own translations. These modifications do not imply criticism of existing English versions, to which we are indebted, but rather reflect the principle that there is never only one "correct" or definitive translation; multiple possibilities exist and some may be more appropriate in different contexts. References to Nichiren's writings in this volume refer to the four-volume *Shōwa teihon Nichiren Shōnin ibun* (Shōwa-era Critical Edition of Nichiren Shōnin's Writings), edited by the Reseach Institute for Nichiren Doctrinal Studies of Risshō University (Risshō Daigaku Nichiren Kyōgaku Kenkyūjo) and published at Minobu-san Kuonji in Yamanashi Prefecture, Japan (1952–1959; rev. 1988).

TWO BUDDHAS
Seated Side by Side

Authors' Introduction

In the vast literature of Buddhism, the *Lotus Sūtra* stands as one of the most inspiring, and the most controversial, of Buddhist texts. As a Mahāyāna sūtra, a sūtra of the "Great Vehicle" tradition, the *Lotus Sūtra* was not accepted by the Buddhist mainstream of its own time as "the word of the Buddha" (*buddhavacana*). It is not accepted as the word of the Buddha by the Theravāda traditions of Sri Lanka and Southeast Asia today. But in East Asia, especially in China and Japan, perhaps more than any other text, the *Lotus Sūtra* has come to define what distinguishes the Mahāyāna from the teachings that preceded it. Indeed, one might say that the *Lotus Sūtra* both explains that difference and then seeks to explain it away, asserting that the Mahāyāna and the earlier tradition both sprang from the Buddha's single intent.

Arguably, the *Lotus Sūtra* has been the most influential Buddhist scripture in East Asia. It has been read, recited, copied, enshrined, and explained. It has been the subject of intense doctrinal debates. Two influential Buddhist schools—the Tiantai (Kor. Cheontae; J. Tendai) school originating in China and the Hokke (Lotus) or Nichiren sect in Japan—are based on it. The *Lotus Sūtra* has also permeated the larger religious culture, and its parables, imagery, and teachings have inspired centuries of poetry and artwork.[1] It was the first Mahāyāna scripture to be translated from Sanskrit into a Western language (Eugène Burnouf, *Le lotus de la bonne loi*, 1852), and its study has helped to shape the modern scholarly discipline of Buddhist Studies. It is one of very few Buddhist scriptures (along with the

Diamond Sūtra, the *Heart Sūtra,* and a few others) to have gained sufficient fame in the English-speaking world to be widely known by an English title.

The fame of the *Lotus Sūtra* in the West has grown over the last half century, not only through academic Buddhist Studies, but also through the activities of *Lotus*-based practice groups. Soka Gakkai International (SGI), which claims a membership of several million households worldwide, is perhaps the best-known group. This lay Buddhist organization traces its origins to the thirteenth-century Japanese monk Nichiren, who argued that the *Lotus Sūtra* is the pinnacle of the Buddha's teachings, superseding all other sūtras. Other lay societies based on the *Lotus Sūtra* are Risshō Kōseikai and Reiyūkai. There are also traditional Nichiren Buddhist orders that include both clerics and laity, such as as Nichirenshū, Nichiren Shōshū, Honmon Butsuryūshū, Kenpon Hokkeshū, and Nipponzan Myōhōji. Tendai Buddhism has a presence in the West, and there are also unaffiliated *Lotus* practitioners.

There is now a growing body of English-language scholarship, both books and articles, on the *Lotus Sūtra.* These include studies of particular themes in the *Lotus* (such as "skillful means," a term that forms the title of one of the sūtra's twenty-eight chapters); examination of its literary forms (such as the sūtra's famous parables); analyses of its doctrines; and historical studies of its associated schools and practices. There are sociological treatments of new religious movements based on the *Lotus Sūtra,* and studies of *Lotus*-based art. There are also books in English written from an "insider" perspective, aimed at encouraging the faith and practice of *Lotus* devotees. English-language commentaries on the sūtra to date generally fall into this last category. What has not appeared thus far is a detailed guide, written from a scholarly perspective, to the sūtra's individual chapters. The first aim of this study is to provide such a guide.

A chapter-by-chapter road map through the *Lotus Sūtra* is something helpful to have; the sūtra is not transparent. Its teachings are not presented in a clear, discursive fashion but, rather, unfold through parables, fantastic events, and mythic imagery. This can be frustrating to the modern reader, who sometimes fails to see how extraordinary the sūtra really is. The autobiography of the Japanese Zen master Hakuin (1686–1769) provides a similar example. Recounting his early efforts to study the Buddhist teachings, Hakuin wrote:

> People who are suffering in the lower worlds [of rebirth], when they rely on others in their efforts to be saved, always ask that the *Lotus Sūtra* be recited for them. There must indeed be profound and mysterious doctrines in this sūtra. Thereupon I picked up the *Lotus Sūtra* and in my study of it found that, other than the passages that explain that there is only one vehicle and that all phenomena are in the state of nirvāṇa, the text was concerned with parables relating to cause and effect. If this sūtra had all these virtues, then surely the six Confucian classics and the books of all the other schools must be equally effective. Why should this particular sūtra be so highly esteemed? My hopes were completely dashed. At this time I was sixteen years of age.[2]

But sixteen years later, after long years of meditative training and the experience of awakening, Hakuin wrote, "One night some time after, I took up the *Lotus Sūtra*. Suddenly I penetrated to the perfect, true, ultimate meaning of the *Lotus*. The doubts I had held initially were destroyed and I became aware that the understanding I had obtained up to then was greatly in error. Unconsciously I uttered a great cry and burst into tears."[3]

Without expecting its readers to burst into tears, this volume explores the rich contents of each of the sūtra's chapters, a richness that is difficult to appreciate by simply reading the text in translation without supporting explanation. The authors of the *Lotus Sūtra* were deeply learned in the language of Buddhism, and the text is filled with all manner of allusions to, and radical reinterpretations of, the Buddha's teachings. A second goal of this book, therefore, is to focus on what was at stake in the compilation of a Mahāyāna sūtra—what it meant to compose a revelation of a new teaching, to legitimize that revelation as the Buddha's words, and then to use it as a polemic against the established tradition. Readers accustomed to the traditional claim held by many devotees, that the *Lotus Sūtra* is the teaching of the historical Buddha expounded in the last eight years of this life, may initially find this perspective challenging. We suggest, however, that one's appreciation of the brilliance and power of the *Lotus Sūtra* is only enhanced when the historical circumstances of its composition are taken into consideration. That is, the genius of the *Lotus Sūtra* becomes fully apparent only when one engages with the kinds of questions the compilers themselves were compelled to address

The phrase "two buddhas seated side by side" (Jpn. *nibutsu byōza*), the title of our book, occurs in medieval Japanese writings and refers to a defining moment in the *Lotus Sūtra,* when Prabhūtaratna, a buddha of the distant past, suddenly appears at the *Lotus* assembly, vibrant and alive within his stūpa, to bear witness to the sūtra's truth. He then invites the buddha of the present, Śākyamuni, to enter the stūpa and share his seat. The scene of the two buddhas seated together overturns two conventional ideas. The first is that only one buddha can appear in the world at a time. The second is that once a buddha has passed into nirvāṇa and his relics have been entombed in a stūpa, he is inaccessible. This scene, which exemplifies the mythic imagery by which the *Lotus* conveys its radical message, has been represented in painting and sculpture for more than fifteen hundred years. A Chinese example, commissioned in 609 by a filial daughter on behalf of her deceased parents, appears on the cover of this volume. Interpretations of the two buddhas seated side by side are discussed in Chapter Twelve.

The Role of Commentary

Despite its influence, exactly what the *Lotus Sūtra* means has remained elusive. Over the centuries, great scholar-monks have penned thousands of pages of commentary in an attempt to explain it. Sermons, didactic tales, literary appropriations, artistic depictions, even the applications of *Lotus* teachings in the lives of practitioners could also be considered "commentary," broadly defined. In one sense, the present volume is yet another commentary, with motivations and aims both shared by, and different from, the scores of commentaries that have come before.

Commentary, and the status of commentary, are vital issues in religions that are based upon texts. One thinks, for example, of debates in Islam over the "closing of the gates of *ijtihad*," that is, the question of whether legal interpretation had been exhausted by the great jurists of the past, or whether it was still possible to exercise original or independent reasoning in legal issues not specifically covered by the Qur'an, Hadith, or scholarly consensus.

In Buddhism, one could perhaps say that, in a certain sense, all scripture is commentary. That is, all Buddhist traditions hold that the Buddha's enlightenment was complete, that he attained complete knowledge of the state of liberation and the path to it during his meditation on that full-moon night. Thus, everything that he spoke thereafter was in a sense an articulation of that experience, adapted for the audience he was addressing. This is one reason why the events immediately following the Buddha's enlightenment, the period of forty-nine days in which he savored the experience of his enlightenment without speaking, is the focus of so much interest in the tradition. Should he teach? If so, whom should he teach? And what should he teach them? These questions appear in the earliest renditions of the story of the Buddha's awakening, and they reappear, with important refinements, in the second chapter of the *Lotus Sūtra*. So important was this question of what the Buddha first taught after his enlightenment that one of the most important Mahāyāna sūtras, the *Flower Garland* (*Avataṃsaka*), presents itself as the Buddha's very first teaching, assigning that pride of place to itself.

The various accounts of the Buddha's enlightenment, from those in the Nikāya traditions of mainstream Buddhism, to the various accounts in the Mahāyāna sūtras, and later the tantras, all acknowledge that the Buddha adapted his teachings to his audience, that he did not teach the same thing to everyone. This immediately raises some questions: If the Buddha accommodated what he taught to the needs and abilities of his audience, what did he really mean? What was his true teaching, unadulterated and unmodified? Is it something that can even be spoken? And, if so, when did he speak it, and to whom? These questions gave rise to the long-standing distinction between those teachings that are final and definitive (*nītārtha*), and those requiring further explication (*neyārtha*), though there has often been disagreement over which was which. Questions about the Buddha's true intent have also historically placed a burden on the commentator, who must not only explain what the words mean but also determine whether the Buddha "really" meant them. Yet, who, other than a buddha, can make such a determination?

These questions have haunted the tradition of Buddhist commentary from the beginning, so much so that the authors of some Mahāyāna sūtras had the Buddha address them himself. One such text is the *Saṃdhinirmocana Sūtra,* whose title confronts the problem directly; it means "Explanation of the [Buddha's] Intention." Here it is explained that the Buddha turned the wheel of the dharma not once but three times, with the first two turnings being "provisional" and the last turning being "definitive." However, the most famous and influential case of the Buddha commenting on his own teachings appears in the *Lotus Sūtra,* where Śākyamuni announces that his previous teaching of three vehicles leading to liberation had been an accommodation. In fact, there is but one vehicle, and it will convey all beings to buddhahood.

Historically, the Buddhist tradition has *not* regarded all scriptures as commentary: the sūtras hold a special status as the Buddha's word. By definition, a commentary composed by someone who is not a buddha cannot be anything new; it can only be an elaboration of the Buddha's enlightenment, as expressed in the sūtras. This lends at least the appearance of literary conservatism to Buddhist commentary, where innovation has sometimes been condemned as a presumption, not praised as a virtue. And yet Buddhist commentary has often been a profoundly creative endeavor, a major vehicle by which interpreters introduced and disseminated their own original insights, even while appearing to hew closely to the words of the sūtras and to humbly explicate their meaning. Buddhist commentary therefore forms a huge and essential element of the Buddhist canon, often of equal or (in Tibet, for example), of greater influence than the sūtras themselves. Indian Buddhist monks composed hundreds of commentaries, drawing from the refined categories of Sanskrit scholasticism to attach to the name of a sūtra (or another commentary) words like *ṭīkā, bhāṣya, vyākhyā, vṛtti, pañjikā,* and *vārttika,* all rendered rather blandly into English with a single word: commentary. Chinese commentaries on the *Lotus* and other sūtras were produced in great numbers, especially during the fifth through tenth centuries. Through commentary, and other forms of interpretation as well, the sūtras were given innovative readings and made to speak to issues specific to the interpreter's own time and place. Thus, a third aim of the current volume is to explore this living interface between text and commentary in Buddhism, using the *Lotus* as an exemplar.

Rather than taking on the impossible task of cataloging the long tradition of commentary on the *Lotus Sūtra* across Asia, we focus on the Japanese figure Nichiren (1222–1282), who stands among the greatest of the *Lotus Sūtra* interpreters. Nichiren lived roughly a thousand years after the *Lotus Sūtra*'s compilers in India, at the extreme opposite edge of Asia. By that time, through the work of East Asian exegetes, the *Lotus Sūtra* had come to be understood as providing the key that revealed the diverse body of Buddhist teachings to be unified in a single, underlying salvific program. Many people of Nichiren's age, however, understood themselves to be living in an era of decline predicted in Buddhist scriptures, a time when the burden of human delusion would be heavy, and enlightenment would be difficult to achieve. Massive natural disasters, civil strife, and the threat of Mongol invasion seemed to confirm this prophecy. Pitting himself against opponents who argued that the *Lotus Sūtra* was too profound for the deluded persons of this evil era, Nichiren asserted that only the *Lotus* represented the Buddha's ultimate message, a message that could lead even the most sinful and ignorant to liberation.

Nichiren's fierce insistence on the sole efficacy of the *Lotus Sūtra* has not endeared him to modern scholarly commentators, who have often dismissed him as narrow and intolerant. Yet another aim of our volume is to show how Nichiren's reading of the *Lotus Sūtra* made compelling sense in the context of his received tradition and his understanding of his own time; it illustrates how much can be at stake in the interpretation of scripture. Through his example, we demonstrate how what *Lotus* followers regard as an ancient and timeless revelation came to be deployed in a specific time and place—thirteenth-century Japan—in an effort to understand, and to transform, that time and place. Focusing on Nichiren allows us to provide a kind of case study of how an ancient Buddhist text was appropriated by someone in a very different historical and cultural context to address questions undreamed of by the sūtra's compilers.

This volume takes the form of a chapter-by-chapter discussion of the twenty-eight chapters of the *Lotus Sūtra*. We consider the significance of each chapter from the perspective of two historical moments: what it may have meant in the first centuries of the Common Era in the Indian cultural sphere as the *Lotus Sūtra* came to take its present form, and how it was read by Nichiren in Japan roughly a thousand years later. Rather than divide the volume into two sections, the first commenting on the *Lotus Sūtra* itself and the second introducing Nichiren's reading, we have intentionally alternated our discussion of the *Lotus* text with Nichiren's comments in each chapter, to avoid as much as possible a somewhat artificial division between the original text and Nichiren's later interpretations. For devotees of the *Lotus Sūtra*, text and interpretation have been inseparable—in effect, parts of the same scripture—as has been the case with many great religious texts over the course of history.

The *Lotus Sūtra* in India

Although the Buddha's precise dates remain contested, current scholarly thinking places him roughly in the fifth century BCE.[4] According to traditional accounts, he lived for eighty years. Like other teachers of his time, the Buddha did not leave written teachings. The teachings or sūtras of the Buddha (the Sanskrit term *sūtra* means "aphorism"), like the Hindu Vedas, were memorized and recited. The first evidence of Buddhist sūtras being committed to writing did not appear until some four centuries after his death, and then not in India but in Lanka (present-day Sri Lanka) to the south and in Gandhara in what is today parts of Afghanistan and Pakistan to the north.

Around the time that the texts previously transmitted orally were being recorded on palm leaves in the south and birch bark in the north, something new occurred, for reasons that scholars do not entirely understand. Groups of monastics began to compose their own sūtras, representing these not as their own compositions but as records of the Buddha's teaching, although he had passed into nirvāṇa centuries before. These texts, which would eventually become known as "the Mahāyāna sūtras," present a different vision of the Buddha and of the path than that espoused by the mainstream Buddhist tradition—which is sometimes disparaged in these works as the "lesser vehicle" (Hīnayāna). For the mainstream, the goal of Buddhist practice was nirvāṇa, stopping the wheel of birth and death by eradicating craving and delusion. The Mahāyāna sūtras extol the ideal of the bodhisattva, who seeks to liberate all beings from suffering and rebirth by following the long path to buddhahood. Produced over the course of several centuries, they constitute a highly disparate group of texts. An early group, the "perfection of wisdom" or *prajñāpāramitā* sūtras (which include the *Diamond* and *Heart* sūtras), is renowned for its exposition of the doctrine of emptiness (*śūnyatā*); the *Lotus Sūtra*, which was completed somewhat later, proclaims a new vehicle that will carry all beings to buddhahood. New findings have overturned or complicated earlier theories about the origins of the Mahāyāna. For example, characterizations of the Mahāyāna as a distinct school or sect, or as promoted chiefly by the Buddhist laity, have been rejected. One intriguing line of inquiry suggests that the Mahāyāna sūtras may have been shaped in part by visualization meditation, in which practitioners envisioned themselves as being in the presence of a buddha and hearing his teaching.[5] Given both the complexity and fragmentary nature of the evidence, scholars have become increasingly reluctant to make general statements, yet we may note one crucial historical fact: almost all of the Mahāyāna sūtras purport to be the word of the historical Buddha, yet none is. They are later works that introduce important innovations in Buddhist thought, even while devising elaborate strategies to demonstrate their authenticity as the Buddha's words; they legitimate the new by representing it as old.

One way to think about the Mahāyāna is not as an internally consistent movement, but as an intertwining of texts made up of threads of varying circumference, weight, and texture. Among those threads, none is more luminous than the *Lotus Sūtra*, in part because of its influence and in part because so many things that we associate with "the Mahāyāna" are found there. Yet it is also a distinctive text with its own psyche and its own legacy of influence and interpretation. Indeed, the brilliance of the sūtra only becomes clear when one considers (or at least imagines) the circumstances of its composition, and the questions its authors wrestled with.

Little is known about the origins of the *Lotus Sūtra*. It was compiled somewhere in the Indian cultural sphere, which reached from what is now Sri Lanka in the south to Afghanistan in the north. The earliest Chinese translation was made in 286, from which we may assume that some version or versions of it were circulating before that date. Like many Buddhist sūtras, the *Lotus Sūtra* evolved over time, possibly quite a long period of time. By analyzing various elements of the sūtra, including its language and the contents of its translations in Chinese, scholars speculate that the *Lotus Sūtra* as we have it today passed through at least three major stages in its compilation. Chapters Two through Nine represent the earliest stratum, focusing on the teachings of the one vehicle and of skillful means. At the next stage, Chapter One, entitled "Introduction," was added, as well as Chapters Ten through Twenty-Two (except for Chapter Twelve, "Devadatta").[6] These chapters focus on the bodhisattva path, the transmission of the sūtra to the future, and the revelation of the Buddha's inconceivable lifespan, set forth in Chapter Sixteen. One artifact of this stage of the compilation process is that the end of Chapter Twenty-Two reads like the conclusion of a sūtra. In the final stage, the remaining portions of the *Lotus Sūtra* as we now know it were gradually added: Chapter Twelve was inserted in the middle, while Chapters Twenty-Three through Twenty-Eight, which chiefly deal with individual bodhisattvas, were added at the end. Several of these chapters seem to have circulated independently.[7]

The *Lotus Sūtra* was certainly known in India. However, like other Mahāyāna sūtras, it was regarded among the established Indian Buddhist schools as spurious, a late work that only pretended to be the word of the Buddha. We know that the *Lotus Sūtra* circulated widely from the more than thirty surviving Sanskrit manuscripts or manuscript fragments. These have been classified into three main lineages, based on the locations where they were discovered: Nepal, Gilgit (in present day Pakistan), and Central Asia.[8] The *Lotus Sūtra* is counted as one of the "nine doctrines" (*navadharma*) of the Newar Buddhist community in Nepal. Its importance can also be gauged by its citation in other works, including compendia of sūtra passages by such famous figures as Nāgārjuna, Śāntideva, and Atiśa. However, other sūtras are more frequently cited in these works; the *Lotus* is but one of many Mahāyāna sūtras and did not enjoy any particular renown.[9] Even among the Mahāyāna schools, its famous doctrine of a single vehicle was not universally accepted.[10]

Another way that scholars measure the influence of a text is by the number of its commentaries. For example, eight Indian commentaries on the *Heart Sūtra* have survived. There is only one Indic commentary on the *Lotus Sūtra*, attributed to the famous Yogācāra master Vasubandhu (late fourth to early fifth century), preserved in Chinese. However, because no Sanskrit manuscripts or Tibetan translations are known, its attribution to Vasubandhu has been questioned.[11] There is a single commentary on the *Lotus Sūtra* preserved in the Tibetan Buddhist canon, ascribed to one Pṛthivībandhu. However, this commentary is a translation into Tibetan not from Sanskrit but from Chinese and is in fact the work of the famous Chinese monk Ji or Kuiji (632–682).[12]

The *Lotus Sūtra* in East Asia

In India, the Buddhist community had some sense of the historical development of the tradition. The fact that so many texts—sūtras and, later, tantras—were posthumously ascribed to the Buddha could be seen as a legitimizing move, an acknowledgment that their authors knew, at least in a strict historical sense, that these texts were not his teachings. Or perhaps it reflects a genuine conviction that, in some way, they were. But whether or not one accepted the Mahāyāna sūtras as the Buddha's word, it was widely acknowledged that they had appeared long after his passage into nirvāṇa (the period of four hundred years was often mentioned). For their opponents, the sūtras were newly composed; for their proponents, they were newly revealed to the world of humans, having—for example—been hidden and safeguarded for centuries by gods and nāgas.

Things were very different in East Asia. The Mahāyāna sūtras were already being produced when Buddhism first entered China. The Chinese, at least initially, had little sense of the historical progression of the tradition, of what had transpired over the previous four centuries. Under the circumstances, the Mahāyāna sūtras were particularly appealing. Their teachings of nonduality resonated with indigenous notions of an integrated, holistic cosmos, while the bodhisattva ideal paralleled Chinese philosophical notions of human perfectibility. And the *Lotus Sūtra,* said to have been the Buddha's ultimate and final teaching, in which he explains his teaching method within the context of his traditional life story, came to hold a special prominence. Here Śākyamuni proclaims that the *Lotus Sūtra* not only supersedes all that he has taught before, rendering all his other teachings provisional, but also that it is the primordial teaching, taught by all the buddhas since the timeless past.

It was in China that the *Lotus Sūtra* assumed the textual form in which it came to be known throughout East Asia. Six Chinese translations were made, of which three survive: those by Dharmarakṣa in 286; by Kumārajīva in 406; and by Jñānagupta and Dharmagupta in 601, a version that largely reproduces Kumārajīva's while including some additional material. Of these, Kumārajīva's translation, *Miaofa lianhua jing* (J. *Myōhō renge kyō*, "Sūtra of the Lotus Blossom of the Wonderful Dharma"), proved by far the most popular. All English translations of the sūtra that have been made from Chinese (seven at the time of this writing, not counting revisions or multiple editions of the same translation) are based upon it. According to his biography, Kumārajīva (344–413), a learned scholar-monk from Kucha in Central Asia, vowed that after his death, his tongue, with which he had expounded the meaning of the Buddhist sūtras, would remain unburnt in the crematory fire, and indeed, although the flames consumed his body, his tongue remained untouched.[13] This story expresses the confidence that Kumārajīva's translations faithfully captured the Buddha's intent. It was also in China that the *Lotus Sūtra* became "threefold," being grouped together with an introductory sūtra, the *Sūtra of Immeasurable Meanings* (*Wuliang yi jing*, *T* no. 276), possibly a Chinese apocryphon, and the *Sūtra of the Practice of Visualizing the Bodhisattva Samantabhadra* (*Foshuo guan Puxian pusa xingfa jing*, *T* no. 277).

Celebrated for its promise of eventual buddhahood for all, the *Lotus Sūtra* became the focus of widespread devotional practices not confined to any particular school: just as the sūtra itself enjoins, it was copied, recited, enshrined, and lectured upon for a range of this-worldly and transcendent aims.[14] Its parables and fantastic scenes inspired painting and sculpture, and so-called miracle tales celebrated its salvific powers. At the same time, the *Lotus Sūtra* received sustained attention from scholar-monks, who discovered in it a path toward resolving a fundamental question that had plagued early Chinese Buddhists.

As noted above, the sūtras were introduced into China at random, and it soon became apparent that they did not necessarily agree and sometimes even contradicted each other. Yet for the Chinese, these were all the teachings of a single figure, the historical Buddha, Śākyamuni, and were thus assumed to share a single, underlying salvific message. Commentators saw as their overriding task the uncovering of a sequence, order, or fundamental organizing principle that would show how the manifold Buddhist teachings related to one another and make clear their essential unity. These attempts led to rival systems of doctrinal systematization or *panjiao*.

Perhaps the most influential figure in this systematizing endeavor was Zhiyi (538–597), revered as the patriarch of the Chinese Tiantai school of Buddhism, whose work profoundly influenced East Asian Buddhist thought and practice. Zhiyi is credited with two *Lotus Sūtra* commentaries: the *Profound Meanings of the Lotus Sūtra* (*Miaofa lianhau jing xuanyi*; hereafter, *Fahua xuanyi*, *T* no. 1716), an elucidation of the sūtra's major principles, and the *Words and Phrases of the Lotus Sūtra* (*Miaofa lianhau jing wenju*; hereafter, *Fahua wenju*, *T* no. 1718), a commentary on specific passages, both compiled by his disciple Guanding (561–632) from the latter's notes on Zhiyi's *Lotus Sūtra* lectures.[15] Zhiyi drew on the *Lotus Sūtra*'s claim that the Buddha's various teachings were all his "skillful means," or teaching devices, preached in accordance with the capacity of different individuals but all ultimately united in the fundamental principle of the one vehicle.

What was that fundamental principle? Zhiyi described it as the "threefold truth," or "threefold discernment," of emptiness, conventional existence, and the middle. Discerning all phenomena as "empty," lacking self-essence or independent existence, frees the practitioner from attachment to desires and intellectual constructs. It collapses all categories, hierarchies, and boundaries to reveal an absolute equality and nondifferentiation. This insight corresponds to the wisdom of persons of the two vehicles of the "Hīnayāna," those who seek the goal of nirvāṇa, stopping the wheel of birth and death, as well as the wisdom of novice bodhisattvas. However, from a Mahāyāna perspective, it is one-sided. Though empty of fixed substance, all things nonetheless exist conventionally in dependence upon causes and conditions. The discernment of "conventional existence" reestablishes discrete entities and conceptual distinctions as features of commonsense experience but without false essentializing or clinging; it frees the practitioner to act in the world without bondage to it. This corresponds to the wisdom of more advanced bodhisattvas. Finally, phenomena are neither one-sidedly empty nor conventionally existing but exhibit both aspects simultaneously: at each moment, every existent, without losing its individual character, permeates and contains all others. This insight, termed "the middle," encompasses both poles of understanding—emptiness and conventional existence—without dissolving the tension between them. The bodhisattva path culminates in the simultaneous discernment of all three truths as integrated in one.

Zhiyi analyzed the Buddhist teachings in their entirety according to how they lead to the understanding of the threefold truth, dividing them into four strands. The tripiṭaka teaching, corresponding to the so-called Hīnayāna, sets forth basic teachings such as the four noble truths and the impermanence of all phenomena, leading to renunciation of *saṃsāra*. The shared teaching, common to both Hīnayāna and Mahāyāna, stresses the truth of emptiness, that all things are without fixed substance. And the distinct or separate teaching, taught solely for bodhisattvas, emphasizes the return from discernment of emptiness to the phenomenal world, allowing bodhisattvas to cultivate the wisdom necessary to negotiate specific circumstances in saving others. These three strands of teaching each set forth partial aspects of the threefold truth and emphasize a gradual, sequentialist approach to cultivating their respective insights. Only the fourth, the "perfect teaching," reveals the integrated threefold truth all at once, in its entirety. This is the one vehicle spoken of in the *Lotus Sūtra*. Thus, the threefold truth for Zhiyi not only expresses how the *Lotus Sūtra* encompasses the three vehicles in the one vehicle, but also makes clear the underlying structure of the entire Buddhist system of thought and practice.[16]

Chinese doctrinal classification systems tended to adopt some presumed chronological sequence for the Buddha's teaching, moving from shallow to profound. Early commentators disagreed as to whether the *Flower Garland* (*Avataṃsaka*) *Sūtra*, the Mahāyāna *Nirvāṇa* (*Mahāparinirvāṇa*) *Sūtra*, or the *Lotus Sūtra* represented the Buddha's highest teaching. The Tiantai school that claimed Zhiyi as its founder developed a highly influential chronology, dividing the presumed fifty years of the Buddha's teaching career into "five periods" with the *Lotus Sūtra* as its culmination (see discussion in Chapter Four). In this schema, the Buddha first prepared the way through provisional teachings, and in the last eight years he expounded his ultimate message in the *Lotus* and *Nirvāṇa* sūtras. This claim was supported by a passage from the *Sūtra of Immeasurable Meanings*, regarded as an introductory scripture to the *Lotus*, which states, "For more than forty years I have expounded the dharma in all manner of ways through adeptness in skillful means, but the core truth has still not been revealed."[17]

Because of what we now know about the long process by which the Buddhist canon was compiled, classification schemes such as the "five periods," —chronological sequences by which the Buddha himself supposedly set forth the entirety of the sūtras—can no longer be viewed as based in historical fact. Nonetheless, as efforts to systematize the whole of the Buddhist teachings and place them within an overall soteriological program, they represent a monumental achievement.

The Tiantai system provides room for both an inclusive reading of the *Lotus Sūtra,* as encompassing all teachings within itself, and a hierarchical or even exclusive one, in which the *Lotus Sūtra* supersedes all others. Zhiyi himself did not view the *Lotus Sūtra* in exclusive terms, because each sūtra, being suited to persons of a particular orientation, has its own role to play in the Buddha's grand soteriological design and could thus not be categorically designated as higher or lower.[18] However, later Tiantai thinkers such as the sixth patriarch Zhanran (711–782), who lived in a time of increased sectarian rivalry, organized the sūtras into a hierarchy with the *Lotus Sūtra* at the apex.[19] We can find both perspectives in the writings of later Tiantai thinkers in China and Japan.

Nowhere has the *Lotus Sūtra* flourished as in Japan. Monastics and lay devotees alike recited and copied it, not only for the supreme goal of buddhahood, but also for a range of other benefits including healing and prosperity, peace in the realm, and the well-being of the deceased. As on the continent, scholar-monks wrote doctrinal commentaries, lectured upon, and debated its teachings; artists depicted its narratives in painting; and literati celebrated its virtues in tales and poetry. It was also the central scripture of the influential Tendai school established by the monk Saichō (766/767–822), who had journeyed to China and brought back Tiantai teachings. Saichō envisioned a grand synthesis that would unite the diverse strands of Buddhist doctrine and practice under the umbrella of the one vehicle of the *Lotus*. Enryakuji, the temple complex that he founded on Mount Hiei north of the imperial capital of Heian-kyō (today's Kyoto), became a leading center, not only of Buddhism, but of learning more broadly.

As we have seen, Zhiyi and other Chinese Tiantai thinkers drew on the *Lotus Sūtra* to integrate the disparate Buddhist teachings into a coherent whole and to explain how all phenomena, being empty of independent substance, interpenetrate and "contain" one another in an interrelated holistic cosmos. Saichō and later Japanese Tendai thinkers took these ideas in new directions. One was the claim that practicing the *Lotus Sūtra* enables one to realize buddhahood "quickly." We find some basis for this in the *Lotus* itself, and the idea had already been proposed in the Chinese Tiantai tradition. Zhiyi's teacher Huisi (515–577), for example, had written that *Lotus* practitioners awaken spontaneously and without proceeding through sequential stages of practice,[20] and Zhiyi, as we have seen, saw the possibility of sudden and full awakening to the threefold truth in its entirety as what distinguished the "perfect teaching" from the "distinct teaching": where bodhisattvas of the provisional Mahāyāna must practice for three incalculable eons to achieve full awakening, practitioners of the sudden and perfect teaching, exemplified by *Lotus Sūtra*, can do so directly. Saichō also understood the *Lotus* as the "great direct path" that enabled the realization of buddhahood in only two or three lifetimes, or in some cases, in this very lifetime.[21]

Saichō's later followers incorporated esoteric Buddhist teachings (J. *mikkyō*) into their *Lotus Sūtra* interpretation, a development that distinguished Japanese Tendai from its continental forebear and promoted ideas of the *Lotus Sūtra* as offering rapid attainment. Saichō had received an esoteric initiation in China and established an "esoteric course" as one of two training programs on Mount Hiei, the other being traditional Tendai doctrine and practice. His later disciples—scholar-monks such as Ennin (794–864), Enchin (814–891), and Annen (841–?) further interpreted the *Lotus* as an esoteric scripture. The buddha of the esoteric teachings is not the historical buddha Śākyamuni but the cosmic buddha who is timeless and omnipresent: all forms are his body, all sounds are his voice, and all thoughts are his mind, although the unenlightened do not realize this. Through the performance of the secretly transmitted "three mysteries"—the performing of mudrās or ritual gestures, the chanting of mantras, and the ritual use of maṇḍalas—the esoteric adept was said to unite his body, speech, and mind with those of cosmic Buddha, thus "realizing buddhahood with this very body" (*sokushin jōbutsu*). Esoteric Buddhism contributed to the rise, in Japan's medieval period, of the Tendai doctrine of original enlightenment (*hongaku hōmon*). According to this doctrine, buddhahood is not a distant goal but the true status of all things: the purpose of practice is not to "attain" buddhahood as a future aim but to realize that one is a buddha inherently. These developments all helped to shape the context in which Nichiren would read the *Lotus Sūtra*.

Nichiren as Interpreter

The Japanese Buddhist teacher Nichiren (1222–1282), arguably the *Lotus Sūtra*'s most famous interpreter, lived and taught in a historical and cultural milieu quite different from that of the sūtra's original compilers. As Buddhism spread through the Sinitic world, the *Lotus* had come to be widely revered as Śākyamuni Buddha's highest and final teaching, and Nichiren asserted that only this sūtra represented his complete message. Like his contemporaries, Nichiren believed he was living in the age of the Final Dharma (J. *mappō*), a degenerate era when people are burdened by heavy karmic hindrances and liberation is difficult to achieve. Now in this evil era, he claimed, only the *Lotus Sūtra* leads to buddhahood; other teachings had lost their efficacy and must be set aside. Nichiren taught a form of *Lotus* practice accessible to all, regardless of social class or education: chanting the sūtra's *daimoku,* or title, in the formula *Namu Myōhō-renge-kyō.*[22] By chanting the daimoku with faith in the *Lotus Sūtra,* he said, one could realize buddhahood in this very lifetime. And, as faith in the *Lotus Sūtra* spread, the ideal buddha land would be realized in the present world.

We have chosen Nichiren as an example of a *Lotus Sūtra* interpreter for three reasons. First, Nichiren drew freely on traditions of *Lotus* exegesis that had preceded him and reworked them into his own, highly innovative reading. Though the entire history of the *Lotus Sūtra*'s reception across East Asia cannot be addressed in this short volume, examining Nichiren enables us to learn much about prior interpretations. A second reason is the extraordinary range of his influence. Nichiren's following developed into one of Japan's major Buddhist traditions, the Hokkeshū (Lotus sect), or Nichiren sect, as it later came to be called, which includes multiple branches and subsects. Today more than forty religious organizations in Japan, both traditional temple institutions and lay movements, trace their origins to Nichiren. Several have substantial followings in other parts of Asia, in Africa, and in the West. It is no exaggeration to say that Nichiren's followers dominate *Lotus Sūtra* practice today. And third, Nichiren offers an instructive case study in the hermeneutics, or principles of interpretation, by which great teachers have reinterpreted their tradition's sacred scriptures to meet the needs of their own time and place. Nichiren's reading, like all readings, was not a pure encounter with the text of the sūtra but was mediated both by his received tradition and the social, political, and religious currents of his own time. Some aspects of his interpretation may not immediately resonate with contemporary readers, particularly, his claim for the exclusive truth of *Lotus Sūtra,* which can grate on modern sensibilities. Indeed, Nichiren challenges us, to a degree that other Buddhist thinkers may not, to step outside our own assumptions and enter his conceptual world, an effort essential to any good historian of religion. What follows is an outline of Nichiren's life and of several main points in his reading of the *Lotus Sūtra,* offered as a foundation for the more detailed discussion that follows in the individual chapters.

Nichiren was born in a small fishing village on the eastern coast of Japan. He drew his following, not from among the elites of the capital in Kyoto, but from mid- and lower-ranking warriors and farmers of the eastern provinces. He was ordained around age twelve (counted ordinally, by East Asian convention) at a temple known as Kiyosumidera (a.k.a. Seichōji), an important center in eastern Japan of esoteric Buddhist learning and mountain ascetic practice. Little is known of his early life beyond a passion for study. He studied Tendai, Shingon, and other traditions and was initiated into esoteric lineages. As a boy, he prayed to the bodhisattva Ākāśagarbha (J. Kokūzō), the chief object of worship at the temple, to become the wisest person in all Japan. "Before my eyes," he wrote, "the bodhisattva manifested himself as a venerable monk and bestowed on me a jewel of wisdom like the morning star."[23] Nichiren said he was then quickly able to master the essentials of Japan's eight traditional Buddhist schools as well as the new Zen and *nenbutsu* movements. Dissatisfied with the limited resources of his home temple, he traveled extensively for further study, both to Kamakura, site of the Bakufu, the shogunate or military government, and across the country, to the major temples of the Kyoto and Nara regions. His earliest surviving essay, written when he was twenty-one, suggests that he already took the *Lotus Sūtra* to be the sole teaching of universal buddhahood; his subsequent studies enhanced and deepened this conviction. Throughout, he was guided by the words of the *Nirvāṇa Sūtra*—regarded in Tendai circles as a restatement of the *Lotus*—to "rely on the dharma and not on the person."[24] For Nichiren, this meant that one should rely on the sūtras rather than the works of later commentators or the opinions of contemporary teachers, however eminent. And among the sūtras, one should rely above all on the *Lotus,* which is complete and final, and not others, which are incomplete and provisional. It is essential to bear in mind that for Nichiren, as for many of his contemporaries, the sūtras were literally the Buddha's words; the stages of his fifty-year teaching career as mapped out in the Tendai doctrinal classification system represented historical truth; and the ranking of particular scriptures in the Tendai hierarchy of teachings directly mirrored their degree of salvific power. With this background, here we will introduce some key features of Nichiren's approach to the *Lotus Sūtra.*

Nichiren saw the *Lotus Sūtra* as all-encompassing, containing the whole of Buddhist truth within itself. All other sūtras reveal but partial aspects of that truth. Or, in Tendai terminology, the *Lotus Sūtra* is "true," while all other sūtras are "provisional." What this meant for Nichiren in practical terms was that the *Lotus Sūtra* alone enables all persons without exception to become buddhas. Nichiren grounded this claim in the "three thousand realms in a single thought-moment" (*ichinen sanzen*), a principle first articulated by Zhiyi and discussed in greater detail in Chapter Two. In essence, this principle means that at each moment the smallest phenomenon ("a single thought-moment") and the entire cosmos ("three thousand realms") mutually pervade and encompass one another. Where Zhiyi had introduced this idea only briefly, Nichiren developed it as the very foundation of his thought.

Ichinen sanzen is a complex and challenging concept, and in his doctrinal instruction, Nichiren frequently concentrated on one of its key component principles: the mutual inclusion of the ten dharma realms (*jikkai gogu*). Traditional Buddhist cosmology divides saṃsāra or the realm of rebirth for unenlightened beings into a hierarchy of six paths: hell dwellers, hungry ghosts (*preta*), animals, demigods (*asura*), humans, and gods (*deva*). Above these, Tendai doctrine places four more realms characterized by ascending levels of awakening: the two realms of the *śrāvakas* and *pratyekabuddhas*, who cultivate the aims of detachment and cessation of desire set forth in the so-called Hīnayāna teachings, aiming for the goal of nirvāṇa; bodhisattvas, who strive for the liberation of all beings; and fully realized buddhas. In contrast to the buddha realm, which represents enlightenment, the other nine realms represent various levels of delusion, or states not yet fully awakened. Being empty of fixed, independent existence, all ten interpenetrate, meaning that each realm contains all ten within itself. Specifically, this means that the Buddha and all living beings are not separate; the buddha realm does not exist apart from oneself. Nichiren explains this in simple terms: "As to where hell and the Buddha exist: some sūtras say that hell lies beneath the ground, while others say that the Buddha dwells in the west. But close investigation shows that both exist within our five-foot body. For hell is in the heart of a man who despises his father and makes light of his mother, just as flowers and fruit are already present within the lotus seed. What we call 'buddha' dwells in our mind, in the same way that stones contain fire and that jewels have value intrinsically."[25]

For Nichiren, the *Lotus Sūtra* alone fully revealed the inherence of the buddha realm in all nine realms of unenlightened beings: By chanting its title, Namu Myōhō-renge-kyō, which instantiates the wisdom of all buddhas, even the most deluded person, he said, can manifest the buddha realm directly. Nichiren likened this to fire being produced by a stone taken from beneath the depths of water or a lamp illuminating a place that has been dark for millions of years.[26]

Though he understood its truth to be universal, Nichiren saw the *Lotus Sūtra* as especially relevant to his own place and time: Japan at the beginning of the Final Dharma age. This idea can be traced to the Japanese Tendai founder Saichō, who argued that Japan had a special karmic connection to the *Lotus Sūtra*. Saichō understood himself to be living shortly before the arrival of mappō and wrote that now was the time when people's religious capacity was suited to the one vehicle of the *Lotus*.[27]

Buddhist sūtras suggest that as the world moved farther and farther away from the time of the historical Buddha, his teachings would be refracted through an increasingly flawed mode of understanding; people would grow ever more deluded and liberation would become harder to achieve. In East Asia, this decline was said to span three successive periods: the age of the True Dharma (*shōbō*), the age of the Semblance Dharma (*zōbō*), and the age of the Final Dharma (*mappō*). Although chronologies differed, a rough consensus in Japan held that the first two ages had lasted a thousand years each and that the Final Dharma age had begun in 1052.[28]

From a scholarly perspective, mappō represents a discourse, not a historical reality. Buddhism in early medieval Japan was thriving: Buddhist institutions, learning, arts, and culture all flourished, and a wealth of new interpretations arose. Nonetheless, the idea that the age was in decline provided a ready explanation for political troubles and natural disasters; Buddhist teachers appropriated the idea of mappō in different ways to advance competing agendas. Some urged that because the times were degenerate, practitioners should be all the more conscientious in carrying out traditional Buddhist disciplines such as maintaining precepts, practicing meditation, and studying scriptures. Others, of whom Nichiren is one, drew on notions of mappō to legitimize innovations in Buddhist thought and practice.

For Nichiren, the problem of mappō was not simply a general decline of human capacity but a widespread rejection of the *Lotus Sūtra* in favor of incomplete, provisional teachings such as Pure Land, Zen, and the esoteric teachings, which he deemed to be no longer efficacious in the present era. Nichiren first formulated this argument in debate with followers of Hōnen (1133–1212), the founder of the Japanese Pure Land sect (Jōdoshū). Hōnen had taught that people living now in the *mappō* era were too ignorant and burdened by evil karma to achieve liberation through their own exertions in traditional Buddhist disciplines. Rather, Hōnen urged, people should set aside all other practices and solely chant the nenbutsu, the name of the buddha Amitābha (J. Amida), relying on the power of Amitābha's compassionate vow to save all who placed faith in him. By entrusting themselves wholeheartedly to Amitābha, they could be born after death in his Pure Land of Utmost Bliss (Skt. Sukhāvatī; J. Gokuraku Jōdo), said to lie far away in the western quadrant of the cosmos. There they could hear Amitābha preach the dharma directly and attain liberation. Birth in a buddha's pure land was understood as a shortcut along a bodhisattva's long path to enlightenment, and from well before Hōnen's time, people of all social ranks had aspired to birth after death in Amitābha's realm and carried out a variety of practices—reciting and copying sūtras, chanting mantras, performing esoteric rituals, keeping the precepts, and commissioning Buddhist paintings and statues—to achieve that goal. Among such practices, the chanted nenbutsu (*Namu Amida-butsu*) was accessible even to the poor and illiterate. Hōnen was by no means the first teacher to recommend it as particularly suited to sinful persons in the latter age, but he was the first to insist that the nenbutsu alone is efficacious and that all other practices should be rejected. Hōnen's later followers, with whom Nichiren engaged, criticized the *Lotus Sūtra* especially as too profound for the deluded people of this era. Those who attempted to practice it, they said, were like a small boy trying to wear his grandfather's shoes or a weakling trying to bend a stout bow or wear heavy armor. Such persons were bound to fail in their practice, thus losing the precious opportunity afforded by their human birth, and would fall after death into the lower realms. Rather, Hōnen's followers maintained, one should set aside the *Lotus* in this lifetime and chant the nenbutsu instead, achieve birth in Amitābha's pure land, and attain the awakening of the *Lotus Sūtra* there.

Nichiren fiercely opposed this argument. For him, Hōnen's focus on human limitations ignored the Buddha's own distinction between true and provisional teachings. The *Lotus* was the sūtra of which Śākyamuni himself had said, "For more than forty years I have expounded the dharma in all manner of ways through adeptness in skillful means, but the core truth has still not been revealed," and, "Having openly set aside skillful means, I will teach only the highest path" (45).[29] Precisely because the *Lotus Sūtra* is profound, Nichiren argued, it can save even the most depraved individuals. He also maintained that the nenbutsu belonged to the lesser category of provisional Mahāyāna and did not represent the Buddha's final intent. He likened it to the scaffolding erected in building a large stūpa: once the stūpa (the *Lotus Sūtra*) has been completed, the scaffolding (the nenbutsu) should be dismantled.

Like Hōnen, Nichiren taught a universally accessible mode of practice, grounded in faith and centered on the chanting of a single phrase. But despite these outward similarities, the doctrine and attitude underlying the two practices differ radically. Rather than promising enlightenment after death and in a distant realm, the daimoku as taught by Nichiren offers direct access to a dimension in which the self opens to pervade the universe, and buddhahood is realized "in this body." In his teaching, mappō is accordingly revalorized as the moment when the "perfectly encompassing path" of immediate enlightenment becomes accessible to all.

The Mission of Propagation

In Nichiren's understanding, abandoning the true teaching in favor of provisional ones not only cut off the path to buddhahood for individuals, but had dire consequences for society. Japan in his day was ravaged by calamities, including famine, epidemics, earthquakes, and the threat of invasion by the Mongols, who had already conquered much of Asia. Nichiren blamed these disasters on widespread rejection of the *Lotus Sūtra*, a theme he developed in many of his writings. The most famous example is his admonitory treatise *Risshō ankoku ron* ("On Establishing the True Dharma and Bringing Peace to the Realm"), which he submitted to the Kamakura Bakufu in 1260. In it Nichiren rebuked officials for their support of monks who promoted incomplete teachings that, from his perspective, were no longer efficacious. He also cited passages from sūtras enumerating the disasters said to befall a country whose ruler fails to protect the true dharma and allows it to be neglected. These calamities, such as epidemics, violent and unseasonable storms, crop failure, famine, and ominous astrological portents, Nichiren noted, had all recently occurred in Japan. Only two disasters mentioned in the sūtras—internal revolt and foreign invasion—had not yet transpired. Unless the situation were rectified, he argued, those disasters would surely materialize as well. (A rebellion led by the shogunal regent's half-brother in 1272, and the Mongol invasion attempts of 1274 and 1281, seemed to bear out these predictions.) Conversely, Nichiren asserted that if the people as a whole embraced the *Lotus Sūtra*, the buddha land would be realized here in this world.

Nichiren's criticism of other Buddhist teachings drew the ire of Buddhist leaders, government officials, and ordinary devotees. Shortly after he submitted the *Risshō Ankoku ron*, a mob attacked his dwelling, forcing him to flee. The following year, he was arrested and exiled to the Izu peninsula. Reprieved two years later, he resumed his proselytizing in Kamakura and the surrounding provinces; on one occasion, his party was attacked, and he himself was wounded. As the country readied its defenses in preparation for a Mongol attack, Nichiren intensified his efforts, expanding his critique of provisional teachings to include Zen, the esoteric teachings, and movements to revive observance of the traditional Buddhist precepts. In the ninth month of 1271, possibly as part of the Bakufu's effort to rally the country's defenses by subduing dissidents, Nichiren was arrested a second time and nearly beheaded; ultimately, he was again banished, this time to the remote island of Sado in the Sea of Japan. There he endured hunger, cold, and the hostility of locals, but he produced some of his most important writings. Summoned back in 1274 by Bakufu officials who thought he might have some insight into when the Mongols would attack, Nichiren declared—accurately, as it turned out—that they would strike within the year. He renewed his remonstrances that disaster could be forestalled only by withdrawing support from other teachings and embracing the *Lotus Sūtra* alone. The Bakufu, however, was in no position to endorse only one form of Buddhism, even had they been persuaded by his argument. Realizing that he would not be heeded, Nichiren withdrew to Mount Minobu in Kai province (Yamanashi prefecture), where he devoted his last years to writing and training disciples to carry on the task of propagation for the future.

For Nichiren, preaching the exclusive truth of the *Lotus Sūtra* was not only about leading individuals to enlightenment, but also about saving the country and establishing an ideal buddha land in this world, a task he came to see as his personal mission and responsibility. In declaring the supremacy of the *Lotus Sūtra*, he found it necessary to rebuke attachment to other, provisional teachings; in consequence, he encountered repeated antagonism. Nichiren was often beset by danger and privation. Out of this experience, he developed what might be called a soteriology of undergoing persecution. The *Lotus Sūtra* itself speaks of the hostility that will confront its devotees in a latter evil age. Nichiren and his followers therefore understood the persecutions they faced as both fulfilling the sūtra's prophecies and confirming the veracity of their mission to propagate it. Nichiren also taught that to endure hardships and opposition in spreading faith in the *Lotus Sūtra* is to repay one's debt to the Buddha, eradicate one's past evil karma, fulfill the bodhisattva's mandate to sacrifice even one's life, if need be, to save others, and guarantee one's future buddhahood. Indeed, one could say that Nichiren's teaching on buddhahood has two temporal modes: immediately manifesting the all-encompassing buddha realm in the act of chanting the daimoku, and realizing buddhahood as an unfolding process in devoting oneself to the daimoku's propagation.

In the contemporary world, where the violence and suffering brought about by religious conflict are so starkly evident, Nichiren's emphasis on the exclusive truth of the *Lotus Sūtra* and his assertive mode of proselytizing sometimes provoke antipathy, as they fly in the face of ideals of tolerance and religious pluralism. Both traditional temple organizations and long-established lay groups of Nichiren Buddhism tend to be more accommodating and to take a milder approach in spreading their teachings, in keeping with Nichiren's admonition that the method of propagation should accord with the times. Nichiren, however, lived in a very different world, where his conviction of the *Lotus Sūtra*'s sole efficacy in the age of the Final Dharma demanded resolute opposition to other Buddhist forms. This stance sharply differentiated him from the Buddhist mainstream of his day. Though it drew hostility, it may well have enabled his fledgling community to survive beyond his lifetime by carving out a unique religious identity.

Nichiren in the Present Volume

Nichiren is known to us today chiefly from his own writings, which comprise more than four hundred doctrinal essays, extracts, charts and outlines, and personal letters to his followers. A remarkable number of his works have survived, including more than a hundred in his own hand. We are also able to glean information from surviving maṇḍalas that he inscribed for his followers as well as records of their conferral. In addition,

Nichiren kept a personal copy of the *Lotus Sūtra,* still extant, which he annotated with passages drawn from other sūtras and Buddhist commentarial literature, inserting them in the margins, between the lines, and on the reverse side of the pages. These passages offer additional insight into Nichiren's understanding of the *Lotus.*

However, Nichiren himself did not leave a systematic, chapter-by-chapter explication of the *Lotus Sūtra.*[30] In China, exegetes such as Zhiyi, Jizang, and others had produced line-by-line commentaries on the *Lotus,* and some Japanese scholar-monks continued to write commentaries of this kind. But at the same time, another interpretive approach emerged, which was to build upon the earlier commentarial tradition by singling out individual passages, phrases, or images to elicit new meanings or emphases.[31] This is an approach we often find in Nichiren, and it is well suited to his fundamental interpretive principle: that the entire *Lotus Sūtra* is contained within its daimoku or title, and that chanting the daimoku opens the buddha realm to everyone without exception. One could say that, for him, the various passages of the *Lotus Sūtra* serve to illuminate aspects of the daimoku. This volume, therefore, does not present a systematic commentary from Nichiren on the individual chapters of the *Lotus Sūtra* but, rather, takes each chapter as a point of departure for introducing aspects of his thought.

Nichiren also illustrates broader processes of religious interpretation that we find beyond the specific contexts of medieval Japan, the *Lotus Sūtra,* or Buddhism itself. Where the authors of scholarly treatments such as the present volume strive to step outside their contemporary assumptions and enter into the original context and intent of a particular text's compilers, readings produced by those speaking from within religious traditions often seek, consciously or otherwise, to interpret their tradition in ways that directly address their own time and place. There is never a pure, unmediated encounter between reader and text, as readers bring to their interpretations both the legacy of previous readings as well as their own, present concerns. Thus, one cannot pick up the text of the *Lotus Sūtra* and immediately discover the teachings of Zhiyi or Nichiren; nowhere does the *Lotus* explicitly state, for example, that "this sūtra perfectly embodies the threefold truth" or that "in the age of the Final Dharma, one should chant Namu Myōhō-renge-kyō." Rather, such readings are shaped by centuries of interpretation. All readers of religious texts engage in this sort of hermeneutical triangulation, in which they navigate between the scriptures of their tradition, their received interpretive tradition, and the specific demands of their own time and circumstances. In this process, some elements are reasserted, others are allowed to lapse, and still others are invested with new meanings, sometimes in surprising ways. Nichiren drew, not only upon the *Lotus Sūtra* itself, but upon his Tendai heritage, elements drawn from esoteric Buddhism and other traditions, and his perception of the needs of people in Japan in his day. We should not be surprised, then, when his readings differ in emphasis and meaning from the *Lotus Sūtra* text. Nor should we be surprised when Nichiren dwells at length on a passage that that strikes the modern reader as insignificant, or when he passes without comment over a passage where the modern reader finds deep meaning. This same process has taken place in the way that Nichiren's later followers have read and reread his teachings up until today. In this way, the *Lotus Sūtra*'s history of interpretation offers insight not only into its own reception, but also into that of religious texts more broadly.

With this background in mind, we invite the reader to begin.

CHAPTER ONE

Introduction

The *Lotus Sūtra* begins, like almost all Buddhist sūtras, with the statement, "Thus have I heard" (3). This is meant to indicate its authenticity, as something heard by the narrator from the Buddha himself. The narrator is typically considered to be Ānanda, the Buddha's cousin and personal attendant, the monk who was most often in the Buddha's presence and thus heard his many teachings. When Ānanda agreed to serve as the Buddha's attendant, he asked that the Buddha repeat to him any teachings that he might not have been present to hear. According to tradition, after the Buddha's death, a council of five hundred enlightened monks was convened to compile his teachings. Ānanda was asked to recite all of the sūtras that he had heard; he is said to have heard 84,000 teachings, which took seven months to recite. He began his recitation of each sūtra with the phrase, "Thus have I heard."

The words "Thus have I heard" at the beginning of the *Lotus Sūtra* are thus hardly surprising, except for the fact that Ānanda did not hear the *Lotus Sūtra*. In fact, scholars are unsure as to exactly what Ānanda heard, as nothing that the Buddha taught was written down for some four centuries after his death. Although accounts of the so-called first council at which Ānanda's prodigious memory was on display have likely been highly mythologized, most scholars assume that at least some of the teachings preserved in the early canons derived from the Buddha himself. The *Lotus Sūtra*, however, was not composed until long after the Buddha's, and Ānanda's, time. As we shall see, the *Lotus Sūtra* is obsessed, perhaps above all, with its own legitimation, with an almost palpable anxiety to prove that it was spoken by the Buddha. That obsession is evident from the first three words of the Sanskrit text: *evaṃ mayā śrutam*, "thus have I heard."

The next standard element of a Buddhist sūtra is a statement of the location where the Buddha delivered the discourse. There are a number of standard places, including Jetavana, a grove in the city of Śrāvastī, as well as the Gabled Hall in the Great Wood near Vaiśālī. Many sūtras are said to have been taught on Vulture Peak (Gṛdhrakūṭa), near the city of Rājagṛha in the kingdom of Magadha. Traditional etymologies say that it was so named because it is shaped like the head of a vulture or because many vultures inhabited a nearby charnel ground. Translations from the Chinese or Japanese often render this name as Eagle Peak. In a second effort at legitimation, the preaching of the *Lotus Sūtra* (like the Perfection of Wisdom sūtras) is set at Vulture Peak.

A third element in the opening to a sūtra is a description of the audience. Here the *Lotus Sūtra* again follows the conventional form, stating that the audience comprises twelve thousand monks, all of whom have achieved the state of the *arhat*, or "worthy one," someone who has followed the path to its conclusion, has destroyed all causes for future rebirth, and will enter final nirvāṇa at death. To provide specificity, twenty-one of these twelve thousand are mentioned by name. They include the Buddha's most famous disciples, such as Mahākāśyapa, who would convene the first council to compile the teachings after the Buddha's death; Mahāmaudgalyāyana, the monk foremost in supernatural powers; Śāriputra, the monk foremost in wisdom; and Rāhula, the Buddha's only son, conceived before he renounced the world. Also in attendance is the Buddha's foster mother Mahāprajāpatī, who had convinced him to establish the order of nuns and who had become a nun, and an arhat, herself. She is accompanied by six thousand attendants. Also present is Yaśodharā, the Buddha's former wife, who is also a nun and an arhat. Another two thousand monks are also in attendance, some who have reached the rank of arhat and others who have not.

Up to this point, the members of the audience would be entirely familiar to those who knew the canon, the texts accepted as authoritative by the Buddhist mainstream. What is different is the numbers. Works in the Pāli canon, for example, do not include such multitudes when describing the audience of a sūtra. Readers of the text who had visited the sacred sites would know that Vulture Peak is more hill than peak; it is difficult to imagine a crowd of twenty thousand monks and nuns seated at its small summit, or how the members of such a huge assembly could hear the Buddha. The size of the *Lotus Sūtra*'s audience is the first sign of something extraordinary. A second sign is a second constituency within the audience: eighty thousand bodhisattvas.

In the early Buddhist tradition, and in what scholars have come to call "mainstream Buddhism" (that is, non-Mahāyāna), there are three paths to enlightenment. The first is the path of the *śrāvaka* or disciple (literally, "listener"), one who listens to the teachings of the Buddha, puts them into practice, and eventually achieves the state of the arhat, entering final nirvāṇa at death. The second is the path of the *pratyekabuddha*, or "solitary enlightened one." *Pratyekkabuddhas* are rather enigmatic figures in Buddhist literature, said to prefer a solitary existence, achieving their liberation at a time when there is no buddha in the world. Having achieved their enlightenment, they do not teach others. The third path is that of the bodhisattva, a person capable of achieving the state of an arhat but who instead seeks the far more difficult and distant goal of buddhahood, perfecting himself over many billions of lifetimes so that he may teach the path to liberation to others at a time when it has been forgotten. Thus, a bodhisattva only achieves buddhahood at a time when the teachings of the previous buddha have faded entirely into oblivion, a process that takes many millions of millennia. Different versions of the tradition say that Śākyamuni Buddha, the buddha who appeared in India some two thousand five hundred years ago, was the fourth, the seventh, or the twenty-fifth buddha to appear in our world during the present cosmic age. There is a bodhisattva, Maitreya, said to be waiting in the Tuṣita ("Satisfaction") heaven to be the next buddha, who will appear in our world when the teachings of our buddha have been completely forgotten, something that will not occur for millions of years. Śākyamuni and other, prior buddhas were bodhisattvas before their enlightenment. In the present age, mainstream Buddhism essentially recognizes only a single bodhisattva: Maitreya. The audience of the *Lotus Sūtra,* however, has eighty thousand bodhisattvas. The sūtra tells us that these eighty thousand bodhisattvas have "paid homage to countless hundreds of thousands of buddhas" (3), far more than four, seven, or twenty-five. The text lists eighteen of these bodhisattvas by name. They include two who would become the most famous in the Mahāyāna pantheon: Avalokiteśvara and Mañjuśrī. And they include the only bodhisattva whose name would have been recognized and whose existence would have been accepted by all: again, Maitreya. Thus, on the first page of the sūtra, a reader familiar with the canon would have been comforted by the familiar opening phrase and the familiar setting, only to be dumbfounded, and perhaps confounded, by the size and composition of the audience, an audience that grows even further as one reads on, with all manner of gods and demigods arriving from their various heavens, each with hundreds of thousands of attendants. Also present is one human king, Ajātaśatru, apparently after he had repented the murder of his father, the Buddha's patron and friend, Bimbisāra, king of Magadha.[1]

With the audience having been enumerated, the Buddha then teaches a Mahāyāna sūtra identified in Sanskrit as *Mahānirdeśa*. However, nothing of the content of that teaching is provided, and *mahānirdeśa* is a generic term that simply means "great instruction." Kumārajīva's Chinese translation, however, renders this as "a Mahāyāna sūtra named *Immeasurable Meanings*," and by the fifth century, a text purporting to be this very sūtra was circulating in China, also with the name *Sūtra of Immeasurable Meanings* (Ch. *Wuliang yi jing*), said to have been translated by a monk named Dharmāgatayaśas. No Sanskrit original, or reference to the Sanskrit original, has been located, nor are any other translations attributed to Dharmāgatayaśas, leading scholars to consider the text to be a Chinese apocryphon, a work composed in China that purports to be not only of Indian origin but spoken by the Buddha himself. It achieved canonical status in China, where it is regarded as the first of three sūtras comprising the so-called threefold *Lotus Sūtra*. The text itself is short, not quite thirty pages in English translation, and has only three chapters. The first describes the bodhisattvas present in the assembly and reports their lengthy praise of the Buddha. In the second, the Buddha praises the importance of the *Sūtra of Immeasurable Meanings* and then gives the actual teaching, which is that, although buddhas teach immeasurable meanings, they all originate from a single dharma, which is without form. Also in the chapter the

Buddha says, "For more than forty years I have expounded the dharma in all manner of ways through adeptness in skillful means, but the core truth has still not been revealed."[2] East Asian commentators would find great meaning in this statement, for it serves to position the *Lotus Sūtra* as the Buddha's final teaching. The third and longest chapter is devoted to ten benefits accruing to those who hear one verse of this sūtra or keep, read, recite, and copy the sūtra.

After expounding this sūtra, we read, the Buddha then enters a state of deep meditation (*samādhi*). In the Mahāyāna sūtras, such states often have specific names, and this one is called "abode of immeasurable meanings" (5). This causes various celestial flowers to rain from sky. The audience is filled with joy.

The body of a buddha is famously adorned with the thirty-two marks of a superman (*mahāpuruṣa*), among which is a small tuft of white hair between his eyebrows, called the *ūrṇā*. In the Mahāyāna sūtras, the Buddha often shoots a beam of light from it, and he does so here at the beginning of the *Lotus Sūtra*. The light illuminates eighteen thousand worlds in the east, extending as far up as Akaniṣṭha, the highest heaven of the Realm of Form, and extending as far down as Avīci, the lowest and most horrific of the many Buddhist hells. The light reveals all of the beings who inhabit these realms, all the buddhas who are teaching there, as well as the monks, nuns, male lay disciples, and female lay disciples who are practicing their teachings. The audience can see bodhisattvas following the bodhisattva path and buddhas who have passed into final nirvāṇa, together with the jewel-encrusted stūpas that enclose their relics.

As we have noted, Maitreya will be the next buddha. He has reached the end of the bodhisattva path and, like all future buddhas, spends his penultimate lifetime as a god in Tuṣita heaven, the fourth of six heavens of the Realm of Desire, where he awaits the appropriate moment to be born in the world of humans, achieve buddhahood, and teach the dharma. As such, Maitreya, having perfected himself over many lifetimes, should be endowed with wisdom surpassed only by the Buddha himself. Yet, in one of the inversions used so skillfully in the *Lotus Sūtra,* Maitreya is here made to play the fool. He does not understand why the Buddha has performed this miracle of illuminating vast reaches of the cosmos. And so he asks a wiser bodhisattva, indeed, the bodhisattva of wisdom himself, Mañjuśrī, "What is the reason for this marvelous sign, this great ray of light that illuminates the eighteen thousand worlds in the east and renders visible the adornments of all the buddha worlds?" (6). As noted above, Maitreya was the only bodhisattva of the present time familiar to the non-Mahāyāna, mainstream tradition of Buddhism. But he does not understand the Buddha's miracle and so he is made to ask a bodhisattva unknown to that mainstream. Here again, this would give the traditional reader pause. The question that would typically open a sūtra is a question addressed to the Buddha from an unenlightened person. Here, the question is asked by an advanced bodhisattva, a bodhisattva a mere one lifetime away from buddhahood, and it is addressed to another bodhisattva, one not part of the mainstream Buddhist tradition. As we shall see, such things occur throughout the *Lotus Sūtra,* where something or someone familiar appears in a way that also seems unfamiliar, evoking recognition but also hesitation. Something is not quite right; indeed, the ground has shifted, and conventional expectations no longer apply.

But before asking his question, as the text says, "Thereupon the bodhisattva Maitreya, wanting to elaborate the meaning of this further, spoke to Mañjuśrī in verse" (6). Over the next seven pages, Maitreya asks, in verse, why the Buddha has emitted a ray of light from between his eyebrows. One wonders why Maitreya here in effect bursts into song, a rather redundant song, a pattern that occurs regularly throughout the first twenty-one chapters of the sūtra. However, this is not *The Lotus Sūtra: The Musical*. Instead, the verses may provide an important clue to the text's origins, a clue that is invisible in translation, as Eugène Burnouf pointed out in 1844.

The *Lotus Sūtra* is written chiefly in what the Indologist Franklin Edgerton called "Buddhist Hybrid Sanskrit," that is, Sanskrit containing grammar and vocabulary common to Indian vernaculars of the period. Much scholarly debate has surrounded the relative dating of the verse and prose sections. One theory has maintained that, although presented in the *Lotus* text as "elaborations" on the prose, at least in the oldest stratum of the sūtra, the verse sections may have been compiled first, with the prose portions being added later.[3] Whatever may be the case, to the dismay of generations of undergraduates, one cannot simply skip over the verse sections. One loses little of the plot by doing so but sacrifices much of the richness of the text. In the case of Maitreya's speech here, the bodhisattva describes in often moving detail all of the things that he sees occurring in the various worlds illumined by the Buddha's light.

In response to Maitreya's question about why the Buddha has illuminated the worlds, Mañjuśrī responds that he has seen this happen before. That is, he remembers something that Maitreya does not, suggesting that the power of his memory to encompass distant space and time—one of the markers of enlightenment in Buddhism—surpasses even that of Maitreya. It also suggests that Mañjuśrī has been cultivating the bodhisattva path far longer even than Maitreya, who was said to be but one lifetime away from achieving buddhahood. This is but one of many moments in which the *Lotus Sūtra* reverses conventional hierarchies by revealing hitherto unimagined expanses of the past.

Mañjuśrī goes on to tell a rather elaborate story about a buddha named Candrasūryapradīpa ("Lamp of the Moon and Sun") who lived incalculable eons, or *kalpas*, in the past. He was followed by another twenty thousand buddhas in succession, all named Candrasūryapradīpa. Before the last Candrasūryapradīpa renounced the world to seek the way, he fathered eight sons. At the end of his life, Candrasūryapradīpa taught a sūtra called *Immeasurable Meanings* and then entered a state of deep meditation; flowers rained down from the sky. Then he emitted a ray of light from his *ūrṇā*, the tuft of hair between his eyebrows. After that, he taught a bodhisattva named Varaprabha and his eight hundred disciples, in a discourse that lasted for sixty intermediate eons. The name of that discourse was the *White Lotus of the True Dharma* (*Saddharma-puṇḍarika-sūtra*, rendered as *White Lotus of the Marvelous Law*, in the Kubo–Yuyama translation), that is, the *Lotus Sūtra*. He then passed into final nirvāṇa. Varaprabha preserved and taught this *Lotus Sūtra* for eighty intermediate eons, and served as the teacher of Candrasūryapradīpa's eight sons, each of whom would become a buddha. The last of the eight became a buddha named Dīpaṃkara. Among Varaprabha's eight hundred disciples was a somewhat avaricious man named Yaśaskāma ("Fame Seeker"), who recited the sūtras but forgot most of what he recited. However, over his lifetimes, he had paid homage to many billions[4] of buddhas.

In Buddhist literature, when the Buddha tells a story of the distant past, he often ends the story by identifying members of his present circle as the contemporary incarnations of the figures in the story. Mañjuśrī does this here, explaining that in a past life, he had been the esteemed Varaprabha, and Maitreya, the next buddha, had been the rather disreputable Yaśaskāma. Based on what he had witnessed so many eons ago, Mañjuśrī concludes that the Buddha is about to teach the *Lotus Sūtra*.

There is much to ponder here, as the *Lotus Sūtra* makes a powerful claim for its own authority. The sūtra, which no one has ever heard before, is not new. In fact, it is very old, so old that it has been all but forgotten. It was taught many eons ago, by a buddha so ancient that his name does not appear in the standard list of the previous buddhas. The only familiar name in the story is Dīpaṃkara (16), the first buddha in the list of twenty-five buddhas of the past, according to the Pāli tradition.[5] In that tradition, it was at the feet of Dīpaṃkara that Sumedha, the yogin who would one day become Śākyamuni Buddha, vowed to follow the long bodhisattva path to buddhahood. It was Dīpaṃkara who prophesied that Sumedha would become a buddha named Gautama. Hence, the first buddha known to the collective memory of the tradition was the last son of the last buddha Candrasūryapradīpa to become enlightened. This means that the story told by Mañjuśrī is about events in a past so distant that no record of them exists. In other words, prior even to the time of the buddha Dīpaṃkara, under whom the buddha of our world, Gautama or Śākyamuni, first took his bodhisattva vows, another buddha, Candrasūryapradīpa, taught the *Lotus Sūtra*. Furthermore, Candrasūryapradīpa was Dīpaṃkara's father, placing him in a position of authority, both in age and in lineage, to the first buddha named by the tradition. The *Lotus Sūtra* is therefore older than any teaching previously known.

The bodhisattva Varaprabha, the teacher of Dīpaṃkara, was Mañjuśrī in a previous life, meaning that a bodhisattva in the audience of the present buddha was, at least at one time, superior to this previous buddha. And the bodhisattva who is honored by the mainstream tradition as the future buddha, Maitreya, turns out to have been his least worthy disciple. The inversion of authority with which the *Lotus Sūtra* proclaims its priority here not only makes the best of bodhisattvas the least of bodhisattvas, but also explains what happened in the distant past to make it so. In Mañjuśrī's response we also encounter the first instance of a device that occurs in many Mahāyāna sūtras but which is employed most famously, and most head-spinningly, in the *Lotus*: self-reference. In this, the first chapter of the *Lotus Sūtra*, Mañjuśrī explains that in the distant past, the buddha Candrasūryapradīpa taught the *Lotus Sūtra*.

The literary device of *mise en abyme*, in which a work makes reference to itself, is familiar to readers of such modern authors as Borges and Calvino. It has a much longer history. In Chapter XXIX of Part Two of *Don Quijote*, the knight errant and his servant and squire Sancho Panza encounter a duke and duchess who have read *Don Quijote* and are familiar with their previous adventures. Also, they overhear travelers at an inn regaling each other with stories of Don Quijote that do not appear in the novel. Don Quijote confronts them and points out their error, telling them that he never did the things they said he did. In the *Odyssey*, Odysseus is present at the court of Alcinous when the blind poet Demodocus sings first of the feud between Achilles and Odysseus at Troy and later of the Trojan Horse, each time causing Odysseus to burst into tears, betraying his identity. In medieval and Renaissance paintings of the Annunciation, Mary is often depicted reading, with a book in her hand or on a nearby table, as Gabriel enters with the news that she will give birth to the messiah. That book is most often a codex rather than a scroll, although the codex was not in use in Palestine at the time of Jesus. But this is merely an anachronism. In the fifteenth-century Merode Altarpiece, Mary has two texts on her table: a scroll, meant to be the Old Testament, and a codex, meant to be the New Testament, although the New Testament, in which the story of the Annunciation is told in the Gospel of Luke, could not have existed until after the birth, death, and resurrection of the child that Gabriel had come to announce.

However, Cervantes wrote Part Two of *Don Qijote* a full decade after he wrote Part One, after Part One had become a sensation and after another author had published a sequel, to Cervantes' great indignation. And while the story of Achilles that Demodocus sings occurs in the *Iliad,* the story of the Trojan Horse does not appear there. Like Don Quijote, Odysseus is present when his own tale is told, but those tales are not *Don Quijote Part Two* or the *Odyssey*. And in the case of the Virgin Mary, that Mary is reading a book that had not yet been written serves any number of purposes, including as a visualization aid to medieval women who imagined themselves as present in the scene.[6]

Something much stranger occurs in the *Lotus Sūtra,* raising the question of who is speaking, who is the "I" of "Thus have I heard"? At this point in the text, Śākyamuni Buddha has not yet spoken, but when he eventually teaches the *Lotus Sūtra,* does he include the first chapter? And when Candrasūryapradīpa taught the *Lotus Sūtra* so many cosmic ages ago, did he include the first chapter, set, from his perspective, in the far distant future? Like *mise en abyme* in which an object is placed between two mirrors, causing the object to be reduplicated into smaller and smaller forms, the *Lotus Sūtra* constantly refers to itself, placing it not at the abyss, but at the very origin of enlightenment. It is at this point that the reader asks the question that haunts the reading: What is the *Lotus Sūtra*?

Roughly a thousand years after the *Lotus Sūtra*'s compilation, in an entirely different cultural sphere, the Buddhist teacher Nichiren maintained that now in the time of mappō, the entire sūtra was encompassed in its daimoku or title, and that chanting the title was the chief practice of the *Lotus Sūtra* for the present era. "Whatever sūtra he expounded," Nichiren wrote, "the Buddha assigned it a title expressing its ultimate principle."[7] Today we know that the historical Buddha did not preach, let alone name, the *Lotus Sūtra*, but the idea that a sūtra's title embodies its essence was well established in Nichiren's time. One of the great scholar-monk Zhiyi's two *Lotus Sūtra* commentaries, the *Profound Meaning of the Lotus Sūtra* (Ch. *Fahua xuanyi*, J. *Hokke gengi*), devotes the greater part of its space to interpreting the five characters *myō*, *hō*, *ren*, *ge*, and *kyō* (as pronounced in Japanese) that comprise the *Lotus Sūtra*'s title in Kumārajīva's translation. The practice of chanting the title of the *Lotus Sūtra* also predates Nichiren. Before lecturing on a sūtra, the lecturer would intone its title, and the audience of *Lotus Sūtra* lectures in premodern Japan would have heard the daimoku in that context. Narrative literature of the latter Heian period contains occasional examples of people reciting the title of the *Lotus Sūtra*. Namu Myōhō-renge-kyō was also the mantra employed in the Tendai esoteric *Hokke hō* or Lotus rite. Esoteric notions of mantras as "meditation containers" that encapsulate the powers of awakened states were an important source for Nichiren's thinking about the daimoku.[8]

We have already seen how, when Maitreya asks Mañjuśrī to explain the meaning of the earth shaking, the flowers falling from the sky, and the ray of light emitted from the Buddha's forehead that illuminates the eastern part of the universe, Mañjuśrī expresses his confidence that Śākyamuni Buddha, like the buddhas of prior ages just before they entered final nirvāṇa, will now preach a sūtra called *White Lotus of the True Dharma* (*Saddharma-puṇḍarika-sūtra*). This was the first time, Nichiren wrote, that sentient beings of this world had heard the name of the *Lotus Sūtra*.[9] This introductory chapter marks a convenient place in the present study to say more about Nichiren's understanding of the *Lotus Sūtra*'s title.

First, we might consider the individual words that make up the title. *Myō* has the connotations of "wonderful," "marvelous," and "inconceivable." The use of this character in the title was Kumārajīva's innovation; an earlier translation by Dharmarakṣa (230?–316) uses *shō* (Ch. *zheng*), meaning "true" or "correct." Fayun (467–529), an early Chinese commentator on the *Lotus Sūtra*, took *myō* (*miao*) to mean "subtle" as opposed to "crude" or "coarse." Zhiyi argued that *myō* has both a relative and an absolute meaning. From a relative standpoint, *myō*, denoting the perfect teaching, is superior to all others, which by comparison are incomplete. But from an absolute standpoint, *myō* is perfectly encompassing; there is nothing outside it to which it could be compared. This reading laid the groundwork for later understandings of the *Lotus Sūtra* as both superior to, and at the same time inclusive of, all other teachings.

Nichiren said that *myō* has three meanings. The first is to open, meaning that it opens the meaning of all other sūtras. "When the Buddha preached the *Lotus Sūtra*, he opened the storehouse of the other sūtras preached during the preceding forty-some years, and all beings of the nine realms were for the first time able to discern the treasures that lay within those sūtras," he wrote. Second, *myō* means "perfectly encompassing"; each of the 69,384 characters of the sūtra contains all others within itself. "It is like one drop of the great ocean that contains water from all the rivers that pour into the ocean, or a single wish-granting jewel that, although no bigger than a mustard seed, can rain down all the treasures that one might gain from all wish-granting jewels." And third, *myō* means "to restore to life," meaning that it revives the seeds, or causes, of buddhahood in those who have neglected or destroyed them.[10]

Renge means "lotus blossom," and the Sanskrit *puṇḍarīka* indicates a white lotus. Lotuses grow in muddy water to bloom untainted above its surface and thus represent the flowering of the aspiration for awakening in the mind of the ordinary, deluded person. The lotus plant also produces flowers and seedpods at the same time. To Chinese Tiantai patriarchs, as well as medieval Japanese Tendai interpreters, this suggested the simultaneity of "cause" (the nine realms, or states of those still at the stage of practice) and "effect" (the buddha realm or state of buddhahood), meaning that all ten realms are mutually inclusive. Nichiren draws on the analogy of the lotus to stress his claim that the *Lotus Sūtra* enables the realization of buddhahood in the very act of practice. As he expressed it: "The merit of all other sūtras is uncertain, because they teach that first one must plant good roots and [only] afterward become a buddha. But in the case of the *Lotus Sūtra,* when one takes it in one's hand, that hand at once becomes a buddha, and when one chants it with one's mouth, that mouth is precisely a buddha. This is just like the moon being reflected on the water the moment it rises above the eastern mountains, or like a sound and its echo occurring simultaneously."[11]

The last character, *kyō,* means "sūtra." *Kyō* in the title of the *Lotus Sūtra,* Nichiren said, encompasses all the teachings of all buddhas throughout space and time.[12] *Namu,* which prefaces the title in chanting, comes from Sanskrit *namas,* meaning "reverence," "devotion," or "the taking of refuge." Ultimately, Nichiren took it as expressing the willingness to offer one's life for the dharma. Nichiren made clear, however, that the significance of the daimoku does not lie in its semantic meaning. The daimoku, he said, is neither the text nor its meaning but the intent, or heart, of the entire sūtra.[13] He defined it alternately as the seed of buddhahood, the father and mother of all buddhas, and the "three thousand realms in a single thought moment in actuality" (*ji no ichinen sanzen*)—a concept to which we will return in Chapter Sixteen. Nichiren's interpretation of the entire *Lotus Sūtra* is grounded in his understanding that the "heart" of the entire sūtra is the wonderful dharma, instantiated in its title, which encapsulates the awakened state that buddhas attain and which opens that buddhahood to all who chant it, however meager their moral virtue or understanding. "To practice only the seven characters Namu Myōhō-renge-kyō might seem narrow," he said, "but because those characters are the teacher of all buddhas of the past, present, and future; the leader of all the bodhisattvas in the ten directions; and the compass for all sentient beings on the path of attaining buddhahood, that practice is actually profound."[14]

In developing his teachings about the daimoku of the *Lotus Sūtra,* Nichiren drew upon and adapted earlier traditions of *Lotus* interpretation. Chinese exegetes had often employed a technique known as "analytic division" (Ch. *fenke*) or parsing that purported to uncover categories of meaning implicit within a particular sūtra, and thus, to reveal the Buddha's true intent. Zhiyi, for example, divided the *Lotus Sūtra* into two sections: the first fourteen of its twenty-eight chapters, he said, represent the "trace teaching" (Ch. *jimen,* J. *shakumon*), which presents Śākyamuni Buddha as a "trace" or manifestation, that is, a historical figure who lived and taught in this world, while the second fourteen chapters constitute the "origin teaching" (*benmen, honmon*), which presents Śākyamuni as the primordial buddha, awakened since the inconceivably remote past. The intent of the trace teaching, Zhiyi said, lies in opening the three vehicles to reveal the one vehicle, while the intent of the origin section is to reveal the Buddha's original awakening in the distant past. Nichiren also regarded these as the two great revelations of the *Lotus Sūtra*. For him, the trace teaching revealed buddhahood as a potential inherent in all beings, while the origin teaching presented it as a reality fully manifested in the Buddha's life and conduct. Nichiren saw the core of the trace and origin teachings as Chapters Two and Sixteen, respectively, and urged his followers to recite these chapters as part of their daily practice.

Chinese commentators also typically divided sūtras into three parts: an introductory section, the main exposition, and a "dissemination" section, urging that the sūtra be transmitted to the future. Zhiyi divided the *Lotus Sūtra* accordingly: Chapter One of the *Lotus Sūtra* represents "introduction"; Chapters Two through the first part of Seventeen represent the "main exposition"; and the latter part of Chapter Seventeen and the remaining chapters represent "dissemination." Zhiyi further divided each of the sūtra's two exegetical divisions, the trace and origin teachings, into these three parts.[15] Nichiren expanded this threefold analysis in two directions. Zooming out, as it were, he applied it to the entirety of the Buddha's teachings: all teachings that preceded the *Lotus Sūtra* are "introduction"; the threefold *Lotus Sūtra* is the "main exposition"; and the *Nirvāṇa Sūtra,* which Tendai tradition regards as a restatement of the *Lotus Sūtra,* represents "dissemination." Zooming in, he identified all the teachings of all buddhas throughout space and time, including the trace teaching of *Lotus Sūtra,* as preparation, and the daimoku, Namu Myōhō-renge-kyo, the heart of the origin teaching, as the main exposition. Nichiren did not say explicitly what "dissemination" would mean in that case. His later disciples put forth various explanations, for example, that it referred to the spread of Namu Myōhō-renge-kyō in the mappō era.[16]

Nichiren was initially moved to remonstrate with government authorities by the suffering he had witnessed following a devastating earthquake in 1257. It was then that he composed and submitted his treatise *Risshō ankoku ron,* his first admonishment to persons in power. Initially he saw that earthquake as collective karmic retribution for the error of neglecting the *Lotus Sūtra.* But over time it came to evoke for him the shaking of "the whole buddha world" (5) in the "Introduction" chapter presaging Śākyamuni's preaching of the *Lotus.* Thus the 1257 quake assumed for him a second meaning as a harbinger of the spread of the daimoku of the *Lotus Sūtra,* the teaching for the Final Dharma age. "From the Shōka era (1257–1259) up until the present year (1273) there have been massive earthquakes and extraordinary celestial portents," he wrote. ". . . You should know that these are no ordinary auspicious or inauspicious omens concerning worldly affairs. They herald nothing less than the rise or decline of this great dharma."[17] Just as the quaking of the earth had presaged the Buddha's preaching of the *Lotus Sūtra,* a violent earthquake had preceded his own dissemination of the sūtra and the practice of chanting its daimoku. This is but one example of how Nichiren read the events of his own life and times as mirrored in the *Lotus Sūtra.*

CHAPTER TWO

Skillful Means

It is only in the second chapter of the *Lotus Sūtra* that the Buddha finally speaks. Most sūtras depict the Buddha preaching in response to a question from one or more of his auditors, but in the *Lotus Sūtra,* the Buddha arises from meditation (*samādhi*) and begins to speak spontaneously. Chinese commentators took this to mean that the *Lotus Sūtra* was not a teaching accommodated to his listeners' understanding, but directly expressed the Buddha's own insight. Śākyamuni begins by praising the wisdom of the buddhas, which he says is far beyond that of *śrāvaka*s and *pratyekabuddha*s. This is because buddhas, during their billions of past lives as bodhisattvas, trained under countless buddhas. Thus, "they have perfected this profound and unprecedented dharma, and their intention in adapting their explanations to what is appropriate is difficult to understand" (23). Śākyamuni goes on to say that he has taught the dharma using "skillful means" (*upāya*) so that beings might rid themselves of attachment. He has been able to do this because all of the buddhas "have attained mastery of skillful means, wisdom, and insight" (23). For modern readers of Mahāyāna sūtras, such statements may not seem particularly radical; "skillful means" is one of the most famous and common terms in the Mahāyāna lexicon.[1] However, in the context of the polemics that underlie so much of the *Lotus Sūtra,* the term "skillful means" is most consequential. Indeed, it is one of the reasons that the sūtra is so highly esteemed. But before examining the

Buddha's opening remarks more closely, let us consider to whom he spoke them.

One might expect that he would address his remarks to Maitreya or to Mañjuśrī, the two interlocutors in the sūtra up to this point, and both also bodhisattvas. But he speaks instead to the monk Śāriputra. In the mainstream Buddhist tradition, that is, the monastic majority, who were not Mahāyāna followers, Śāriputra was renowned as the wisest of the Buddha's disciples. Prior to becoming a disciple of the Buddha, he met a Buddhist monk and asked him what his teacher taught. When the monk demurred, saying that he was a beginner and thus unable to explain it in detail, Śāriputra asked for a summary. The monk replied with a single verse, "Of those things produced by causes, the Tathāgata has proclaimed their causes and also their cessation. Thus the great ascetic has spoken."[2] Merely by hearing those words, Śāriputra achieved the first level of enlightenment, the stage of the stream-enterer. According to tradition, the *abhidharma*, the part of the canon dealing with technical analysis of doctrine, was first taught by the Buddha to Śāriputra. Śāriputra was also one of the few monks whom the Buddha sanctioned to deliver discourses, so that some sūtras are spoken by Śāriputra rather than the Buddha.

Śāriputra is a śrāvaka and an arhat, having achieved the profound wisdom necessary to destroy all ignorance and to enter final nirvāṇa upon his death. In the mainstream tradition, the Buddha is also called an arhat because he has achieved that same wisdom and will enter *parinirvāṇa* at death. The primary difference between a buddha and an arhat in the early tradition appears to have been that a buddha discovers the path to nirvāṇa without relying on a teacher, while an arhat must rely on the Buddha's teachings to do so. A buddha also possesses certain supernormal powers that an arhat may not have, but both were held to partake equally in the liberating insight that is the goal of the Buddhist path. Because Śāriputra was the wisest of the arhats, one often asked to speak for the Buddha, there should not, from the perspective of the Buddhist mainstream, be a substantial difference between the wisdom of the Buddha and the wisdom of Śāriputra; there should not be something of substance that Śāriputra fails to understand, that is, not until these first remarks of Śākyamuni in the *Lotus Sūtra*. In another case of inversion, Śāriputra, like Maitreya in the preceding chapter, is perplexed.

At the conclusion of his opening comments, the Buddha says, "Enough, O Śāriputra, I will speak no further. Why is this? Because the dharma that the buddhas have attained is foremost, unique, and difficult to understand. No one but the buddhas can completely know the real aspects of all dharmas—that is to say their character, nature, substance, potential, function, cause, condition, result, effect, and essential unity" (23–24). Yet, the character, nature, substance, etc. of all dharmas is exactly what the Buddha had presumably taught to Śāriputra when he conveyed to him the *abhidharma* years earlier. These are things that Śāriputra understands better than any of the Buddha's disciples. But now in the *Lotus Sūtra*, the Buddha declares that only buddhas understand these things. (This statement would be cited often over the centuries to excuse the many who would find the *Lotus Sūtra* difficult to understand.) When the Buddha reiterates these points in verse, he says so explicitly: "Even if this whole world were filled with those such as Śāriputra, and they tried together to comprehend it, they still would not be able to understand completely the wisdom of the buddhas" (25).

The Buddha's statement is understandably disconcerting to Śāriputra and the other famous arhats in the audience. They had thought that there was a single liberation, nirvāṇa, which they believed that they had already achieved, yet Śākyamuni now says that the buddhas' wisdom is so profound that they cannot possibly comprehend it. They also do not understand why the Buddha is praising something they have never heard of before, something called "skillful means." At the time of the *Lotus Sūtra*'s composition, "skillful means" had not yet become a standard element of the Buddhist lexicon. Thus, on behalf of the assembly, Śāriputra asks the Buddha to explain why he has said these things, but the Buddha responds that he will not do so because the answer would be too astounding to gods and humans. It is only when Śāriputra asks a third time that the Buddha agrees to teach something that is impossible for the unenlightened to understand. But before he begins his explanation, one of the most remarkable scenes in Buddhist literature takes place: five thousand monks, nuns, and male and female lay disciples stand up, bow to the Buddha, and walk out. The sūtra explains that they did so because they were arrogant, "thinking that they had attained what they had not attained and had realized what they had not realized" (30). One does not generally walk out on the Buddha; the reason that they did so must be sought.

The *Lotus Sūtra*, like all Mahāyāna sūtras, is an apocryphal text, composed long after the Buddha's death and yet retrospectively attributed to him. To establish its authenticity, the *Lotus Sūtra* must produce its own community of faith, but it must also respond to its enemies, those who declare, with some historical justification, that the *Lotus Sūtra* is a fraud, a work that only pretends to be the word of the Buddha. This seems, in fact, to have been a frequent charge leveled by mainstream monastics against the Mahāyāna sūtras. When prominent monks and nuns of the Buddhist community in India, where the *Lotus Sūtra* first appeared, declared it to be spurious, noting, correctly, that it was not to be found anywhere in the various collections that had been compiled in the centuries since the Buddha's death, the proponents of the *Lotus Sūtra* had to respond. They could not claim that the sūtra appeared in the existing collections, because it did not. How could the *Lotus Sūtra* have been spoken by the Buddha without others knowing about it? One implicit explanation is that before the Buddha could teach the sūtra, five thousand members of the audience stood up and walked out. They did not know about the *Lotus Sūtra* because they were not there to hear it. If these arrogant monks and nuns had only stayed, they would have heard the Buddha preach the *Lotus Sūtra*. (Although we are now partway through the second chapter, the *Lotus Sūtra* has apparently not yet begun.) One could also see this mass exit as a criticism of those mainstream monastics who rejected the *Lotus Sūtra*. "The roots of error among this group had been deeply planted, and they were arrogant," we are told, and the Buddha himself is made to dismiss them as "useless twigs and leaves" (30).

Perhaps the sūtra begins now, when the Buddha, having finally agreed to preach, tells Śāriputra that it is very rare that a buddha teaches the true dharma (*saddharma*) that he is about to teach, as rare as the *uḍumbara* flower (a flower said to bloom once every three thousand years). It is noteworthy that the Buddha says that he is going to teach the "true dharma." This is the term that Mañjuśrī had used to describe what Candrasūryapradīpa had taught so long ago. And this, of course, is the term that appears in the full Sanskrit title—a title rarely used in English—of the *Lotus Sūtra*: "White Lotus of the True Dharma."

The teaching of the Buddha is of course called the dharma. The term *saddharma* means "true dharma" or "right dharma" and is widely used in Buddhist literature. Because *dharma* is a generic term for a doctrine or teaching, especially a religious doctrine, in ancient India, *saddharma* was sometimes used to distinguish the teaching of the Buddha from that of non-Buddhist teachers. Here, however, it means a doctrine that is more true, more correct, more real, than the doctrines that the Buddha has previously taught. The Buddha clearly implies that he is about to teach something new, although we know from the first chapter that it had also been taught by the buddhas of the distant past. It seems then, that this is the first time that Śākyamuni is going to teach the true dharma. In the Indian versions of the Buddha's life story, Prince Siddhārtha leaves the palace at age twenty-nine and then practices asceticism for six years, finally achieving enlightenment at the age of thirty-five. In Chapter Fifteen of the *Lotus Sūtra,* Maitreya says that more than forty years have passed since the Buddha achieved enlightenment. Thus, he is more than seventy-five years old when he preaches the *Lotus*. His teaching of the "true dharma" occurs late in his life.

This true dharma is both simple and shocking. Although the Buddha taught many doctrines using various skillful means, in fact, Śākyamuni declares, buddhas appear in the world for but one reason: to lead all sentient beings to buddhahood. Although he had in the past taught three paths or vehicles—the path of the śrāvaka, the path of the pratyekabuddha, and the path of the bodhisattva—in fact, there is but one vehicle, the buddha vehicle (*buddhayāna*). Everything that the buddhas teach is ultimately for that single purpose. Because the Buddha knows the inclinations and capacities of sentient beings, he uses various skillful means to teach them, yet he is leading them, however circuitously, to a single goal: buddhahood. Different Mahāyāna sūtras treat the status of arhatship—the goal of the mainstream tradition—in different ways, for example, as a lesser but still viable goal (as in *The Inquiry of Ugra*) or as an outright misunderstanding on the part of the Buddha's disciples (as in the *Vimalakīrti Sūtra*). There was a shared consensus, however, that persons of the first two vehicles, in liberating themselves from rebirth by achieving the goal of nirvāṇa, were thereby excluded from achieving the buddhahood that is gained on the bodhisattva path. The *Lotus Sūtra* is distinct in asserting that the apparent threefold division of the teaching into the distinct vehicles of śrāvakas, pratyekabuddhas, and bodhisattvas is only apparent: ultimately, all are following the bodhisattva path and will eventually become buddhas. This "revival" of śrāvakas, causing them to realize that they are actually bodhisattvas, was identified early on by Chinese exegetes as a crucial feature of the *Lotus*.

Because the notion of universal buddhahood now seems so obvious to those familiar with the Mahāyāna, it is difficult to imagine how radical this declaration of a single vehicle would have been in its own time. Up until this point, in the mainstream tradition, the goal of the Buddhist path was to become an arhat. The achievement of buddhahood was far more difficult, and the path to buddhahood was far longer; only the rarest of individuals in a given cosmic age was capable of undertaking that task. The arhat's path to nirvāṇa was shorter and easier. Furthermore, there was no need for many buddhas as long as the teaching of a single buddha remained known in the world; hence the idea that there is only one buddha in the world at a time. Here, the Buddha is therefore saying something new. While his disciples had thought that they were following the path of the two vehicles culminating in nirvāṇa, in reality, that was the Buddha's "skillful means," taught in order to guide them to the bodhisattva path. This revelation could not be ignored; Śākyamuni declares that those who claim to be arhats and yet do not accept that the buddhas "lead and inspire only bodhisattvas" (31) are not true arhats, nor are they true disciples of the Buddha.

He further declares that those who claim to be arhats and do not aspire to buddhahood are arrogant. It is impossible that a true arhat should not accept this dharma. He makes an exception for those who might become arhats after his death; such individuals might not believe in the single buddha vehicle because, after the Buddha has passed into nirvāṇa, it will be difficult to find people who preserve, recite, and understand the *Lotus Sūtra*. We have here again a barb directed at the opponents of the *Lotus Sūtra*. At the time of the text's composition, centuries after the Buddha's death, there would have been those who denied its authenticity. The sūtra, setting itself in the final years of the Buddha's life, explains that such people are merely ignorant of his true intent.

When the Buddha reiterates all this in verse, he provides a more detailed explanation of why he had taught three vehicles in the past, why, up until now, he had never said that all beings will follow the path to buddhahood, and why he is saying so now. Bringing the second chapter to its conclusion, this long verse section is one of the most powerful passages in the sūtra. Śākyamuni declares that the buddhas themselves have followed the bodhisattva path to buddhahood and, because they have achieved the supreme state themselves, they would not teach an inferior path to others; it would be ungenerous to do so. Yet if the Buddha taught the single vehicle to everyone, many would be confused and be unable to accept it because their merit is meager, as they have wandered for eons in the lower realms of saṃsāra. "That is why, O Śāriputra, I devised the method of teaching the way to extinguish all sufferings through nirvāṇa. Even though I taught nirvāṇa, it is not the true extinction" (37).

Not only Śākyamuni, we learn, but all buddhas of the past, present, and future have taught and will teach three vehicles as skillful means, but their true aim is to lead all beings to the single vehicle.

Other passages in the *Lotus Sūtra* describe the hardships of the bodhisattva path. But here we learn that gaining entry to the path is remarkably easy. The Buddha begins by making the standard claim that those who perform the six perfections (*pāramitās*) of giving, ethics, patience, effort, concentration, and wisdom—the so-called bodhisattva deeds—will attain the path of the buddhas. This is familiar doctrine in both the mainstream and Mahāyāna traditions. But then, in one of the most moving passages in the sūtra, he promises the same attainment for those who perform the far easier act of merely paying homage to stūpas. Even little children "who have drawn a buddha image with a blade of grass or a twig, brush or fingernail, such people, having gradually accumulated merit and perfected great compassion, have certainly attained the path of the buddhas" (39). The same is true for those who pay homage by making music or even make a low-pitched sound with their voice. "Those who, even with distracted minds have offered a single flower to a painted image will in due time see innumerable buddhas. Or those who have done obeisance to images, or merely pressed their palms together, or raised a single hand, or nodded their heads, will in due time see immeasurable buddhas" (40). For a tradition that by this time had already developed an architectonics of enlightenment notable for both its precision and its complexity, such declarations are revolutionary.

But why did the Buddha not teach the single vehicle until now? This crucial question was faced not only by the compilers of the *Lotus,* but by early Mahāyāna teachers more broadly. If, as they maintained, the Buddha had indeed intended others to follow the bodhisattva path as he had done, then why had he not said so? Why had he instead taught the path of the two vehicles, of śrāvakas and pratyekabuddhas, leading to nirvāṇa? To explain this, the *Lotus Sūtra* returns to the scene of the Buddha's enlightenment. It was here that the Buddha understood the nature of reality in its entirety. To offer a new vision of reality, and a new path to its realization, Buddhist authors retell the story of the Buddha's enlightenment. This retelling has occurred over the centuries of the history of Buddhism, and it occurs in the *Lotus Sūtra.*

According to a well-known account, after the Buddha achieved enlightenment under the Bodhi Tree, he remained in its vicinity for forty-nine days, relishing the experience and subsisting only on its power; he consumed no food during that time. He reflected that what he had realized was too profound for others to understand and that he should perhaps pass into final nirvāṇa without teaching. At this point, the god Brahmā descended from his heaven to implore the Buddha to teach, arguing that there were some "with little dust in their eyes" who would understand.

The *Lotus Sūtra* presents this scene, but with typical Mahāyāna excess; Brahmā is accompanied by other gods and hundreds of thousands of attendants, who entreat the Buddha to teach. And in the *Lotus Sūtra,* the Buddha's initial reluctance to teach is recast in terms specific to the *Lotus* itself: If he teaches the single buddha vehicle, many will reject it, causing them to be reborn as animals, hungry ghosts, or in the hells. He therefore should not teach but instead should enter nirvāṇa, that is, he should die, immediately. But then it occurs to him that he should teach something that many can accept; he should teach three vehicles, using skillful means, as the buddhas of the past had done. And, indeed, the buddhas of the ten directions immediately appear in order to endorse his decision.

In the standard version of the story, the Buddha surveys the world to determine who might have little dust in their eyes. He decides that his two old meditation teachers should be the first recipients of his teaching but then realizes that they have recently died. The next most deserving are the five ascetics with whom he had practiced various forms of self-mortification for six years, before they abandoned him for deciding that extreme asceticism is not the path of enlightenment. He discerned that they were living in a deer park near Vārāṇasī and set out to find them. When the Buddha arrived, he gave his first sermon, where he laid out the middle way, the four noble truths, and the eightfold path.

In the *Lotus Sūtra,* the Buddha tells this story in brief. But he says that when he encountered the five ascetics, he realized that what he wanted to explain to them could not be put into words; and so, employing skillful means, he used words like *nirvāṇa, arhat, dharma,* and *saṃgha*—words that for others represent the foundation of the Buddha's teaching. The Buddha goes on to explain to Śāriputra that now he is happy and fearless. He has set aside skillful means and teaches only the path to buddhahood. He predicts that, having heard this, the twelve hundred arhats in the audience and all the bodhisattvas will become buddhas.

Here we see the author or authors of the *Lotus Sūtra* displaying their remarkable rhetorical and doctrinal dexterity. They take the famous story of the Buddha's reluctance to teach and give it an entirely new meaning. In the original story, fearing that he will be misunderstood, the Buddha hesitates to teach at all. In the retelling, it is not that the Buddha is reluctant to teach at all after his enlightenment; he is reluctant to teach the unalloyed truth of the buddha vehicle. He is quite willing to teach something less than that truth, adapted to the limited capacities, the clouded eyes, of his audience. It is only in the *Lotus Sūtra* that the Buddha finally conveys the full content of his enlightenment. This retelling has important implications for the narrative of the tradition. In mainstream Buddhism, the first sermon to the group of five ascetics is a momentous event in cosmic history, as the Buddha for the first time turns the wheel of the dharma. In the *Lotus Sūtra,* that momentous event is reduced to a mere accommodation for those whose understanding is immature. Only in the *Lotus Sūtra* is the Buddha's true teaching revealed for the first time.

The *Lotus Sūtra* may be the first Buddhist text—and certainly the most famous Buddhist text—to acknowledge, at least tacitly, its own belatedness. It sets forth doctrines that had not been set forth before. The sūtra itself must explain this. And so we read in Chapter One that the *Lotus Sūtra* had been taught in the distant past; its present exposition only seems late because no one but Mañjuśrī can remember when a previous buddha taught it ages ago. Here in Chapter Two, the text acknowledges its belatedness in a different way. In other sūtras, the Buddha rarely comments on his earlier teachings. His comments on the past tend to be limited to past lives, when he recounts events in the previous rebirths of himself or others; sometimes he refers to past events in this existence, such as his life as Prince Siddhārtha in the palace or his practice of asceticism. We will learn in Chapter Fifteen that the *Lotus Sūtra* is being set forth late in the Buddha's life, some forty years after the Buddha's enlightenment (226), not long before his passage into final nirvāṇa. Here in Chapter Two, he provides a commentary on his own earlier teachings, looking back on the teaching of what he had taught long ago, accounting for it, and almost renouncing it. Central to this retelling is the claim that had befuddled Śāriputra and the other arhats: that the apparent division of the Buddha's teaching into three vehicles was the Buddha's "skillful means" that lead ultimately to the one buddha vehicle. In the words of the great Chinese exegete Zhiyi, the *Lotus* "opens the three vehicles to reveal the one vehicle." The sūtra's initial declaration of this teaching appears here in the second chapter and is further elaborated in Chapters Three through Nine by means of parables and other explanations. In Zhiyi's analysis, these eight chapters together constitute the "main exposition" section of the sutra's first half or trace teaching (*shakumon* in Japanese). They may also represent the earliest stratum of the sūtra's compilation.

In its original context, the message of the "one buddha vehicle" first articulated in Chapter Two was directed from the marginal Mahāyāna movement toward the Buddhist mainstream, that is, the majority of monks and nuns who counted themselves as śrāvakas and aspired to the arhat's nirvāṇa. But a thousand years later, in medieval Japan, the Mahāyāna was the mainstream; that is, Japanese Buddhism was entirely Mahāyāna, and there were no śrāvakas, except those mentioned in texts. Largely through the influence of the *Lotus*-based Tendai Buddhist tradition, the idea that buddhahood is at least in theory open to all had gained wide currency. In Nichiren's reading, the thrust of the *Lotus Sūtra*'s one-vehicle argument therefore shifts in significant ways. No longer is it about opening buddhahood to specific categories of persons previously excluded, that is, to people of the two lesser vehicles. Rather, it is about opening buddhahood as a reality for all beings, in contrast to what Nichiren deemed purely abstract or notional assurances of buddhahood in other, provisional Mahāyāna teachings. Recall that, in the Tendai tradition in which Nichiren had been trained, the *Lotus Sūtra* is "true" and all others are "provisional," meaning that the *Lotus Sūtra* is complete and all-encompassing, while other teachings are accommodated to their listeners' understanding and therefore partial and incomplete. For Nichiren, now in the age of the Final Dharma, only the *Lotus Sūtra* embodied the principles by which Buddhist practitioners could truly realize enlightenment. Drawing on his Tendai roots, he described these principles as the "mutual encompassing of the ten realms" and the "single thought-moment that is three thousand realms," which we discussed briefly in the Authors' Introduction. These principles are, undeniably, somewhat complex. But to understand why Nichiren believed that the *Lotus Sūtra* alone offered access to the Buddha wisdom, we must delve into them more deeply. Let us begin by considering a single sentence, whose interpretation lies at the heart of much Tendai doctrine and also of Nichiren's.

In the opening passage of Chapter Two, Śākyamuni declares that only buddhas can "completely know the real aspects of all dharmas—that is to say, their character, nature, substance, potential, function, cause, condition, result, effect, and essential unity" (24). No extant Sanskrit version of the *Lotus* contains precisely this wording. Though Kumārajīva may have worked from an unknown Sanskrit version of the *Lotus*, as some scholars have suggested, the expression "true aspects of the dharmas" appears to have been coined by him and occurs in several of his translations. His Chinese translation of the *Dazhi du lun* ("Treatise on the Great Perfection of Wisdom," *T* 1509) also contains close counterparts to the list of the ten aspects in this passage from the *Lotus Sūtra*. Thus, several scholars have suggested that the passage reflects Kumārajīva's understanding.[3]

In the East Asian commentarial tradition, this passage is referred to as the "ten suchnesses" or "such-likes" (J. *junyoze*) because each of the "real aspects" is preceded in the Chinese text by the words "suchness" or more literally "like such" (*nyoze*). "Such" or "suchness" (*tathatā* in Sanskrit) is one of many terms for reality in Buddhism, denoting that a buddha perceives things just as they are, without imposing reifying concepts or descriptions. In their translation, Kubo and Yuyama call these ten the "real aspects" of the dharmas or phenomena, but one could also refer to them collectively in the singular as the "real aspect" shared by all phenomena. By punctuating this passage that enumerates the "ten suchnesses" in three different ways, Zhiyi derived the threefold truth (outlined in the Authors' Introduction to this volume) of emptiness, conventional existence, and the middle.[4] To this day, the passage is often ritually recited three times, representing the threefold truth and its threefold discernment.

What do "character, nature, substance, potential . . . and essential unity" actually mean? Here we will bracket the intentions of the sūtra's compilers and focus on the Chinese commentarial tradition. Zhanran, Zhiyi's later disciple, explains that these ten can be grouped in three modalities—form, mind, and causality—that characterize all existents. "Character," which could also be translated as "mark," "sign," or "aspect," is what can be seen externally; in the case of a person, it denotes one's outer appearance. "Nature" is internal, what belongs to that person intrinsically. "Substance" denotes the union of these two as a particular individual; each existent, in Tendai thought, has both physical and mental aspects. "Potential" is the capacity for action, while "function" is the exertion or display of that potential. These two suchnesses thus pertain to space. "Cause, condition, result, [and] effect" refer to the dimension of causality, and therefore, time. "Causes" are volitional acts, or karma. "Conditions" are the circumstances that condition actions. "Result" is the potential karmic consequence inherent in a volitional act, and "effect" is its eventual manifestation. All ten are "essentially unified," or ultimately consistent. For example, the character, nature, function, causes, and results of a denizen of hell will reflect and perpetuate misery; those of a bodhisattva will express insight and compassion.

On the basis of this passage, Zhiyi formulated a grand, architectonic concept that came to be called the "single thought-moment entailing three thousand realms" (*ichinen sanzen*). In a famous passage, he writes: "Now a single thought [literally, "one mind"] comprises ten dharma-realms, and each dharma-realm also comprises ten dharma-realms, giving a hundred dharma-realms. A single realm comprises thirty kinds of worlds; hence a hundred dharma-realms comprise three thousand kinds of worlds. These three thousand are contained in a single moment of thought. Where there is no thought, that is the end of the matter, but if there is even the slightest thought, it immediately contains the three thousand [realms]."[5]

This is a crucial passage and requires some unpacking. Briefly, the "three thousand realms" denotes "all dharmas" or "all phenomena." In that sense, the number "three thousand" might be considered somewhat arbitrary. Nonetheless, it refers to a constant set of patterns that for Zhiyi constituted the "real aspect of the dharmas." The ten dharma-realms, from hell to buddhahood, have already been introduced. Because each one contains all ten within itself, there are a hundred realms, each endowed with the ten suchnesses. The resulting thousand realms each entail another "three realms" or three aspects of living beings: (1) the "five aggregates (*skandhas*)," or momentary mental and physical constiuents that unite temporarily to form living beings; (2) living beings considered as individuals belonging to one or another of the ten realms, such as hell dwellers, hungry ghosts, humans, and others; and (3) the insentient container worlds, or environments, that living beings inhabit.

In translating, we often say "three thousand realms *in* a single thought-moment" because that is natural English, but, strictly speaking, it is not correct. As Zhiyi goes on to explain: "Were the mind to give rise to all phenomena, that would be a vertical [relationship]. Were all phenomena to be simultaneously contained within the mind, that would be a horizontal [relationship]. Neither horizontal nor vertical will do. It is simply that the mind is all phenomena and all phenomena are the mind. . . . [This relationship] is subtle and profound in the extreme; it can neither be grasped conceptually nor expressed in words. Therefore, it is called the realm of the inconceivable."[6]

In essence, the most minute phenomenon (a single thought-moment) and the entire cosmos (three thousand realms) are mutually encompassing: the one and the many, good and evil, delusion and awakening, subject and object, self and other, and all sentient beings from hell dwellers, hungry ghosts, and animals up through buddhas and bodhisattvas as well as their corresponding insentient environments—indeed, all things in the entire cosmos—are inseparable from the mind at each moment. However, only in the state of buddhahood is this fully realized. Zhanran comments, "You should know that person and land both encompass three thousand realms in one thought-moment. Thus, when we attain the way, in accordance with this principle, our body and mind at each instant pervade the dharma-realm."[7]

Nichiren took the *ichinen sanzen* concept that Zhiyi had briefly delineated and made it the foundation of his teaching. For Nichiren, *ichinen sanzen* was "the father and mother of the buddhas."[8] He often referred to it in its "short form," so to speak, as the mutual inclusion of the ten dharma realms (also discussed above in the Authors' Introduction to this volume). Because the "ten suchnesses" (referred to at the beginning of the "Skillful Means" chapter) and the mutual inclusion of the ten realms are both concepts integral to the single thought-moment that is three thousand realms, the one implied the other, and Nichiren could take "the real aspect of all dharmas" or the ten suchnesses as pointing to the mutual inclusion of the ten realms. For him, this teaching was unique to the *Lotus Sūtra* and was what qualified it as the "wonderful dharma." In one passage, he writes: "The sūtras that the Buddha preached for more than forty years before the *Lotus* do not set forth the mutual inclusion of the ten realms. And because they do not set forth the mutual inclusion of the ten realms, one cannot know the buddha realm within one's own mind, and because one does not know the buddha realm within one's own mind, the buddhas do not manifest externally either. . . . But now with the *Lotus Sūtra,* the buddha realm within the nine realms was opened, and those who had heard the Buddha's forty and more years of preaching—bodhisattvas, persons of the two vehicles, and ordinary beings of the six paths—could for the first time see the buddha realm within themselves."[9]

Like other Buddhists of his day, Nichiren understood the six paths as actual cosmological realms into which beings are born repeatedly in accordance with their deeds, and the four holy paths of śrāvakas, pratyekabuddhas, bodhisattvas, and buddhas, as higher states achieved through cultivation. But at the same time, he understood all ten realms as lying "within ourselves." In his major treatise "On the Contemplation of the Mind and the Object of Worship" (*Kanjin honzon shō*), Nichiren explains this by way of illustration. When one looks at another person's face, they appear sometimes ecstatic, sometimes furious, and sometimes calm, or they might wear expressions of foolishness or perversity. Rage, he explains, is the hell realm; greed, the realm of hungry ghosts; foolishness, the realm of beasts; perversity, the *asura* realm; joy, the heavenly realm; and calm, the human realm. The four holy paths do not appear outwardly but can be known by introspection. Our understanding that all things are insubstantial and fleeting reflects the realms of the two vehicles of śrāvakas and pratyekabuddhas within our own mind. The affection that even a hardened criminal feels for his wife and children is an expression of the inner bodhisattva realm. Because the nine realms within one's own mind can thus be demonstrated, Nichiren says, one should believe that the buddha realm is present as well.[10]

In the above quotation, "seeing" the Buddha in one's mind might suggest a specific cognition or insight, but for Nichiren, this meant chanting the daimoku, the expression of faith in the *Lotus Sūtra*. Though he encouraged study and intellectual understanding of the Buddhist teachings, the benefits of the daimoku, he said, are the same whether chanted by a wise person or a foolish one. He illustrated this by the analogies of fire that burns without intent to do so, or a newborn infant nourished unknowingly by its mother's milk.[11] At the beginning of the present chapter, when Śākyamuni Buddha first begins to speak, his opening words are: "Profound and immeasurable is the wisdom of the buddhas" (23). "What is this wisdom?" Nichiren asks. "It is the embodiment of the real aspect of all dharmas, the ten suchnesses realized by the Buddha. What is that embodiment? It is Namu Myōhō-renge-kyō."[12]

The interpenetration of ten realms reveals that, in principle, there is no difference between an ordinary person and a buddha; both embody the three thousand realms in a single thought-moment. But in ordinary, deluded persons the buddha realm remains dormant and unrealized, and they are trapped by suffering. In the case of a buddha, the buddha realm is fully expressed; that is, all the other nine realms are illuminated, elevated, and redirected by it to work in an enlightened way. For Nichiren, this fully realized state was embodied in the daimoku. We could say that chanting the daimoku aligns or "syncs" the ten realms and three thousand realms of the practitioner with those of the Buddha, enabling direct realization in the very act of practice.

This second chapter of the *Lotus Sūtra* represents the Buddha as declaring, "I will now definitely expound the truth" (26) and "having openly set aside skillful means, I will teach only the highest path" (45). These statements, together with the passage from the *Lotus Sūtra*'s introductory scripture, *Sūtra of Immeasurable Meanings*—"For more than forty years I have expounded the dharma in all manner of ways through adeptness in skillful means, but the core truth has still not been revealed"—constituted for Nichiren significant proof that the *Lotus Sūtra* superseded all prior, provisional teachings. They were, he said, like a great wind scattering dark clouds, the full moon appearing in the heavens, or the orb of the sun blazing in the blue sky, revealing the possibility of buddhahood for all.[13]

Zhiyi had taught that the *Lotus Sūtra* has the function of "opening and integrating" (J. *kaie*) the three vehicles within the one vehicle. We have seen above how Nichiren understood this as opening the nine realms to reveal the buddha realm. But what did it mean in terms of practice? Nichiren's contemporaries often freely combined copying and reciting the *Lotus Sūtra* with nenbutsu chanting, esoteric rituals, and other modes of Buddhist devotion. For many Tendai scholars of the day, the distinction between true and provisional teachings did not mean renouncing practices other than the *Lotus Sūtra*. It would indeed be a mistake, they said, to recite other sūtras or chant the names of the various buddhas and bodhisattvas thinking that these represented separate truths. But the one vehicle of the *Lotus Sūtra* integrates all other teachings within itself, just as the great ocean gathers all rivers. Therefore, they claimed, any practice—whether esoteric ritual performance, sūtra copying, or nenbutsu recitation—in effect becomes the practice of the *Lotus Sūtra* when carried out with this understanding. Others, however, disagreed, and none more vocally than Nichiren. To argue his point, he inverted the "rivers and ocean" metaphor. Once integrated into the *Lotus Sūtra*, he said, the nenbutsu, esoteric rites, and other practices lose their identity as independent practices, just as the many rivers emptying into the ocean assume the same salty flavor and lose their original names.[14] Precisely because provisional teachings are integrated into the all-encompassing principle of the one vehicle, they are no longer to be practiced as independent forms. At the same time, however, Nichiren insisted that the daimoku contains all truth and blessings within itself. Because the daimoku is all-encompassing, chanting it would confer all the benefits that the religious practices of his day were thought to produce: this-worldly benefits such as protection and healing, assurance for the afterlife, and buddhahood itself. His aim was not to eradicate the spectrum of religious interpretations, but to undercut their basis in other traditions and assimilate them to the *Lotus Sūtra* alone.

CHAPTER THREE

A Parable

As Chapter Three begins, Śāriputra changes sides. In yet another polemical device, the hero of the so-called Hīnayāna becomes an advocate for the Mahāyāna. He explains that, in the past, he felt excluded when the Buddha gave instruction to bodhisattvas and predicted their eventual buddhahood. He was haunted by the question of why the Buddha would teach an inferior vehicle to him and to the other śrāvakas. But now he realizes that the fault was his. He did not understand that the Buddha was using skillful means and that he would eventually reveal the true teaching. Now he can rejoice in the knowledge that he will one day also attain the many qualities of a buddha's body, speech, and mind. This is the first instance in the sūtra where joy on encountering the *Lotus* is represented as a sign of keen spiritual receptivity and an indication of future buddhahood. Śāriputra confesses, however, that when the Buddha began to proclaim the single vehicle (presumably, in the previous chapter), denying that the nirvāṇa of the arhat was the true nirvāṇa, he experienced a moment of doubt. He wondered whether it was really the Buddha who was speaking or whether it might instead be Māra impersonating the Buddha.

Māra is the Buddhist devil, the deity of death and desire who is the Buddha's chief antagonist, attacking him as he sat in meditation beneath the Bodhi Tree on the night of his great awakening. When Māra and his minions were unable to prevent his enlightenment, Māra urged the Buddha to pass into nirvāṇa as soon as possible, without teaching others. Seeking to keep beings trapped in the cycle of birth and death, Māra appears in many stories and in various guises to turn the Buddha's disciples away from the path. Thus, in Buddhism, a standard way to condemn what is judged to be a heretical teaching is to call it a teaching of Māra, to say that the proponents of such a teaching are followers of Māra, not of the Buddha, that the supposed heretic, or the heretic's teacher, is Māra in disguise. We can imagine that such a charge may well have been leveled against the *Lotus Sūtra*. Thus, the author or authors seek to counter such charges by having Śāriputra, the embodiment of orthodoxy, anticipate them, confessing that for a moment he thought that Māra had taken on the guise of the Buddha and then taught the single vehicle. If Śāriputra, the wisest of the śrāvakas, had such a doubt himself, it is natural that others would share it. But Śāriputra goes on to say, "The Bhagavat teaches the real path, but the Wicked One does not. Therefore, I know definitely that it was not Māra acting like the Buddha" (52).

At the end of Śāriputra's long speech, the Buddha explains that he had taught Śāriputra the true dharma many times in previous lifetimes, but Śāriputra had forgotten it. "Now, because I want you to remember the path that you practiced according to your original vow in the past, I will teach the śrāvakas the Mahāyāna sūtra called the *Lotus Sūtra,* the instruction for the bodhisattvas and the treasured lore of the buddhas" (53). Apparently, here in the middle of Chapter Three, the *Lotus Sūtra* still has not started. Also noteworthy here is the indication—the first in the sūtra—that Śākymuni has been teaching since before the present lifetime. Again, we see the theme of a forgotten past recalled to memory in the sūtra's narrative.

There is great power in the Buddha's declaration that there is but one vehicle, the buddha vehicle. But in some ways, it is an abstract statement. According to mainstream Buddhist doctrine, merely having the wish to liberate all sentient beings from suffering is not enough to make one a bodhisattva and guarantee one's future buddhahood. Such a person must also receive a prophecy (*vyākaraṇa*) from a buddha in which that buddha predicts where, when, and with what name the person will become a buddha in the future. Śākyamuni, for example, in a prior life is said to have received such a prophecy from the buddha Dīpaṃkara. In one of the pivotal moments in the *Lotus Sūtra,* Śākyamuni Buddha now makes such a prophecy for Śāriputra, predicting that immeasurable eons hence, he will become a buddha named Padmaprabha ("Lotus Light") in a land named Viraja ("Free from Dust") during an eon called Mahāratnapratimaṇḍita ("Adorned with Great Jewels"). His lifespan will be twelve intermediate eons. The audience rejoices at the Buddha's prediction, and the gods rain down flowers from the heavens.

As noted previously, the teaching of the Buddha is called "turning the wheel of the dharma," and he is said to have first turned the wheel when he taught the middle way, the four truths, and the eightfold path to the group of five ascetics in the Deer Park in Sarnath, outside Vārāṇasī. The Buddha having set the wheel of the dharma in motion, it turned throughout his life, as he taught the dharma until his passage into nirvāṇa. But at this point in the *Lotus Sūtra,* after the prediction of Śāriputra's buddhahood, the gods confirm what the Buddha has already implied: that he has now again turned the wheel of "the subtlest, utmost, and greatest dharma" (57). This is a consequential claim, implying that what the *Lotus Sūtra* teaches surpasses and supersedes the teachings that have come before. We should note that a later sūtra, the *Saṃdhinirmocana*, states that the Buddha turned the wheel of the dharma a third time, and some claim that the Buddhist tantras are a fourth turning. The world awaits the fifth wheel.

Rejoicing at the prediction of his future buddhahood, Śāriputra asks the Buddha why he appears to be contradicting what he had said in the past. The twelve hundred arhats in the audience believed that they had attained nirvāṇa. "Yet now, in the presence of the Bhagavat, they have heard what they have never heard before and have fallen into doubt" (58). The Buddha responds, rather testily, that he has already explained that buddhas teach the dharma using skillful means. But perhaps realizing that this single statement is not enough, he embarks on the first, and most famous, parable in the *Lotus Sūtra,* and perhaps in Buddhist literature.

An elderly wealthy man has a large house, which, despite his affluence, is in serious disrepair. In the lengthy description of the house in the verse portion of the parable, it is filled with all manner of vermin and monsters, a scene worthy of a horror movie. The man has many children, who are playing in the house. A fire breaks out, and the father is at a loss as to how to take all of his children to safety; the house has a single entrance, and there is no time for him to carry them out one by one. He calls to them to run out of the house, but the children are so engrossed in their games that they disregard his warning; what is worse, they do not even know what "fire" is. So the father devises a plan to lure the children out of the burning house. Knowing that they like different kinds of toys, he tells them that waiting outside are three kinds of carts: one pulled by a sheep, one by a deer, and one by an ox. The children rush out of the house to safety, demanding their carts. However, the father gives them each just one kind of a cart, a magnificent cart decorated with jewels, flower garlands, fabrics, and pillows, each pulled by a strong and swift white ox. He is able to give each of his children the best of carts because of his great affluence. The children, filled with delight, climb onto their carts.

Having told the tale, the Buddha asks Śāriputra whether the father lied to the children when he promised them three kinds of carts. Śāriputra replies that it was not a lie. The father was trying to save his children's lives. It would not have been a lie even if there had been no cart. But the father not only saved his children, he gave them each a better cart than the one he promised.

The elements of the allegory are not hard to parse, but the Buddha explains them at some length. He is the father of the world (there is no mention of a mother); the father's wealth is the Buddha's wisdom. The dilapidated house is saṃsāra, aflame with the afflictions of desire, hatred, and ignorance. Sentient beings, the Buddha's children, are beset with attachments, blithely at play in a world of sorrow, unable to recognize the dangers that surround them. If the Buddha were to proclaim the one buddha vehicle, they would not understand. The Buddha therefore does not reveal the full truth but instead uses skillful means to teach three vehicles; the Sanskrit word *yāna*, translated in Buddhist contexts as "vehicle," is a generic term for any form of conveyance, including a cart. The three are the śrāvaka vehicle, the pratyekabuddha vehicle, and the bodhisattva vehicle. Once his disciples have entered these vehicles and overcome their attachment to the world, the Buddha reveals to them the single vehicle, the great vehicle, the Mahāyāna.

This seems clear enough; but it is unclear whether the one cart, the cart pulled by the ox, was one among the three that the father promised or was an entirely different one, for when the children arrive to claims their carts, the single cart that they find is far grander than anything the father described as he tried to lure them from the flames. This question is not simply a matter of the father's rhetoric. If the single cart that the children find is one of the three that the father originally promised, then the one vehicle is the bodhisattva vehicle, a vehicle that will carry all beings on the long path to buddhahood. In that case, the other two vehicles are "skillful means," and the Mahāyāna represents the full truth that is the buddha vehicle. But if the splendid oxcart given to the children is entirely different from the oxcart that the father had promised, then the one vehicle is something other than the bodhisattva vehicle, raising the possibility that the Mahāyāna itself might be a "skillful means." Thus, the one vehicle is a vehicle that transcends the other three and, in a sense, is the goal itself. Passages in the *Lotus Sūtra* can be found to support either interpretation, and the issue was debated by East Asian exegetes, among whom it became known as the "three carts or four carts" controversy. Those in the latter camp, which included Zhiyi and other prominent Tiantai thinkers, took the position that there were four vehicles, and that in the *Lotus Sūtra* the Buddha does not simply reveal that there is but one vehicle, but that it is a vehicle whose existence he had never revealed before. The ramifications of this debate were quite complex and included attempts to reconcile the two positions.[1]

The verse reiteration of the parable concludes with the most disquieting passage in the *Lotus Sūtra*, where the Buddha describes in grisly detail the horrible fate that awaits those who reject the *Lotus Sūtra*. He begins by telling Śāriputra that the sūtra should only be taught to the wise; those of superficial awareness will not be able to comprehend it and will only be confused. Even Śāriputra, the wisest of the arhats, is only able to understand the sūtra through faith. The sūtra should thus never be taught to the arrogant and lazy, for if they disparage the sūtra, they will "destroy the seed of the Buddha in the entire world" (76), and they will go to hell when they die.

The Buddhist cosmos contains an elaborate system of hells, located beneath the earth. The hells are reserved for those who commit various sins, including the standard crimes of murder, rape, and robbery. The hells tend to be populated by the followers of other religions; the Buddha's disciple Maudgalyāyana would often use his supernormal powers to travel to the hells, where he would find the teachers of other religions. He would then return to inform the followers of their masters' fates. Buddhists are rarely consigned to hell if they keep their vows and do not commit any of the ten nonvirtuous deeds. The most miserable of the Buddhist hells, located at the bottom of the stack of eight hot hells, is called Avīci, or "Incessant." Here the suffering is the worst and the lifespan is the longest before one is eventually reborn elsewhere. That hell is typically reserved for those who commit one of the five heinous sins in Buddhism: killing one's father, killing one's mother, killing an arhat, wounding the Buddha, and causing a schism in the monastic community.

At the end of the third chapter, the Buddha explains that those who disparage the *Lotus Sūtra* and who "despise, hate, and hold grudges against the people who recite, copy, and preserve it" (77) will be reborn in Avīci when they die. After eons in hell, they will then be reborn as dogs with leprosy or as snakes eaten by insects. If they are reborn as humans, they will be crippled, stupid runts, blind, deaf, and humpbacked. No one will believe what they say and their breath will be foul. The threats go on for three pages (the Buddha says it would take more than an eon to describe all the consequence of disparaging the sūtra), suggesting, among other things, that there must have been some opposition to the early reception of the teachings that would become the *Lotus Sūtra*. There must have been many whom the devotees of the *Lotus* imagined, and perhaps hoped, were destined to these variously horrible fates. There is a certain "us versus them" mentality in the chapter's conclusion. The Buddha exhorts Śāriputra to take care in deciding to whom the sūtra should be revealed. The stakes are high.

In the *Lotus Sūtra*'s narrative, Śāriputra is the first śrāvaka to receive the Buddha's prediction of his future buddhahood. "When Śāriputra heard this," Nichiren wrote, "he not only cut off the illusions arising from primal ignorance and reached the stage of the true cause [for liberation] but was acclaimed as the [future] tathāgata Padmaprabha [Lotus Light]. . . . This was the beginning of the attainment of buddhahood by all beings of the ten realms."[2] For Nichiren, as discussed earlier, the *Lotus Sūtra*'s message that persons of the two lesser vehicles could attain buddhahood was not about extending this possibility to a group of previously excluded individuals but, rather, established the mutual inclusion of the ten realms as the ground that, for the first time, opened buddhahood as a real possibility to anyone.

We have seen how Zhiyi divided both the trace and the origin teaching into introductory, main exposition, and dissemination sections. Within the trace teaching, or the first fourteen chapters, Chapters Two through Chapter Nine represent the main exposition. They set forth and restate from multiple perspectives the idea that the buddhas come into the world with a single intent, to lead all beings to buddhahood, and that the seeming divergences among their teachings—such as the division into śrāvaka, pratyekabuddha, and bodhisattva paths—merely represent the "skillful means" by which they lead persons of different capacities toward supreme enlightenment. Most of the *Lotus Sūtra*'s famous parables occur in these chapters. By Nichiren's time, educated people were often familiar with these stories, and the *Lotus Sūtra*'s message that all could attain buddhahood was widely accepted—although how that buddhahood was to be achieved and how long it might take were subjects of debate. Nichiren himself sometimes alludes to these parables in advocating the daimoku as the path of realizing buddhahood in the present age, but he rarely dwells on them at length.

Nichiren makes only limited reference to the parable of the burning house that occupies most of this chapter's narrative. In a few passages, he refers to the great cart drawn by a white ox metaphorically as the vehicle that will carry *Lotus Sūtra* practitioners to the "the pure land of Vulture Peak," that is, the realm of enlightenment, or as a war chariot that he rides in a great dharma battle between true and provisional teachings.[3] He does not provide an extended discussion of the parable itself. Rather, as we go through these initial chapters of the *Lotus*, we will see how Nichiren drew out the significance of other passages that might not seem central to the sūtra's narrative but that assume considerable importance in his reading, a reading that was shaped by the sūtra's reception history, by his contemporary circumstances, and by his own perspective.

For example, in interpreting the parable of the burning house, the Buddha says to Śāriputra: "Now this triple world is my property and the sentient beings in it are my children. There are now many dangers here and I am the only one who can protect them" (72). Nichiren interpreted this passage as expressing Śākyamuni Buddha's three virtues of sovereign, teacher, and parent, which are mentioned briefly in a commentary on the *Nirvāṇa Sūtra* by Zhiyi's disciple Guanding

(561–632).[4] Nichiren asserted repeatedly that only Śākyamuni Buddha of the *Lotus Sūtra* possesses these virtues with respect to all beings of the present, Sahā world: He protects them, like a powerful ruler; he guides them, like an enlightened teacher; and he extends compassionate affection to them, like a benevolent parent. In contrast, other buddhas, such as Mahāvairocana (J. Dainichi), Bhaiṣajyaguru (Yakushi), or Amitābha (Amida), have no such connection to this world-sphere: "The buddha Amitābha is not our sovereign, not our parent, and not our teacher."[5] This reading enabled Nichiren to depict the devotion to the buddha Amitābha, so popular in his day, as the unfilial act of honoring a stranger above one's own parent, or as even a form of treason, such as venerating the ruler of China or Korea over the ruler of Japan.[6]

What particularly drew Nichiren's attention in the "Parable" chapter was the long segment of the final verse section detailing the horrific karmic retribution incurred by those who disparage the *Lotus Sūtra* (76–80). The act of "disparaging the dharma" (S. *saddharmapratikṣepa*, J. *hōbō*, also translated as "slandering" or "maligning" the dharma) was considered so grave a sin that in East Asia it was sometimes appended to the list of the five heinous deeds. The term occurs frequently in the Mahāyāna sūtras, where it often means maligning the Great Vehicle scriptures; in its Indic context, it was probably intended to counter the mainstream Buddhist criticism that the Mahāyāna was not the Buddha's teaching.

Japanese Buddhists, however, understood theirs to be a "Mahāyāna country." Unlike the situation faced by the *Lotus Sūtra*'s compilers, no one questioned the Mahāyāna's legitimacy. Nichiren therefore took the term "dharma slander" in a different sense, to mean rejecting the *Lotus Sūtra* in favor of provisional teachings. He had first leveled this accusation against the followers of Hōnen, who taught that one should set aside all practices other than the nenbutsu as too profound for the capacity of ordinary persons of the Final Dharma age and rely solely upon the buddha Amitābha's compassionate vow to achieve birth after death in his pure land. Nichiren was by no means the only person to condemn Hōnen's exclusive nenbutsu teaching as "disparaging the dharma." Other critics, however, based their objections on the widely held premise that the Buddha had taught multiple forms of practice for persons of different capacities; claiming exclusive validity for one practice alone was "disparaging the dharma" because it rejected the multitude of other Buddhist teachings and practices such as keeping the precepts, meditation, esoteric ritual performance, reciting sūtras, and so forth.

Nichiren's criticism had a different thrust: namely, that the Pure Land teachings were provisional and therefore unsuited to the present time, the age of the Final Dharma. They did not set forth the mutual inclusion of the ten realms that enabled all persons to realize buddhahood here in this world, in this body, but instead deferred it to another realm after death. By his time, a generation or so after Hōnen, exclusive nenbutsu followers were specifically urging people to abandon the *Lotus Sūtra,* which they claimed was too profound for people in this benighted era. In Nichiren's view, this was disparaging the dharma. To discourage people from practicing the *Lotus Sūtra* because it was beyond their capacity was far worse than direct verbal abuse of the sūtra, because it threatened to drive the *Lotus* into obscurity, closing off the one teaching powerful enough to liberate people of the present evil age. "The *Lotus Sūtra* is the eyes of all the buddhas," he wrote. "It is the original teacher of Śākyamuni Buddha, master of teachings. One who discards even a single character or brush dot commits a sin graver than killing one's parents ten million times or shedding the blood of all buddhas in the ten directions."[7]

Nichiren's understanding of dharma slander included not only verbal disparagement, as the term suggests, but the mental act of rejection or disbelief. As he declared, "To be born in a country where the *Lotus Sūtra* has spread and neither to have faith in it nor practice it, is disparaging the dharma."[8] In other words, one could be guilty of "disparaging the dharma" without malign intent, even without knowledge that one was doing so, simply by following a teacher who had set the *Lotus* aside in favor of lesser, provisional teachings. Nichiren initially leveled this charge against Hōnen's followers but later expanded it to include both Shingon and Tendai adepts who subordinated the *Lotus Sūtra* to the esoteric teachings; practitioners of Zen, who emphasized its "wordless transmission" over the Buddhist scriptures in general; as well as movements to revitalize precept observance, which based themselves on precepts grounded in provisional teachings.

Like his contemporaries, Nichiren embraced the idea that human beings are an integral part of the cosmos, and their actions affect both society and the natural world. He attributed the disasters confronting Japan during his lifetime—famine, epidemics, earthquakes, and the Mongol threat—to this fundamental error of "disparaging the *Lotus Sūtra*." Rejection of the sūtra, in his eyes, would destroy the country in this life; in the future, it would condemn its people to countless rebirths in the Avīci hell. The horrific sufferings described in the verse section of the present chapter were for him not mere rhetorical hyperbole but an actual account, coming from the Buddha's own mouth, of the fate that awaited the great majority of his contemporaries, something that grieved him deeply.

The modern reader may quickly grow impatient with Nichiren's harping on the Avīci hell. People at the time, however, envisioned the hells as actual postmortem destinations and depicted their torments in gruesome detail in narrative scroll paintings and didactic tales. Many thought that, without some form of earnest effort in Buddhist practice, rebirth in the lower realms would be inevitable. Hell had come to stand for the entire samsaric process. Although inflected through his *Lotus* exclusivism, Nichiren's frequent references to frightful karmic retribution in the afterlife were consistent with his larger religious milieu. The resolve to close off that terrible possibility both for himself and others was part of what motivated his aggressive proselytizing.

Buddhist sūtras specify two approaches to teaching the dharma: *shōju*, or leading others gradually without criticizing their present stance, and *shakubuku*, or actively rebuking attachment to false views. The choice between them, Nichiren said, should depend on the time and place. In his view, in Japan at the beginning of the Final Dharma age—a time and place where the *Lotus Sūtra* was being rejected in favor of provisional teachings—the confrontational *shakubuku* method should take precedence over the more accommodating *shōju* approach.

Because the consequences of slandering the *Lotus Sūtra* are so frightful, in the verse section of this third chapter of the sūtra, after summarizing the karmic retribution that would attend that offense, the Buddha admonishes Śāriputra "never to expound this sūtra to those who have little wisdom. . . . You should teach the *Lotus Sūtra* to those who are able to accept it" (80, 81). Some among Nichiren's disciples wondered why he himself failed to follow this injunction. Would one not do better to lead people gradually through provisional teachings, as Śākyamuni Buddha himself had done, rather than insisting on immediately preaching the *Lotus Sūtra* to persons whose minds were not open to it? In Nichiren's understanding, however, the sūtra's warning against preaching the *Lotus Sūtra* to the ignorant had applied only to the Buddha's lifetime and to the subsequent two thousand years of the ages of the True Dharma and the Semblance Dharma, when people still had the capacity to achieve buddhahood through provisional teachings. Now, in the age of the Final Dharma, he argued, no one can achieve liberation through such incomplete doctrines. Therefore, the Buddha had permitted ordinary teachers such as himself to preach the *Lotus Sūtra* directly, so that people could establish a karmic connection with it, "whether by acceptance or rejection." Here Nichiren invoked and assimilated to the *Lotus Sūtra* the logic of "reverse connection" (J. *gyakuen*), the idea that even a negative relationship to the dharma, formed by rejecting or maligning it, will nonetheless eventually lead one to liberation. Persons who have formed no karmic connection to the true dharma may perhaps avoid rebirth in the lower realms but lack the conditions for attaining buddhahood; those who slander the dharma paradoxically form a bond with it. Though they must suffer the fearful consequences of disparaging the *Lotus Sūtra*, after expiating that offense, they will be able to encounter the *Lotus* again and achieve buddhahood by virtue of the very karmic connection to the sūtra that they formed by slandering it in the past. Now, in the age of the Final Dharma, Nichiren maintained, most persons are so burdened by delusive attachments that they are already bound for the hells. "If they must fall into the evil paths in any event, it would be far better that they do so for maligning the *Lotus Sūtra* than for any worldly offense. . . . Even if one disparages the *Lotus Sūtra* and thereby falls into hell, the merit gained [by the relationship to the sūtra that one has formed thereby] will surpass by a billion times that of making offerings to and taking refuge in Śākyamuni, Amitābha, and as many other buddhas as there are sands in the Ganges River."[9] Thus in this age, Nichiren maintained, one should persist in urging people to embrace the *Lotus Sūtra*, regardless of their response, for the *Lotus* alone can implant the seed that bears the fruit of buddhahood.

For Nichiren, convinced as he was that only the *Lotus Sūtra* leads to liberation in the *mappō* era, preaching exclusive devotion to the *Lotus* was not dogmatic self-assertion, but a compassionate act of bodhisattva practice. Whether others accepted the *Lotus Sūtra* or rejected it, telling them of its teaching would implant the seed of enlightenment in their minds and thereby enable them to establish a karmic connection to the sūtra that would someday allow them to realize buddhahood, whether in this lifetime or a future one.

CHAPTER FOUR

Willing Acceptance

The *Lotus Sūtra* is renowned for its seven parables, with that of the burning house being the most famous. Next comes the parable of the wealthy man and his impoverished son. When the *Lotus Sūtra* was first translated into a European language, into French by Eugène Burnouf, he called it the "parable of the prodigal son"—although it has little in common with the famous story in the Gospel of Luke, where a second son demands his birthright, leaves home and squanders it, only to be welcomed back by his loving father, a parable about the redemption of the sinner. The parable here has a much more elaborate plot and a very different meaning.

The chapter begins, however, with four of the most senior arhats—Subhūti, Mahākātyāyana, Mahākāśyapa, and Śāriputra's old friend Mahāmaudgalyāyana—expressing their joy (and thus giving their approval) upon hearing about the true dharma of the single vehicle. They say that they are old and feeble and had assumed that, having attained nirvāṇa, they were incapable of buddhahood and so did not seek it. Indeed, sitting in contemplation of the three doors to liberation—emptiness, wishlessness, and signlessness—they never even imagined that buddhahood was possible. But now, they rejoice at the predictions of Śāriputra's future buddhahood. Hearing these predictions, they say, is like finding a vast treasure that they had never sought.

To illustrate this, the four arhats recount the parable of the wealthy man and his impoverished son. A young man runs away from home and stays away for many years, living a life of poverty. His father searches for him the entire time without success. The father becomes wealthier during this period and despairs that he has no heir to inherit his riches. The son eventually returns to his home city. When he reaches his father's house, the son sees his father seated on a throne and mistakes him for a king or other powerful person; fearing he will be seized for forced labor, he runs away. His father recognizes his son, and sends his attendants to bring him home, but the son faints, thinking that he is being arrested by the king. The father sees all this and has his attendants offer the son a job sweeping up manure in the stables, which he gratefully accepts. The father cannot bear to see his son living in such abject circumstances, so he disguises himself as the head manure sweeper and approaches his son, telling him that because he is a good worker, he will always be provided with food and that he should consider him as his father. The son is grateful for this arrangement and works as a manure sweeper for the next twenty years.

As the father grows old, he knows that he has little time left in which to bequeath his wealth to his son. He hires him to oversee his treasury and tells him to learn everything about its contents. The son does so, although never wanting any of the wealth for himself and continuing to feel inferior. As the father is about to die, he summons his son to meet with the king and other dignitaries and announces that his treasurer is in fact his son, and that he bequeaths his entire fortune to him. The son is overjoyed, saying, "I never even considered receiving this; nevertheless, this treasure house has come into my possession, though unsought and unawaited" (88).

Having told their parable, the old arhats explain its meaning. The Buddha is the loving and wealthy father, and the śrāvakas are the sons. Like him, they are content to sweep away the manure of misconceptions and are happy to have a day laborer's wages of nirvāṇa, never imagining that they were deserving of something more. Understanding their sense of inferiority, the Buddha did not immediately teach them about the Mahāyāna, instead using his skillful means to teach what they could accept as appropriate for them. Just as the son unknowingly managed his father's wealth, the śrāvakas heard the Buddha teach the Mahāyāna and even taught it themselves to others, but they never imagined that it was intended for them. "Even if we heard about the pure buddha lands and leading and inspiring sentient beings, we never rejoiced in it. We felt no eagerness. For days and nights we neither craved for nor were we attached to the wisdom of the buddhas" (96). Now, with the revelation of the single vehicle, the śrāvakas rejoice at the knowledge that they are heirs of the Buddha.

Nichiren makes little direct reference to this parable in his writings. However, it played a key role in the development of the Tiantai schema of the sequence of the Buddha's teachings, which in turn was important to Nichiren's understanding of the *Lotus*.

As mentioned in the Authors' Introduction to this volume, after Zhiyi's time, through the efforts especially of Zhanran and the Korean scholar-monk Chegwan (?–971), the Tiantai school gradually developed a model that divides the Buddha's teaching career into five periods that span fifty years.[1] According to this model, the Buddha began by preaching the *Flower Garland Sūtra* (*Avataṃsaka Sūtra*), a highly advanced doctrine directed solely to bodhisattvas. None of the śrāvakas in the assembly could understand it and were struck dumb, just as the impoverished son was terrified when first forcibly approached by his father's attendants. Seeing that the *Flower Garland* teaching was beyond his auditors' capacity, the Buddha then backtracked and for twenty years preached the *āgamas*, the sūtras of the Buddhist mainstream, emphasizing the four noble truths, the twelve-linked chain of dependent origination, and the goal of nirvāṇa—that is, the teachings sometimes disparaged as the "Hīnayāna." This period corresponds to the wealthy man hiring his son to sweep manure for twenty years. In the third period, seeing that his followers were maturing, the Buddha preached the *vaipulya* or introductory Mahāyāna teachings such as the *Vimalakīrti Sūtra,* which criticize the one-sided emphasis on emptiness and detachment found in the āgamas and instead extol the way of the bodhisattva. This corresponds to the son having "free access to his father's house" yet still living in his own humble quarters (87). In the fourth period, the Buddha preached the *prajñā* or wisdom teachings, which integrate all of his teachings up to that point in the two discernments of emptiness and wisdom by which bodhisattvas both uproot attachment and act compassionately in the world. This corresponds to the wealthy man entrusting the care of his fortune to his impoverished son. Then finally, in the fifth period, during the last eight years of his life, the Buddha set aside the coarse and incomplete provisional teachings of the preceding four periods and preached the perfect teaching that opens buddhahood to all. This teaching is represented by the *Lotus Sūtra,* and—in the Tiantai reading—restated in the *Nirvāṇa Sūtra,* said to have been preached just before the Buddha's passing. This corresponds to the father, now approaching death, publicly acknowledging his son and bequeathing all of his wealth to him. In this way, the parable of the wealthy householder provided a basis for grasping the entirety of the Buddha's teachings as integrated into a single, comprehensive chronological and soteriological agenda, by which he sought to gradually cultivate his followers' capacity until they were mature enough to receive and accept the message of the one buddha vehicle.[2]

The "five periods" and other schemas of this kind represent remarkable achievements as efforts to systematize the Buddhist teachings into a coherent whole. However, text-critical scholarship has now made clear that they cannot be accepted as historically accurate. The Buddhist sūtras were compiled over a long period, and the Mahāyāna sūtras in particular were produced over several centuries, well after Śākyamuni's passing. Nonetheless, it is vital to understand that for Nichiren and his Tendai forebears and contemporaries, the division of the teachings into "five periods" was, in fact, historical reality, a faithful account of how Śākyamuni Buddha had taught, and indeed, of how all buddhas proceed.

Despite its influence, which extended well beyond Tiantai circles, the idea that the Buddha preached provisional teachings for forty-two years and then revealed his true, complete teaching in the *Lotus Sūtra* was not without opponents. In China and later in Japan, rival circles championed the superiority of their own ranking of the sūtras, and the parable of the wealthy householder and his impoverished son sometimes figured in their criticisms. Scholars of the Kegon (Ch. Huayan) school, which is based on the *Flower Garland Sūtra*, argued that their sūtra had been preached to bodhisattvas, while the "Willing Acceptance" chapter of the *Lotus*, on which the Tiantai "five periods" schema is based, was directed to mere śravakas. Scholars of the Hossō (Ch. Faxiang) or Yogācāra school, who championed the *Sūtra on the Explanation of the Intention* (*Saṃdhinirmocana Sūtra*), made a similar argument.

The Hossō school represents an intriguing case, in that its doctrinal position offered a steadfast minority opposition, not only to the Tiantai/Tendai schema of the five periods, but also to the entire notion of buddhahood as a universal possibility. Hossō thought distinguishes two kinds of buddha nature: buddha nature as suchness or principle (J. *ri busshō*), which is universal, and active buddha nature (*gyō busshō*), which is not. Buddha nature as principle is quiescent and does not manifest itself in the phenomenal world; thus its universality does not mean that all beings can become buddhas. Achieving buddhahood depends on the presence of "untainted seeds" originally inherent in the *ālaya* or storehouse consciousness, the root consciousness underlying samsaric existence in which all deeds and impressions are stored as "seeds" or latent potentials, later fructifying in the form of experience. According to Hossō doctrine, individuals can be divided into "five natures" according to what sort of seeds they possess. Some have "active buddha nature," that is, seeds that enable them to practice the bodhisattva way and become buddhas. Others have seeds that allow them to practice the path of the śrāvaka or the pratyekabuddha. These individuals can reach the nirvāṇa of the arhat, but they cannot become buddhas. Another group has a mixture of two or more of these three kinds of seeds: bodhisattva, śrāvaka, pratyekabuddha. Which kind of seed will develop is not predetermined; such persons are therefore said to be of "indeterminate nature." Last, there are those who possess no untainted seeds and thus can never escape saṃsāra. They can, however, better their condition by accumulating merit through Buddhist practice.

Against the *Lotus Sūtra*'s claim that the three vehicles are the Buddha's skillful means while the one vehicle is true, Hossō thinkers put forth this division of human capacity into five natures; they argued that the three vehicles of the śrāvaka, pratyekabuddha, and bodhisattva are true, while the one vehicle is a skillful method, designed by the Buddha to lead persons of the indeterminate group to follow the bodhisattva path and become buddhas, rather than taking the lesser path of the two vehicles. To support this argument, they invoked the *Lotus Sūtra's* theme of "resuscitating" śrāvakas and restoring them to the bodhisattva path—as when the Buddha, in Chapter Three, reminds Śāriputra of his long-forgotten bodhisattva vow (53). Saichō, the Japanese Tendai founder, countered in part by drawing on Huayan (J. Kegon) thinkers to argue that suchness has not only a quiescent aspect as universal principle (*fuhen shinnyo*), but also a dynamic aspect that manifests itself as the concrete forms of the phenomenal world (*zuien shinnyo*). He also maintained that suchness has the nature of realizing and knowing. Thus, there was no need to postulate seeds in the store consciousness of only certain individuals as the cause of buddhahood. Saichō equated suchness in its dynamic aspect with active buddha nature, and because suchness is universal, everyone has the potential to realize buddhahood.

The Hossō school was quite powerful in Japan's Heian period (794–1185). Its main temple, Kōfukuji, was supported by the influential Fujiwara family and represented the chief institutional rival of Enryakuji on Mount Hiei, headquarters of Saichō's Tendai school. Scholar-monks representing the two institutions engaged in formal court-sponsored debates about whether the one vehicle or the three vehicles represented the Buddha's true intent. The controversy continued throughout the Heian period and was addressed by leading Tendai thinkers, such as Genshin (943–1017).[3] By Nichiren's time, the one vehicle idea had carried the day, and even some Hossō thinkers were beginning to accommodate it. Thus, Nichiren himself did not need to argue against the Hossō position, although he mentions it occasionally. Unlike Saichō, however, Nichiren did not ground his own argument that all can attain buddhahood in claims for universal suchness, a term that occurs only rarely in his writings but, rather, in the mutual inclusion of the ten realms. This doctrine also renders irrelevant Hossō and Kegon claims that the *Lotus Sūtra* should be ranked below the *Explanation of the Intention* or *Flower Garland* sūtras because the parable of the wealthy man and his impoverished son, on which the Tendai hierarchy of Buddhist teachings is based, was spoken by śrāvakas. Nichiren wrote, "The four śrāvakas expressed their understanding, saying, 'The most magnificent jewels have been obtained without being sought or awaited' (90). They represent the śrāvaka realm within ourselves."[4] Central to Nichiren's understanding was the idea that, because the ten realms are mutually inclusive, if beings of one realm can attain buddhahood, so can those of any other. In his reading, the initial chapters of the *Lotus Sūtra* open buddhahood not merely to previously excluded śrāvakas, but to all beings.

CHAPTER FIVE

Herbs

The brief fifth chapter begins with the Buddha praising the parable of the rich man and his poor son that the four arhats have recounted. He then responds with one of his own. He describes a land with rich flora, a great variety of grasses, trees, shrubs, and herbs. Dense clouds fill the sky and rain falls on the various plants. The same rain falls evenly on them all, yet they grow at different rates based on their different capacities. The Buddha is like the great cloud and rains down the dharma that has a single character, the character of liberation, dispassion, and cessation. Like the trees and grasses, the variety of sentient beings respond differently based on their capacities; the teaching is the same.

This metaphor of a single truth leading to different results seems at odds with the previous parables, which emphasize the Buddha's ability to perceive the capacities of his disciples and, using skillful means, to adapt his teachings accordingly. To borrow the metaphor of this chapter, the notion of skillful means there would seem to imply a different rain falling on different plants. The central image of this chapter is the variety of sentient beings and how they differ in character, disposition, and capacity, something perceived only by the Buddha. In fact, the chapter seems to acknowledge the tension between the notions of a single vehicle and a plurality of skillful means by explaining that the Buddha first attracts sentient beings with a single resounding statement, "I set free those who have not been freed.

I enlighten those who have not been enlightened and bring calm to those who have not been calmed. I am the one who knows the present and future worlds exactly as they are" (102). When billions of beings hear this single statement and approach the Buddha to hear his teaching, he examines their faculties to determine whether they are sharp or dull and then "explains the teachings according to their capacities in a variety of immeasurable ways, gladdening and benefiting them all. Having heard his teaching, all of these beings are at peace in this world and are born into a good existence in the future" (102).

As before, the Buddha reiterates his teaching in verse, and here again, no attempt is made to resolve any contradiction between a single teaching and a multiplicity of skillful means. In the verse section, the emphasis is strongly on the dharma as having a single flavor, that of liberation and nirvāṇa. Humans and gods are like small herbs; pratyekabuddhas are like medium-sized herbs. Those who think they will become buddhas are like large herbs. Those who know beyond doubt that they will become buddhas are like small trees. Those who have advanced on the bodhisattva path and have saved billions of beings are like large trees. "The Buddha's equal teaching is like the rain of one flavor" (107), fulfilling the entire world yet expressed using skillful means.

The Buddha then reveals to the arhats what he calls "the highest teaching": "There are no śrāvakas who attain nirvāṇa. What you practice is the bodhisattva path; and if you practice it step by step, you will all become buddhas" (108).

In Kumārajīva's translation of the *Lotus Sūtra* into Chinese, the fifth chapter ends here. However, in several Sanskrit manuscripts, the chapter continues. The Buddha reiterates his declaration of a single doctrine, a single vehicle, and a single enlightenment, but with different metaphors, saying that the sun and moon illuminate the beings of the world equally, whether they are tall or short, fragrant or pungent. In the same way, there is only one vehicle. Whether pots hold sugar, butter, or curds, all pots are made of the clay. In the same way, there is only one vehicle.

In the Sanskrit version, we also find another parable, one that does not appear in Kumārajīva's translation and so is not counted among the standard list of seven, namely, the parable of the blind man. A man blind from birth denies the existence of physical forms, the sun, and the moon, and will not be convinced otherwise by those who can see. A wise physician seeks to cure him of his blindness and goes to the Himalayas to find the necessary herbs for the medicine. Through the physician's efforts, the man is cured and admits his error. However, he becomes convinced that he has now seen all there is to see and proclaims that no one's vision is superior to his. A group of sages, endowed with the five super-knowledges (*abhijñā*; translated as "transcendent powers" in the sūtra), overhears him. The five are: the divine eye, or the ability to see at great distances; the divine ear, or the ability to hear at great distances; the knowledge of others' minds, or telepathy; the ability to remember one's former lives; and magical powers, a range of supernormal powers such as the ability to fly, walk through walls, and dive into the earth. It is said that both Buddhists and non-Buddhists can gain these five powers; a sixth power, called "destruction of the contaminants" (*āsravakṣaya*), can only be gained through the Buddha's teachings.

The sages chide him for his arrogance, saying that he is like a man who never leaves his house and cannot see things outside his door. The man is convinced to undertake the meditative practice that will result in attainment of the super-knowledges and eventually comes to see that his new sight was indeed limited in its scope. The Buddha compares the blind man to ignorant sentient beings who are restored to sight by the great physician, the Buddha himself, who teaches them the three vehicles. Those who follow the śrāvaka and pratyekabuddha paths destroy the afflictions and achieve liberation from rebirth. Like the man whose normal sight has been restored, they complacently believe that their vision is complete. Only then does the Buddha challenge them to attain an even deeper insight by following the path to buddhahood.[1]

This parable, although presumably teaching the single vehicle, is different from both the parable of the burning house and the parable of medicinal herbs. Blindness is destroyed forever by restoring sight. But ordinary sight is not destroyed by divine sight; the ordinary is augmented by the divine. By the logic of this particular parable, the nirvāṇa of the arhat would seem to be an expedient device that does in fact exist and continues to be useful, although at a level of insight inferior to that of the Buddha, just as the mainstream Buddhist schools assert. The parable of the blind man, unlike the parables that have preceded it, does not offer a direct challenge to the mainstream tradition.

The promise in this chapter that those who embrace the one vehicle will be "at peace in this world" and in the next, will be "born into a good existence" (102) articulates what most people sought from religion in Nichiren's day: good fortune and protection in their present existence and some sort of assurance of a happy afterlife. Traditionally, as with other religions, people expected from Buddhism not only wisdom and insight, but also practical benefits: healing, protection, and worldly success.[2] Nichiren often cited this passage to assure followers that faith in the *Lotus Sūtra* does indeed offer such blessings. "Money changes form according to its use," he wrote. "The *Lotus Sūtra* is also like this. It will become a lamp in the darkness or a boat at a crossing. It can become water; it can also become fire. This being so, the *Lotus Sūtra* guarantees that we will be 'at peace in this world' and be 'born into a good existence in the future.'"[3]

However, "peace in this world" often seemed to be the very opposite of what Nichiren and his followers experienced. This phrase took on a heightened significance for them during Nichiren's second exile. In 1271, following his second arrest. Nichiren had narrowly escaped being beheaded by Bakufu officials. Tradition holds that he was saved only by a luminous object that streaked across the night sky at the critical moment, terrifying his would-be executioners. He was then banished to the forbidding island of Sado in the Sea of Japan, where his captors possibly intended—as often happened with exiles—that he would die of hunger or exposure. His followers, for their part, had to bear the onus of their association with a teacher who had been branded a criminal and heretic. Functionaries of the military government drew up a list of their names; some were imprisoned or had their lands confiscated. The very survival of his following was threatened.

During the bleak Sado Island years, Nichiren grappled with the question of why, when the *Lotus Sūtra* promises "peace in this world," he should have to undergo such ordeals. He also pondered other doubts, sometimes voiced by his followers: If he was indeed correctly practicing the *Lotus Sūtra,* why didn't the benevolent deities who protect the buddha-dharma intervene to assist him? Why didn't those who persecuted him meet with obvious karmic retribution?

Nichiren addressed these questions in a deeply introspective mode, for example, in his famous treatise *Kaimoku shō* ("Opening the Eyes," 1272), one of his most important writings, written as a testament to his followers in the event of his death. Here he reflects that in prior lifetimes, he himself must have committed offenses against the *Lotus Sūtra* and its devotees and was now enduring his present trials to expiate such offenses, just as iron is cleansed of impurities when forged in a fire. In this context, Nichiren drew upon the six-fascicle *Mahāparinirvāṇa Sūtra,* which states: "By the power of the merit gained by protecting the dharma, one receives lightened [karmic retribution for past offenses] in the present life."[4] In adopting this perspective, Nichiren claimed agency for his sufferings by representing them, not as a trial inflicted upon him by his enemies, but as an ordeal that he had deliberately chosen as an act of expiation. He also encouraged his followers by saying that the hardships they faced had in fact been predicted in the *Lotus Sūtra* itself, and thus confirmed the legitimacy of their practice and the certainty of their eventual buddhahood.

As for why their tormentors failed to experience obvious karmic retribution, Nichiren simply noted that when a person's sins are so weighty as to condemn them after death to the Avīci hell, there may be no sign of retribution in that individual's present life. Alternatively, Nichiren maintained that because people had abandoned the *Lotus Sūtra,* the protective deities, no longer able to hear the true dharma, had abandoned their shrines and returned to the heavens; thus, they could not be counted on to safeguard *Lotus* devotees or to punish their persecutors. Yet his conclusion was a resolve that seeks no explanation for adversity and no guarantee of protection; it is a resolve to simply persevere, whatever may happen: "Let heaven forsake me. Let ordeals confront me. I will not begrudge bodily life. . . . Whatever trials I and my disciples may encounter, so long as we do not cherish doubts, we will naturally achieve buddhahood. Do not doubt because heaven does not extend its protection.

Do not lament that you do not enjoy peace in this world."[5] Nichiren's conviction infused his life with immense meaning and enabled him to assert—in the midst of privation and danger—that he was "the richest man in all Japan today."[6] Nichiren taught his followers that while faith might result in this-worldly good fortune, more importantly, it revealed inner resources of joy and assurance, independent of outward circumstances, that would sustain them through trying times.

Does that mean, then, that Nichiren understood the sūtra's promise of "peace in the present world" only as expressing an inner mental composure? By no means. Its promise was also that of an actual peace to be realized in the outer world through the spread of the *Lotus Sūtra*. Another letter he wrote from Sado reads: "Question: Those who practice the *Lotus Sūtra* as it teaches should be 'at peace in this world.' Why then are you beset by the three powerful enemies [who oppose the *Lotus Sūtra*'s practitioners]?" In this instance, Nichiren responds that teachers of the *Lotus Sūtra* in the past, such as Daosheng, Zhiyi, Saichō—even Śākyamuni Buddha himself—surely practiced in accordance with the *Lotus Sūtra* and yet they endured great trials to communicate its message; meeting hardships does not in and of itself imply flaws in one's practice. Rather, troubles are to be expected in an evil age when the dharma has been obscured and everyone from the ruler down to the common people has turned against the *Lotus Sūtra*. That is why it is all the more important to persevere. He concludes: "When all people of the realm, including the various Buddhist schools, convert to the one vehicle and chant Namu Myōhō-renge-kyō as one, the wind will not thrash the branches nor the rain fall hard enough to erode the soil. The world will be as it was in the ages [of the ancient sage kings] Fuxi and Shennong. In this life, inauspicious disasters will be banished, and people will obtain the art of longevity. You will behold a time when the principle becomes manifest that persons and dharmas neither age nor die."[7]

This is one of the few passages in Nichiren's extant writings that sets forth his vision of an ideal, this-worldly buddha land to be established in the future. It seems to entail a state of harmony with nature, just government, long life, and freedom from catastrophe. Included in the *ichinen sanzen* principle is the idea that sentient beings and their insentient environments are nondual; human actions, whether wise and compassionate or selfish and deluded, shape the world that they inhabit. Thus, for Nichiren, the awakening of the *Lotus Sūtra* was not simply to be experienced subjectively by individual practitioners, but would also find expression as concord, creativity, and fulfillment in the outer world. This conviction gives his teaching a distinctively social dimension. On this basis, he took "peace in this world" to mean not only the unwavering inner wisdom and security established by faith, but also an ideal to be concretely and visibly realized in everyday life.

CHAPTER SIX

Prediction

With Śāriputra having received a prediction of buddhahood in Chapter Three, it is now time for other great arhats to receive their predictions. In this chapter, the Buddha predicts future buddhahood first for Mahākāśyapa, and then for Subhūti, Mahākātyāyana, and Mahāmaudgalyāyana, the four who have displayed their understanding that there is but one vehicle by relating the parable of the wealthy man and his impoverished son. The Buddha first predicts buddhahood for his senior disciple, Mahākāśyapa. Hearing this, three others—Subhūti, Mahākātyāyana, and Mahāmaudgalyāyana—are "all charged with excitement" and implore the Buddha to confer prophecies on them as well, "as though to starving people, waiting for permission to eat" (111, 112).

For each of them, the Buddha predicts the name of the buddha he will become, the name of his land, the name of the eon, and the length of his lifespan. Here we see the meaning of enlightenment shift from the state of an arhat to the state of a buddha. Indeed, in terms of the time required to fulfill the bodhisattva path, enlightenment, or buddhahood, recedes to a point beyond the horizon—but with the millions of intervening lives, beginning with this one, consecrated by the Buddha's prophecy that these present lives are a future buddha's past lives, chapters of a buddha's story and thus sacred history. Having received Śākyamuni's prediction of their future buddhahood, the four declare: "It is as though someone coming from a country suffering from famine were suddenly to find a great king's feast spread before him" (111).

Nichiren explained that these four great śrāvakas "had not even heard the name of the delicacy called ghee," but when the *Lotus Sūtra* was expounded, they experienced it for the first time, savoring it as much as they wished and "immediately satisfying the hunger that had long been in their hearts."[1] Nichiren's reference here to "ghee," or clarified butter, invokes the concept of the "five flavors," an analogy by which Zhiyi had likened the stages in human religious development to the five stages in the Indian practice of making ghee from fresh milk.[2] As we have seen, like other educated Buddhists of his day, Nichiren took the Tendai division of the Buddha's teaching into five sequential periods to represent historical fact. From that perspective, Nichiren sometimes described the sufferings that he imagined the Buddha's leading śrāvaka disciples must have endured during the period when Śākyamuni began to preach the Mahāyāna, seeing their status plummet from that of revered elders to targets of scorn and reproach for their attachment to the inferior "Hīnayāna" goal of a personal nirvāṇa. Some Mahāyāna sūtras excoriate the śrāvakas as those who have "destroyed the seeds of buddhahood" or "fallen into the pit of nirvāṇa" and can benefit neither themselves nor others. Their "hunger" then would have represented their chagrin and regret at not having followed the bodhisattva path and thus having excluded themselves from the possibility of buddhahood.

At the same time, Nichiren imagined them suffering hunger in the literal sense. As monks, they would have had to beg for their food each day. Nichiren imagined that on hearing the śrāvakas rebuked as followers of a lesser vehicle, humans and gods no longer viewed them as worthy sources of merit and stopped putting food in their begging bowls. "Had the Buddha entered final nirvāṇa after preaching only the sūtras of the first forty years or so without expounding the *Lotus Sūtra* in his last eight years, who then would have made offerings to these elders?" he asked. "In their present bodies, they would have known the sufferings of the realm of hungry ghosts."[3] Serious hunger was a condition that Nichiren had experienced at multiple points in his life and with which he could readily sympathize. But when the Buddha preached the *Lotus Sūtra* and predicted buddhahood for the śrāvakas, Nichiren continued, his words were like the brilliant spring sun emerging to dissolve the ice of winter or a strong wind dispersing dew from all the grass. "Because [these predictions] appear in this phoenix of writings, this mirror of truth [i.e., the *Lotus*], after the Buddha's passing, the śrāvakas were venerated by all supporters of the dharma, both humans and gods, just as though they had been buddhas."[4]

Nichiren also commented on the "great king's feast" in connection with memorial prayers that he offered on behalf of followers who had lost family members. In so doing, he evoked associations between the arhat Maudgalyāyana (Ch. Mulian, J. Mokuren), whose attainment of buddhahood is predicted in this chapter of the *Lotus Sūtra,* and Buddhist funerary and memorial rites. Maudgalyāyana was celebrated in the early Buddhist tradition as the Buddha's disciple most accomplished in supernatural powers. After his mother had died, the story goes, Maudgalyāyana scanned the cosmos with his divine eye to see where she had been reborn and found her suffering in the realm of hungry ghosts as retribution for her greed and stinginess when alive. He then attempted to send her magically conjured food, but it burst into flames and scorched her when she tried to eat it. Bewildered, he consulted the Buddha, who advised him to offer a meal to the assembly of monks at the end of the summer monsoon retreat. Maudgalyāyana did so, and with that merit, his mother gained release from the hungry ghost realm. This legend became the basis throughout East Asia of the annual "Ghost Festival" (Skt. Ullambana; Ch. Yulanpen; J. Urabon), in which lay people make special offerings to monks at the close of the summer retreat, a period during which monastics are said to heighten their spiritual powers. The monks in turn perform services to transfer merit to their patrons' deceased relatives, confirming the reciprocal bonds between monastics and laity, the living and the dead.[5] Maudgalyāyana's story was also related to the "ritual for hungry ghosts," a merit offering for those deceased who had no relatives to sponsor services on their behalf. In Japan, this ritual was often performed in conjunction with Urabon, or for persons who had died in battle, of starvation, or under other unfortunate circumstances.

In the original story, Maudgalyāyana cannot assist his mother with his own magical powers; he can only do so by the power of the dharma. The fact that she is saved when he offers a meal to the monastic assembly reflects the widely held idea that the transfer of merit to the deceased is most efficacious when ritually mediated by monastics, especially those earnest in practice and pure in their vows. In the same letter cited above, however, Nichiren presents an alternative explanation, showing how he adapted traditional Buddhist stories to his *Lotus* exclusivism:

> The Urabon service began with the Venerable Maudgalyāyana's attempts to save his mother, Shōdai-nyo, who on account of her miserliness and greed had fallen for five hundred lifetimes into the realm of hungry ghosts. But he could not make her become a buddha. The reason was because he himself did not yet practice the *Lotus Sūtra*, and so he could not lead even his own

mother to buddhahood. But at the eight-year assembly on Vulture Peak, he embraced the *Lotus Sūtra,* chanted Namu myōhō-renge-kyō, and became the Buddha Tamālapattra-candanagandha [Tamālapattra Sandalwood Fragrance]. At that time, his mother became a buddha too.

You also asked about offerings for hungry ghosts. The third fascicle of the *Lotus Sūtra* says, "It is as though someone coming from a country suffering from famine were suddenly to find a great king's feast spread before him." . . . When you make offerings for hungry ghosts, you should recite this passage from the sūtra and also chant Namu Myōhō-renge-kyō.[6]

Claims that one person's religious attainment would simultaneously benefit that individual's family members, sometimes for seven generations in each direction, was common in Nichiren's time. They express a confidence, grounded in Mahāyāna notions of interconnection, that one's own practice affects others across time, space, and the boundaries of life and death. Nichiren here assimilates such ideas to the practice of chanting the daimoku, the title of the *Lotus Sūtra.*

CHAPTER SEVEN

The Apparitional City

This chapter concludes with the fourth of the *Lotus Sūtra*'s seven parables. But it begins with an elaborate story. Incalculable eons ago, and apparently before the time of the buddha Candrasūryapradīpa described in Chapter One, there was a buddha named Mahābhijñājñānābhibhū ("Victorious through Great Penetrating Knowledge"). He had an incredibly long lifespan: five hundred and forty myriads of *koṭi*s of *nayuta*s of eons, with a myriad being ten thousand, a *koṭi* being ten million, and a *nayuta* being one hundred billion. He also spent an unusually long time—the text says one to ten intermediate eons (121)—seated on the terrace of enlightenment (*bodhimaṇḍa*), trying, without success, to achieve buddhahood. Eventually, thirty-three gods prepared a lion throne, one *yojana* (approximately eight miles) tall, beneath the Bodhi Tree. They then paid homage to him, raining down flowers and playing music for ten intermediate eons, after which he attained buddhahood.

Prior to renouncing the world, he had fathered sixteen sons. Hearing of his enlightenment, they set out to pay homage to him, accompanied by their grandfather, who was a king, together with a hundred ministers, and the usual "hundreds of thousands of myriads of *koṭis* of people" (121). The sons implore their father, the Buddha, to turn the wheel of the dharma. He replies that when he achieved enlightenment, billions of worlds quaked in six ways and dark places were illuminated, places that had been dark for so long that the beings living there, seeing each other for the first time, said, "How is it possible that sentient beings have suddenly appeared here?" (124). (The earthquakes and the illumination of dark worlds are standard elements in the description of a buddha's enlightenment.) The quaking and illumination from the great rays of light reached up to the Brahmā world (*brahmaloka*), that is, the first three heavens of the Realm of Form (*rūpadhātu*). This happened in all the worlds of the ten directions (the four cardinal directions, the four intermediate directions, the apogee, and the nadir), beginning in the east, with the gods in that cosmic quarter expressing astonishment at the supernatural light, wondering about its source, assuming that a buddha must have appeared in the world, and then repairing to the terrace of enlightenment to pay homage. There, they circumambulate the Buddha a hundred thousand times, offer him their palaces, and implore him to teach the dharma. This description is repeated somewhat laboriously for the gods in the southeast and the south, with the text saying that the same thing occurred for the other cardinal and intermediate directions as well as the lower regions. The same description is then provided for the gods of the upper regions.

Having been implored by the sixteen princes and the gods of the ten directions, the Buddha agrees to teach the dharma. He begins, as Śākyamuni would eons hence, with the four noble truths. After that, he teaches the twelve links of dependent origination (*pratītyasamutpāda*). After each of his teachings, many beings become free from corruption. The sixteen princes all renounce the world and become novice monks (*śramaṇera*), asking their father to expound the teaching of complete enlightenment. The Buddha agrees, and twenty thousand eons later, he teaches the *Lotus Sūtra* for eight thousand eons, without stopping, in verses equal in number to the sands of the Ganges.

He then enters a state of meditation for eighty-four thousand eons, during which time the sixteen sons teach the *Lotus Sūtra* to sentient beings equal in number to the grains of sand of the Ganges. When Mahābhijñājñānābhibhū rises from his meditation, he praises the sixteen novices for preserving the wisdom of the buddhas, saying that all should pay homage to them.

The scene then returns to the present, where Śākyamuni explains that the sixteen novices all went on to achieve buddhahood and are currently teaching the dharma in the worlds of the ten directions, with two buddhas each in the four cardinal and four intermediate directions. He goes on to identify them by name. The names include two buddhas who would become famous in other Mahāyāna sūtras, Akṣobhya and Amitābha. The Buddha explains that he himself, Śākyamuni, is the sixteenth, living "in this Sahā world" (137).

The point of this long story, like that of the story of another previously unknown buddha of the past, Candrasūryapradīpa, in the first chapter, is to legitimate the *Lotus Sūtra* as an authentic, indeed primordial, text. It would seem redundant to tell yet another long story in which a buddha of the past teaches the *Lotus Sūtra*. However, although both stories seek to legitimate the *Lotus Sūtra*, they do so in slightly different ways. In the first chapter, Mañjuśrī interprets the event in which Śākyamuni illuminates myriad worlds with a beam of light emitted from between his eyes, saying that in a distant previous life, he had witnessed Candrasūryapradīpa do the same thing. Based on that experience, Mañjuśrī is able to speculate, correctly, that Śākyamuni is about to teach the *Lotus Sūtra*. In the present chapter, the speaker is not Mañjuśrī, but Śākyamuni himself, who, speaking as a buddha with full knowledge of the past, present, and future, can tell the story of an even more ancient buddha, Mahābhijñājñānābhibhū, teaching the *Lotus Sūtra* even longer ago. The power of Śākyamuni's testimony is enhanced by the revelation that Śākyamuni was in fact one of Mahābhijñājñānābhibhū's sixteen sons, and so was personally present in the audience when Mahābhijñājñānābhibhū first taught the *Lotus Sūtra*. Śākyamuni provides the eyewitness testimony of a buddha. The difference in the power of authorization is not huge (a tenth stage bodhisattva compared to a buddha); the more important conclusion to be drawn from the story in this chapter is the *Lotus Sūtra*'s persistent obsession with demonstrating its authenticity.

The chapter concludes with a brief parable, one that, despite its simple plot, has weighty doctrinal implications. In the mainstream tradition, at death, a buddha or an arhat enters what is called *parinirvāṇa* ("final nirvāṇa"). All karma has been destroyed by wisdom, and hence all causes for future rebirth have been exhausted. The standard Buddhist image of nirvāṇa, drawn from the etymology of the term, is of a fire going out because its fuel has been completely consumed. The continuum of consciousness that has existed without beginning comes to a permanent end. Part of the Buddhist fixation on the relics of the Buddha, a fixation quite at odds with other Indian traditions of the day where the corpse was considered unclean, may derive from the Buddhist belief that this is all that remains of the Buddha after his death. He is not in heaven, he is also not "in" nirvāṇa because nirvāṇa is not a place; it is the extinction of suffering and rebirth.

This doctrine, so central to the mainstream tradition, is a problem for the *Lotus Sūtra*. If all of the Buddha's disciples are destined for buddhahood, if the nirvāṇa of the arhat is only another example of the Buddha's skillful means, what happens to arhats when they die? And what has become of the many monks who became arhats and passed away before the Buddha, only late in his life, revealed the *Lotus Sūtra* and the doctrine of the single vehicle?

The problem recalls that faced by the early Christian church. If salvation is only possible because of the crucifixion and resurrection of Jesus, what is the fate of all the righteous people who died in human history before that epochal event, such people as Adam and Eve, Abraham, Noah, and all the prophets of the Hebrew Bible? During the early centuries of the church, this dilemma was solved by the doctrine of the "Harrowing of Hell." The Saturday between the crucifixion on Friday and the resurrection on Sunday was not described in the Gospels. It was said, then, that during that time Jesus "descended into Hell" (in the words of the Apostles' Creed), where he redeemed the righteous, a scene commonly depicted in medieval art, with Jesus, wearing his burial shroud and bearing the cross of victory, breaking open the gates of hell and leading the righteous (often led by Adam) to salvation, while trampling the infernal demons underfoot.

In Chapter Two of the *Lotus Sūtra,* the Buddha had voiced the possibility that some among those who will become arhats after he enters *parinirvāṇa* might not believe in the *Lotus Sūtra.* In this chapter, he has a different concern: the fate of those who not only would become arhats after his passing but, apparently not knowing any better, would enter *parinirvāṇa* without having heard the *Lotus.* However, they are not doomed. The Buddha explains, "I will become a buddha in another land with a different name. Although the idea of extinction has awoken in these disciples and they have entered *parinirvāṇa,*[1] in that land they will still seek the wisdom of the buddhas and will then be able to hear this sūtra" (138). From the point of view of classical Buddhist doctrine, both the Buddha and the arhats cease to return, indeed, cease to exist, at the point when they enter *parinirvāṇa*. Thus, what the Buddha describes here is doctrinally impossible. What the *Lotus Sūtra* is claiming, in a radical reinterpretation of the central doctrine of nirvāṇa, is that nirvāṇa as it has been understood, and as the Buddha had described it earlier in his teachings, does not exist, and that those who enter *parinirvāṇa*, either as a buddha or an arhat, do not vanish permanently. In the case of the Buddha, this will be addressed more explicitly in Chapter Sixteen. In the case of the arhats, the Buddha provides a parable.

A group of people sets out on a long and dangerous journey of five hundred *yojanas* in search of treasure. They are led by a wise and skillful guide. Along the way, the party becomes exhausted and decides to turn back. The guide then uses his magical powers to conjure a city three hundred *yojanas* away along the route and convinces the party to continue their journey, saying that they will be able to rest in the city. They arrive and rest until their fatigue is gone. The guide then explains to them that the city is an apparition and that they must press on, as the treasure is near.

The Buddha, of course, is the guide, and the travelers are sentient beings. The treasure is buddhahood. If the Buddha taught only the goal of buddhahood, they would not want to seek it, feeling that the path is too long and difficult. He therefore teaches an easier goal, the two nirvāṇas: the nirvāṇa of the śrāvaka and the nirvāṇa of the pratyekabuddha (essentially the same goal reached by different paths). However, these are illusions; there is only one treasure. And so, when arhats achieve nirvāṇa, thinking that they have reached their goal, the Buddha informs them that the true goal lies ahead.

As inspirational as this parable might be, it is also polemical. The earlier tradition's claim to legitimacy is usurped by the *Lotus Sūtra*, which suggests that what the Buddha had taught before seems to have been a lie, that there is no such thing as the path of the arhat, no such thing as nirvāṇa.

As with Chapter Three, Nichiren's references to this chapter focus, not on the parable from which it takes its name, but on another element entirely, in this case, the story of the buddha Mahābhijñājñānābhibhū.

Nichiren drew three chief conclusions from this narrative. The first is that beings of our own, Sahā world have a karmic connection solely to Śākyamuni Buddha and not to the buddhas of other words. Everything about the dharma known in this world originated with Śākyamuni. None of the great Pure Land teachers, Nichiren said, had ever actually met the buddha Amitābha or renounced the world to practice the way under his guidance. The name Sahā, from the Sanskrit word meaning "to bear or endure," refers to the tradition that this world is an especially evil and benighted place where it is difficult to pursue the Buddhist path—quite unlike the radiant pure lands with which the Mahāyāna imagination populated the cosmos. Thus, Śākyamuni was said to have displayed exceptional compassion in appearing in this world. In the *Greater Amitābha Sūtra* or *Sūtra of Immeasurable Life*, Amitābha Buddha vows to accept into his pure land all who place faith in him except those persons who have committed the five heinous deeds or disparaged the dharma.[2] Nichiren accordingly suggested that these most depraved of evil persons had been excluded from the pure lands of the ten directions and were gathered instead in the present, Sahā world, where Śākyamuni had undertaken to save them. This was the meaning, he said, of Śākyamuni Buddha's statement in Chapter Three, "I am the only one who can protect them" (72). To forsake the original teacher Śākyamuni was a grave error, as the people of this world cannot escape saṃsāra by following any other buddha.[3]

Second, Nichiren drew from the Mahābhijñājñānābhibhū story an understanding of how the Buddha's pedagogical method unfolds over time. Zhiyi had identified three standards of comparison by which the *Lotus Sūtra* could be said to surpass all others. The first, based on Śākyamuni's declaration of the one buddha vehicle in the "Skillful Means" and subsequent chapters, is that it encompasses persons of all capacities. The second, based on the present, "Apparitional City" chapter, is that it reveals the process of the Buddha's instruction from beginning to end.[4] Drawing on the Mahābhijñājñānābhibhū narrative, Zhiyi described this process with the metaphor of "sowing, maturing, and harvesting." That is, the Buddha implants the seed of buddhahood in the mind of his disciples with an initial teaching; cultivates it through subsequent teachings, enabling their capacity to mature; and finally reaps the harvest by bringing those disciples to full enlightenment. As the opening passage of this chapter describes, the buddha Mahābhijñājñānābhibhū lived an immensely long time ago, so long that one could measure it only by grinding a vast number of world systems to dust and using each dust speck to represent one eon. In that distant time, Mahābhijñājñānābhibhū and his sixteen sons planted the seed of buddhahood in the minds of their auditors by preaching the *Lotus Sūtra*. Those who heard the *Lotus Sūtra* from the sixteenth son were born together with him in lifetime after lifetime, as he nurtured their capacity, bringing it to maturity with subsequent teachings over the course of innumerable lifetimes. When that son preached the *Lotus Sūtra* in the Sahā world as Śākymuni Buddha, some were at last able to reap the harvest of enlightenment, while others would do so in the future. In other words, Śākyamuni's resolve to lead all beings to the one vehicle was not merely a matter of this lifetime, but a project initiated in the inconceivably remote past. Indeed, this chapter offers another early hint that Śākyamuni's buddhahood encompasses a time frame far exceeding the present lifetime, a theme that the *Lotus Sūtra* develops in later chapters.

The concept of "sowing, maturing, and harvesting" was developed by Zhanran, who argued that only the perfect teaching of the *Lotus Sūtra* can plant the seed of buddhahood. From this perspective, Śākyamuni's preaching of the *Lotus Sūtra* during his lifetime in India both allowed those who had received the seed of buddhahood from him in previous lifetimes to reap the harvest of enlightenment and also planted that seed in the lives of those who had not yet received it. Nichiren understood this process in terms of how it unfolded after Śākyamuni's final nirvāṇa, and especially in his own time. Like Zhanran, but to a greater degree, he stressed that only the *Lotus Sūtra* plants the seed of buddhahood; all that provisional teachings can accomplish is to cultivate the capacity of persons who have already received that seed by encountering the *Lotus Sūtra* in prior lifetimes. Thus, in the final analysis, buddhahood always has its source in the *Lotus*.

In Nichiren's understanding, during the ages of the True Dharma and the Semblance Dharma, people had been able to achieve buddhahood through provisional teachings such as nenbutsu or Zen because they had already formed a connection to the *Lotus Sūtra* by hearing it from Śākyamuni Buddha in previous lifetimes. But people born in the age of the Final Dharma have not yet formed such a connection and thus cannot benefit from the nenbutsu or other provisional teachings, no matter how earnestly they might practice them, just as one cannot reap a harvest from a field where seeds have never been sown. Now in the age of the Final Dharma, Nichiren taught, it is the daimoku, the essence of the *Lotus Sūtra,* that embodies the seed of buddhahood. "At this time," he wrote, "Namu Myohō-renge-kyō of the 'Fathoming the Lifespan' chapter, the heart of the origin teaching, should be planted for the first time as the seed [of buddhahood]" in the hearts of the benighted persons of the mappō era.[5]

The concept of sowing, maturing, and harvesting suggests a linear process developing over time. Mahāyāna thought traditionally maintained that fulfilling the bodhisattva path requires three incalculable eons. However, as we have seen, Nichiren drew on both Tendai and esoteric notions of realizing buddhahood "with this body" to argue that buddhahood is accessed in the very act of chanting Namu Myōhō-renge-kyō. The daimoku, in other words, is a "seed" that flowers and bears fruit in the very moment of its acceptance. This goes to the heart of how Nichiren understood the Final Dharma age. In the age of the True Dharma and the age of the Semblance Dharma, people practiced according to a linear model, gradually eradicating delusions and accumulating merit, eventually culminating in the attainment of buddhahood after countless lifetimes of practice. But in chanting the daimoku of the *Lotus Sūtra,* the practice for the mappō era, practice and enlightenment, sowing and harvest, occur simultaneously, and buddhahood is realized in this very body. In other words, in the Final Dharma age, the direct realization of buddhahood becomes accessible to ordinary people. Nichiren's claim paradoxically inverts the negative soteriological implications of the benighted mappō era and makes it the ideal time to be alive. "Rather than be great monarchs during the two thousand years of the True Dharma and Semblance Dharma ages, those concerned for their salvation should rather be common people now in the Final Dharma age," he wrote. "It is better to be a leper who chants Namu Myōhō-renge-kyō than to be chief abbot of the Tendai school," the highest position in the religious world of Japan at the time.[6]

A third message that Nichiren drew from the story of the buddha Mahābhijñājñānābhibhū and his sixteen sons was the importance of perseverance in practice. In the "Parable" chapter, Śākyamuni tells Śāriputra that he had once followed the bodhisattva path in prior lifetimes but had since forgotten it. What had caused Śāriputra, this wisest of all śrāvakas, to "forget" and abandon the bodhisattva way? The *Lotus Sūtra* does not tell us, but a story in the *Treatise on the Great Perfection of Wisdom* (*Dazhi du lun*) and other sources fills in the gap. It explains that in the past, Śāriputra had already practiced bodhisattva austerities for sixty eons and was cultivating the virtue of giving or generosity, the first of the *pāramitās* or perfections that a bodhisattva must master on the path to buddhahood. At that point, a certain beggar (in alternate versions, a brahman) asked for one of his eyes. When Śāriputra replied that his eye could not possibly benefit anyone else, the beggar rebuked him, saying that so long as Śāriputra was committed to mastering the practice of generosity, he could not refuse to give what was requested of him. Śāriputra accordingly plucked out an eye and offered it. The beggar sniffed it, flung it to the ground, and stepped on it. Disgusted, Śāriputra concluded that such people were hopeless. At that point, he abandoned the bodhisattva's commitment to saving others and retreated to the śrāvaka's pursuit of personal nirvāṇa.[7] In Nichiren's reading, Śāriputra, deceived by evil influences, had abandoned the *Lotus Sūtra* for provisional teachings and, as a result, had fallen into the Avīci hell, languishing there for vast numbers of eons. Not until he reencountered Śākyamuni Buddha in the present world was he again able to hear the *Lotus Sūtra*, regain the bodhisattva path, and receive a prediction of future buddhahood.[8]

In terms of practice, the account of Śākyamuni Buddha's instruction as unfolding over many lifetimes in the "Apparitional City" chapter assumes a double significance in Nichiren's thought. On the one hand, this account teaches the need to maintain one's own practice of the *Lotus Sūtra*, no matter what hardships or discouragement one might encounter. At the same time, it suggests that teaching the daimoku to others, even if they initially mock or malign it, is always a fruitful effort, establishing for them a karmic connection with the *Lotus Sūtra* and thus ensuring that they will one day achieve buddhahood.

CHAPTERS EIGHT AND NINE

The Five Hundred Disciples Receive Their Predictions *and* The Predictions for Those Who Still Have More to Learn and for Those Who Do Not

Chapter Eight

Now more arhats come forward, requesting prophecies of their buddhahood, beginning with Pūrṇa, a monk renowned as a preacher of the dharma. The Buddha duly predicts his name, the name of his land, the name of his eon, and the length of his lifespan ("immeasurable incalculable eons"). When the Buddha describes the inhabitants of Pūrṇa's buddha land, he notes that there will be no animals, ghosts, or denizens of hell, and no women (149). The rest of the twelve hundred arhats in the audience then ask for prophecies. The Buddha confers a prophecy for each of them, beginning with Ājñātakauṇḍinya. He provides a mass prophecy for five hundred arhats, saying that they will all become buddhas named Samantaprabha ("Universal Light"). The five hundred arhats are sufficiently delighted that they respond with a parable:

When visiting a friend, a man gets drunk and falls asleep. The friend has to leave before the man wakes up, but before leaving, he sews a priceless jewel into the man's garment. The man later wakes up and goes on his way, encountering great hardship in the years that follow. One day, he encounters his friend, who informs him that he has had a priceless jewel in his garment all the time.

The man who passes out drunk are the monks in whom the Buddha had inspired the aspiration to buddhahood, but who had either forgotten it or not understood it. They therefore followed the path of the arhat, undergoing great hardship, and imagined that they had attained nirvāṇa. With his prophecy, the Buddha has now informed them that they are bodhisattvas and that they will achieve buddhahood.

Chapter Nine

The disciples of the Buddha are often divided into two categories: literally "learners" (*śaikṣa*) and "non-learners" (*aśaikṣa*). The latter is a synonym for arhat; they are called "non-learners" because they have completed the path and so have nothing left to learn. The former can mean any other disciples of the Buddha or, in a technical sense, anyone who has achieved any of three ranks on the path prior to reaching the status of an arhat, that is, the ranks of stream-enterer, once-returner, or never-returner. In this chapter, the "learners" among the Buddha's disciples are represented by his cousin and personal attendant Ānanda (who, according to traditional accounts, became an arhat only after the Buddha's death), and the "non-learners" are represented by Rāhula, the Buddha's son. Both receive prophecies of their future buddhahood. Notably, the Buddha, being impartial, waits until the end before conferring predictions on his family members.

Ānanda receives a particularly marvelous prediction, with a very long lifespan and a very long duration of his teaching. This causes some of the bodhisattvas in the audience to be disgruntled, wondering why this monk who is not even an arhat received a better prophecy than they had. The Buddha explains that he and Ānanda had aroused the aspiration for perfect enlightenment in the presence of the same buddha long ago. Ānanda had wanted to preserve the dharma that Śākyamuni would eventually teach. For this reason, he receives this special prophecy. Upon hearing the prophecy, Ānanda is miraculously able to remember the teachings of innumerable buddhas of the past.

This elevation of Ānanda is yet another weapon used by the *Lotus Sūtra* to assert its legitimacy. If Ānanda can remember the teachings of innumerable buddhas of the past, he is certainly able to remember the teachings of Śākyamuni, suggesting that it was indeed Ānanda who says, "Thus have I heard" at the beginning of the sūtra. In the story of the first council in which he recited the sūtras, Ānanda is taken to task by certain senior monks for having encouraged the Buddha to establish the order of nuns, a move that not all (male) members of the saṃgha had approved of. In the centuries that followed, Ānanda would become a beloved figure in the tradition, especially honored by nuns. That he receives a special prophecy in the *Lotus Sūtra* suggests that the authors of the text not only wished to bring him aboard the great ship of the Mahāyāna (as they did with Śāriputra), but perhaps also that they had a particular affection for him.

The Buddha next gives a prophecy of buddhahood for his son and disciple Rāhula, at which point the Buddha's most famed disciples have all received predictions. He then confers still further prophecies on a group of two thousand other śrāvakas, including both those who still have more to learn and those who do not, who will all become buddhas with the same name, Ratnaketurāja ("Jewel Sign King").

The prophecies in these two chapters, whether conferred on individuals or groups, each specify the name of the buddha whom the recipient will become, the name of his buddha land or field of activity, and the length of time that his teaching will endure. For the sūtra's East Asian commentators, such concrete detail lent these predictions a level of credibility beyond any mere abstract assertion that "persons of the two other vehicles can become buddhas." Because the Buddha knows the past, present, and future and never lies, it was certain that his śrāvaka disciples would in fact attain buddhahood just as he had predicted. For Nichiren, based on the premise that all ten realms are included in any one realm, the fact that śrāvakas can become buddhas meant that anyone else can as well. Thus the Buddha's prediction for any one of these figures could be read as a prediction of certain buddhahood for all who embrace the *Lotus Sūtra*, regardless of their status.

In Chapter Eight, to express their understanding of the one vehicle teaching, five hundred arhats who have just received a prediction from the Buddha relate the parable of the jewel hidden in the garment. Like the other parables of the *Lotus Sūtra*, this one was well known to educated Japanese and provided a frequent subject for traditional *waka* poems based on the sūtra, as in this twelfth-century example:

if the wind
  from Vulture Peak
had not blown
  my sleeves inside out—
would I have found
  the jewel
inside the reverse
  of my coat?[1]

Here the poet expresses his recognition that, without the Buddha's preaching of the *Lotus Sūtra*, he would never have discovered the treasure he had possessed all along.

For Nichiren, the daimoku of the *Lotus Sūtra* is what enables that discovery. He writes that living beings "have never for an instant been separated from the wish-granting jewel." Although they could quickly realize buddhahood simply by chanting Namu Myōhō-renge-kyō, being deluded by the wine of ignorance, they do not realize this and are instead satisfied with trivial gains, such as achieving rebirth in the heavens as the gods Brahmā or Indra or the status of rulers or great ministers of state in the human world. But the Buddha taught that these are mere illusory pleasures. Rather, "we should simply uphold the *Lotus Sūtra* and quickly become buddhas."[2] In the sūtra text, the man being "satisfied if he just obtains a very meagre amount" (155) represents the Buddha's disciples accepting the teachings of the two lower vehicles and being content with the arhat's goal of nirvāṇa, not aspiring to the bodhisattva path. It thereby conveys an implicit criticism of the Indian Buddhist mainstream at the time of the sūtra's compilation. Nichiren reorients the parable to suggest that any transient acquisition—including all the wealth, pleasures, and power to be had in the human or heavenly realms—is vastly inferior to realizing buddhahood by embracing the *Lotus Sūtra*.

Commentators have often interpreted the jewel in the garment as the "buddha nature." The *Lotus Sūtra* does not contain the precise term "buddha nature" (Ch. *foxing*; J. *busshō*), perhaps because it had not yet come into use in Indian Buddhism. However, the *Lotus* clearly recognizes the buddha potential in all beings, and Chinese exegetes argued that the concept is there, if not the term itself. The expression "buddha nature" was well known in medieval Japan, and Nichiren uses it occasionally, but he appears to have preferred "buddha realm" (among the ten realms) or "seed of buddhahood" (J. *busshu*). His use of the latter term is quite different from the Hossō idea of untainted seeds in the storehouse consciousness, mentioned in Chapter Four. "Buddha nature" and "seed of buddhahood" are similar in that both indicate the potential for buddhahood, supreme enlightenment, but where "nature" is constant and unchanging, "seeds" can lie dormant, even rot, or germinate and grow in response to conditions; as the *Lotus Sūtra* says, "The buddha-seeds germinate through dependent origination" (41). Thus, Nichiren may have used the term "seed of buddhahood" because he wished to portray buddhahood, not as an abstract potential, but as manifested through specific causes and conditions, that is, by embracing a specific form of practice. In that regard, he sometimes borrows Zhiyi's concept of the "buddha nature as three causes": (1) the innate potential for buddhahood; (2) the wisdom that illuminates it; and (3) the practice that manifests that wisdom. For Nichiren, that practice was chanting Namu Myōhō-renge-kyō, the act that manifests the jewel of the buddha realm hidden within the nine realms of ordinary people. Sometimes he refers to the daimoku itself as the "seed of buddhahood."[3]

According to Zhiyi's parsing, Chapters Two through Nine of the *Lotus Sūtra* comprise the main exposition of the "trace teaching," or *shakumon*, the first fourteen chapters of the *Lotus Sūtra*. These chapters assert that followers of the two "Hīnayāna" vehicles can achieve buddhahood. For the sūtra's compilers, this message subsumed the entire Buddhist mainstream within its own teaching of the one buddha vehicle and extended the promise of buddhahood to a category of persons—śrāvakas and pratyekabuddhas—who had been excluded from that possibility in other Mahāyāna sūtras. In Nichiren's day, however, the idea of the one vehicle, that buddhahood is in principle open to all, represented the mainstream interpretive position, and his own reading therefore has a somewhat different emphasis. For Nichiren, the sūtra's assertion that even persons of the two vehicles can become buddhas pointed to the mutual possession of the ten realms and the three thousand realms in a single thought-moment, without which any talk of buddhahood for anyone, even those following the bodhisattva path, can be no more than an abstraction. The revelation of this universal ground, he said, especially in the "Skillful Means" chapter, constitutes the heart of the *shakumon* portion of the *Lotus*. Nonetheless, he regarded Chapter Two through Chapter Nine, the main exposition section, as having been preached primarily for the benefit of persons during the Buddha's lifetime. The remaining chapters, Chapter Ten through Chapter Fourteen, which constituted the remainder of the trace teaching, he saw as explicitly directed toward those who embrace the *Lotus* after the Buddha's passing, and therefore, as having great relevance for himself and his followers. It is to those chapters that we now turn.

CHAPTER TEN

Expounder of the Dharma

The title of this chapter in Sanskrit is *dharmabhāṇaka,* literally "reciter of the dharma" or "proclaimer of the dharma." In early Buddhism, the discourses of the Buddha were not committed to writing. Instead, they were memorized by monks who specialized in particular sections of the canon; these monks were called "reciters of the dharma," as well as "keepers of the dharma" (*dharmadhara*) and "narrators of the dharma" (*dharmakathika*). With the rise of the Mahāyāna, the term *dharmabhāṇaka* seems to refer to those who preached the Mahāyāna sūtras.

Some scholars consider this chapter to have been added to the end of the original sūtra, which may have ended as early as Chapter Nine. It contains no prophecy, no plot, and no doctrine. It does contain a brief parable, although it is not traditionally counted as one. A thirsty man digging for water knows that if he digs up only dry earth, water is far away. However, when he digs up mud, he knows that water is near. In the same way, bodhisattvas who have not heard the *Lotus Sūtra* are far from enlightenment; for bodhisattvas who have heard it, enlightenment is near.

This chapter is instead a powerful advertisement for the *Lotus Sūtra*. The Buddha addresses his words to Bhaiṣajyarāja ("Medicine King"), a bodhisattva who has not appeared up to this point, except in the list of bodhisattvas in the audience in the first chapter; he will play a dramatic role in Chapter Twenty-Three.

The Buddha begins by saying that if there are those who hear even a single verse or line of the *Lotus Sūtra,* either in the Buddha's presence or after he has passed into nirvāṇa, and rejoice for even a single moment, he will confer on such persons a prophecy of their future buddhahood, another instance of rejoicing on hearing the sūtra as a sign of eventual enlightenment. To memorize, recite, or explain a single verse of the sūtra, or to pay homage to it by offering flowers, incense, fragrant oils, banners, or music, or to simply join one's palms together in reverence to the sūtra, is in effect to have paid homage to billions of buddhas in the past. Those who do these things should be respected throughout the world and should be revered in the same way as the Buddha. After the Buddha has passed away, those who uphold the *Lotus Sūtra* are great bodhisattvas who, voluntarily forgoing the rewards of their own pure deeds, have been born out of compassion in this troubled world to proclaim the sūtra far and wide for sentient beings' sake. They are "ambassadors of the Tathāgata," dispatched by him to carry out his work (165–66). One insightful modern analysis of this passage notes how a certain power is gained by choosing to regard one's present hardships as stemming, not from one's past misdeeds, as standard karma theory would hold, but from a vow compassionately undertaken to benefit others. The commentator argues that this perspective "can change the worldview of persons who really groan under the weight of suffering" and suggests that the *Lotus Sūtra* aims at converting its followers from "persons to be saved" to those who work actively to save others.[1]

The chapter also contains a warning, a warning about the future, but likely directed toward the first audiences of the *Lotus*

Sūtra, offering protection to those who accept it and threatening punishment for those who reject it. The Buddha explains hypothetically that were a disturbed person to disparage him in his presence over the course of an eon, that person would of course incur grave fault. Yet persons who utter a single word disparaging those who recite the *Lotus Sūtra* will incur fault that is far graver. The Buddha says that the sūtras he has taught in the past, now teaches, and will teach in the future number in the countless billions, but of these, the *Lotus Sūtra* is the most difficult to accept and understand. Therefore, the *Lotus Sūtra* should be distributed with care and not taught openly. People show hostility toward the sūtra even in his presence. How much more hostile, he says, will the response be after he has passed into nirvāṇa (169).

Still, those who recite the sūtra will be blessed and protected. In the verse portion that closes the chapter, the Buddha says that after his *parinirvāṇa,* "If there is any expounder of the dharma who recites this sūtra in a secluded, tranquil place where there is no sound of human beings, I will then manifest my body of pure light. If they forget a chapter or a verse, I will teach it to them, enabling them to master it" (173). But how can he do that if he has forever passed away? Not until Chapter Sixteen will we gain a clear answer to this question.

The opening passage of this chapter contains the first mention, recurring throughout the sūtra, of what Chinese exegetes would call the "five practices" or ways of upholding and disseminating the *Lotus Sūtra* after the Buddha's passing. Though English translations vary, the five practices are as follows: (1) to accept and uphold the *Lotus* (to "preserve" it, in the Kubo–Yuyama translation), indicating an underlying faith or commitment; (2) to read it; (3) to recite it from memory (Kubo and Yuyama collapse 2 and 3 as "to recite" the sūtra); (4) to explain it, which would include teaching and interpreting it; and (5) to copy it (165). These were in fact the forms of sūtra practice widely performed in East Asia, where the *Lotus* and other sūtras were enshrined, read, recited, copied, and lectured upon for a range of benefits, including protection of the realm, good fortune in this life, and the well-being of the deceased. These "five practices" together employ all three modes of action (karma): that is, actions of body, speech, and mind. For Nichiren, the first of the five, "accepting and upholding"—preserving—was the most important: "Embracing the *Lotus Sūtra* and chanting Namu Myōhō-renge-kyō at once encompasses all five practices."[2]

Nichiren also stressed to his followers that they themselves are the "ambassadors of the Tathāgata" praised by Śākyamuni Buddha in this chapter, the very people who, in an evil era after the Buddha's passing, will be able to uphold the sūtra and teach it to others. To one individual, borrowing the sūtra's language in this passage, he wrote: "It is rare to receive human birth, but you have done so. You have also encountered the buddhadharma, which is difficult to meet. And within the buddhadharma, you have found the daimoku of the *Lotus Sūtra* and now put it into practice. Truly you have 'already paid homage to tens of myriads of koṭis of buddhas of the past.'"[3]

The idea that one is an "ambassador of the Tathāgata" and has "already paid homage to tens of myriads of koṭis of buddhas" might seem to contradict another of Nichiren's claims, already discussed, that people born into the age of the Final Dharma have never before received the seed of buddhahood. Like most founders of religious movements, Nichiren taught according to his audience and circumstances and did not fully systematize his teachings; this would be one way to account for this apparent inconsistency. But there are also other ways to think about it. Past lives are unknowable, and talk about them by Buddhist teachers is intended to cast light on the present. Thus, we might think of the tension between these two ideas as Nichiren offering his followers alternative perspectives on their practice. To say that one has now received the seed of buddhahood for the very first time engenders gratitude for the rare opportunity of having encountered the daimoku of the *Lotus Sūtra*; to say that one has served countless buddhas in the past and been dispatched to this world as the Tathāgata's ambassador invests one's personal practice with the quality of a noble mission.

Nichiren said of himself that, being an ordinary person steeped in delusion, "my mind is far from that of the Tathāgata's ambassador." But because he had endured great trials for the *Lotus Sūtra*'s sake with his body and chanted its daimoku with his mouth, he continued, "I am like the Tathāgata's ambassador."[4] His claim to legitimacy as the teacher of the *Lotus Sūtra* for the Final Dharma age lay not in superior spiritual attainments, something he never asserted, but in the fact that he had fulfilled the sūtra's own predictions of the hardships its devotees would encounter in a troubled age after the Buddha's passing.

In this chapter, Śākyamuni declares: "There are immeasurable thousands of myriads of koṭis of sūtras I have taught in the past, which I teach now, and which I will teach in the future. Among them, however, this *Lotus Sūtra* is the most difficult to accept and to understand" (169). As a literary device, this statement cleverly preempts possible challenges to the *Lotus Sūtra*'s authority. Other sūtras might claim to be the Buddha's highest teaching, but such claims could always be dismissed by saying that any sūtra might be the "highest" that the Buddha had preached up until that point and yet had been superseded by later ones. The inclusion of both present and future teachings here precludes such a dismissal. East Asian interpreters, however, did not see this claim on the *Lotus Sūtra*'s part as a mere literary device. For Nichiren, it was nothing less than the Buddha's own statement of the relative ranking of the sūtras that he had expounded during his fifty years of teaching.

Nichiren's writings suggest two reasons why the *Lotus Sūtra* is "difficult to accept and to understand." First, as Saichō had noted, the provisional teachings—those preached before the *Lotus Sūtra*—were expounded "according to the minds of others," or in other words, the Buddha had accommodated them to the understanding of his listeners. In contrast, Śākyamuni preached the *Lotus Sūtra* "in accordance with his own mind," revealing his own enlightenment.[5] Nichiren took this to mean the Buddha's insight into the mutual inclusion of the ten realms, or more specifically, the understanding that "our inferior minds are endowed with the buddha realm."[6] For many of Nichiren's contemporaries, who believed that buddhahood was to be attained only after death in the Pure Land, this idea must have seemed deeply counterintuitive. "[Among the ten realms], the buddha realm alone is difficult to demonstrate," he acknowledged. "But having understood that your mind is endowed with the other nine realms, you should believe that it has the buddha realm as well. Do not have doubts about this."[7]

Another reason why the *Lotus Sūtra* is "difficult to accept and to understand" is because those who propagate it may encounter antagonism. "People show great hostility toward this sūtra, even in the presence of the Tathāgata," Śākyamuni declares in the present chapter. "How much more so after the parinirvāṇa of the Tathāgata!" (169). Although cast here in the form of a prophecy of what will happen after the Buddha's demise, this passage may point to opposition from the Buddhist mainstream encountered by the early *Lotus* community. For Nichiren, it foretold the hardships that he and his followers encountered in spreading the *Lotus Sūtra*. Writing from his first exile, to the Izu peninsula, he confessed, "When I first read this passage, I wondered if things would really be so terrible. But now I know that the Buddha's predictions do not err in the slightest, especially since I have experienced them personally."[8] For Nichiren, this sūtra passage carried a double legitimation, both of the *Lotus Sūtra* to which he had committed his life and of his own practice in upholding and propagating the *Lotus*. The passage is cited nearly fifty times in his extant writings.

At the same time, Nichiren saw the "difficulty" of embracing the *Lotus Sūtra* as pointing, not merely to the inevitability of hardships, but also to a guarantee of buddhahood. "To accept [the *Lotus Sūtra*] is easy," he wrote. "To uphold it is difficult. But the realization of buddhahood lies in upholding faith. Those who would uphold this sūtra should be prepared to meet difficulties. Without doubt, they will 'quickly attain the highest Buddha path'" (186).[9]

CHAPTER ELEVEN

The Appearance of the Jeweled Stūpa

One might imagine that the most visually dramatic moment in the *Lotus Sūtra* occurs in the first chapter, when the Buddha emits a beam of light from the tuft of hair between his eyes and illuminates myriad worlds. But the Buddha does things like that quite frequently in the Mahāyāna sūtras. A more visually dramatic moment in the *Lotus* occurs in Chapter Eleven.

The most significant physical structure in the Buddhist world is arguably not the monastery, or even the image of the Buddha. It is the stūpa. According to the *Great Discourse on the Final Nirvāṇa* (*Mahāparinibbāna Sutta*), the Buddha left specific instructions for the disposition of his body after his death. It was to be cremated, with the relics then entombed under a mound built at a crossroads. After his cremation, disputes broke out over which of the groups of the Buddha's followers would receive his remains. In the end, the relics were divided into eight shares to be enshrined by the Buddha's disciples in eight different principalities; the ashes remaining from the crematory fire and the urn used to divide the relics were also treated as holy objects. Ten stūpas were then built.[1] With the Buddha having passed into parinirvāṇa, all that was left were bits of bone recovered from the funeral pyre. These became the most precious substances in the Buddhist world, the only physical remnants of the Buddha's presence.

According to legend, one hundred years after the Buddha's death, the Indian king Aśoka broke open the stūpas, gathered all the relics, and then redistributed them in 84,000 stūpas across his vast realm. Despite this hyperbole, the stūpa would become the most ubiquitous element of the Buddhist landscape. Although displaying great differences in their architectural styles, the pagoda of East Asia, the *chöten* of Tibet, and the *chedi* of Southeast Asia are all stūpas. Paralleling relics as the remains of his physical body, the Buddha's teachings were sometimes referred to as his "dharma body," and a written text was often enshrined in stūpas instead of physical remains. A text frequently chosen for this purpose was the verse in which the monk had summarized the Buddha's teaching for Śāriptura, as related above in Chapter Two: "Of those things produced by causes, the Tathāgata has proclaimed their causes and also their cessation. Thus the great ascetic has spoken."

Stūpas played a central role in the Buddhist economy, both real and symbolic. They were usually relatively simply structures (especially compared with elaborate Hindu temples), mound-shaped forms that seemed to emerge from the landscape. Built using donations from the laity, they would in turn serve as magnets for further donations, becoming sites of pilgrimage and merit making. The control of a stūpa was therefore an important source of economic power for a community of monks.

With the rise of the Mahāyāna, long after the Buddha's passing, the physical texts of Mahāyāna sūtras were themselves sometimes treated as relics, with instructions that they should receive the same reverence typically offered to a stūpa or another kind of shrine called a *caitya*.[2] In the *Diamond Sūtra* (*Vajracchedikāprajñāpāramitā Sūtra*), the Buddha declares, "On whatever piece of ground one elucidates this sūtra, that piece of ground will become worthy of worship, that piece of ground will become worthy of veneration and reverential circumambulation for the whole world with its gods, human beings and demigods, that piece of ground will become a shrine."[3] But not all Mahāyāna sūtras extol the sūtra over the stūpa. Stūpas are repeatedly praised in the *Lotus Sūtra*. And in this chapter, a stūpa is the site for one of the sūtra's most important revelations. Indeed, foreshadowing what is about to happen, in Chapter Ten, the Buddha tells the bodhisattva Bhaiṣajyarāja, "Wherever this sūtra is taught, read, recited, copied, or wherever it is to be found, one should build a seven-jeweled stūpa of great height and width and richly ornamented. There is no need to put a relic inside. Why is this? Because the Tathāgata is already in it" (169).

Chapter Eleven begins, "At that time there appeared before the Buddha a seven-jeweled stūpa, five hundred *yojana*s in height and two hundred and fifty *yojana*s both in length and width, which emerged from the ground and hovered in the air" (175). We recall that a *yojana* was a unit of distance in ancient India, said to be the distance that a yoked team of oxen could pull a cart, or alternatively that the king's army could march in a day. A *yojana* has been variously estimated, with roughly eight miles being a common equivalent. By that calculation, the chapter opens with a massive stūpa, four thousand miles high and two thousand miles wide, emerging from beneath the ground. The stūpa is beautifully adorned with seven types of precious substances, decorated with banners, flags, garlands, and bells, and has the fragrance of sandalwood. Were this not sufficiently earth-shaking, a voice is heard from within the stūpa, declaring, "Splendid!" and praising Śākyamuni's preaching of the *Lotus Sūtra*. A stūpa contains a relic of a buddha, such as a tooth or a charred piece of bone. To hear a voice emanating from one is not simply startling; it is mildly eerie.

A bodhisattva called Mahāpratibhāna ("Great Eloquence"), speaking on behalf of the audience, asks the obvious questions: Why did a huge stūpa just emerge from the earth, and what is that voice? Śākyamuni responds that there is a buddha inside the stūpa. Long ago and in a universe far away, there was a buddha named Prabhūtaratna ("Abundant Jewels"). When he was a bodhisattva, Prabhūtaratna made a vow that when he became a buddha, after his passage into parinirvāṇa, his stūpa would appear wherever the *Lotus Sūtra* was being taught, and he would testify to its truth and would offer praise, saying "Splendid!" The Buddha explains that Prabhūtaratna is inside the stūpa. Mahāpratibhāna then asks whether it would be possible for everyone to see him. Śākyamuni explains that Prabhūtaratna's vow had further stipulated that if a future buddha wished to reveal Prabhūtaratna's form to the assembly, that buddha should first gather together all his magically created forms that are teaching the dharma in the worlds of the ten directions. The astonishing implication of this statement, which passes without further comment, is that all the billions of buddhas teaching the dharma in billions of worlds throughout the universe are in fact emanations of Śākyamuni.

Śākyamuni accordingly sends out a beam of light from the tuft of hair between his eyebrows, extending throughout the ten directions and summoning the buddhas there. But before they arrive, Śākyamuni must prepare seats for them, which involves a complete transformation of the world. In the Mahāyāna sūtras, our world is called the Sahā world. As noted earlier, *sahā* is often said to mean "endurance" or "forbearance," because there are many sufferings to be endured here. This is the buddha field (*buddhakṣetra*) of Śākyamuni, the domain of his salvific activities. It differs from the buddha fields of other buddhas. The buddha field of Śākyamuni is impure because it contains the realms of animals, ghosts, and denizens of hell. It is dirty, and, in what seems to have been most offensive to the ancient Indian sensibility, it is bumpy, with all manner of hills and mountains. Such a world is not a fit place to invite buddhas from throughout the universe; before these buddhas arrive, our world must be prepared.

And so the Sahā world is purified. It becomes completely flat, with no towns, oceans, rivers, mountains, or forests. Its roads are laid out like a chessboard and are bordered with cords of gold. There are jeweled trees and incense, and the ground is covered with blossoms. Furthermore, all the gods and humans in the world, except those seated in the assembly, are temporarily transported to other worlds, presumably to make room for the arriving buddhas. Each buddha brings just one bodhisattva attendant, and each buddha sits on a lion throne under a jeweled tree, but all the seats are filled before all the buddhas of even one of the ten directions arrives. So Śākyamuni twice creates more space by transforming billions of other lands, all made of *vaidurya* (probably chrysoberyl but sometimes regarded as lapis in East Asia), completely flat, and with no animals, ghosts, or denizens of hell, and with the humans and gods temporarily relocated elsewhere.

When all the buddhas have arrived, they each send an attendant forward to offer flowers to Śākyamuni, enquire about his health, and ask that he now open the huge stūpa that is suspended in midair. Śākyamuni rises into the air until he is floating in front of the door of the huge stūpa. With his right finger, he pushes back the bolt. There is a loud creaking sound, as though the gate of a great city were being opened. The door opens, revealing not a relic or a skeleton, but a buddha seated on a lion throne in the posture of meditation, his body whole and undecayed, like the uncorrupted body of a Roman Catholic saint. In light of the standard Buddhist doctrine of nirvāṇa, in which a buddha from the past never returns, this is an astounding sight. Yet something more astounding is about to occur. Prabhūtaratna moves over on his lion throne and invites Śākyamuni to sit down beside him.

One of the most famous texts of the Pāli Buddhist tradition is the *Questions of Milinda* (*Milindapañha*), a work presented in the form of a dialogue between a Greek king named Milinda and a Buddhist monk named Nāgasena. In fact, a king named Menander (Milinda in Indian sources) ruled a region that encompassed parts of modern India, Pakistan, and Afghanistan in the second century BCE, though whether he ever conversed with Nāgasena is open to question. The *Questions of Milinda* was probably composed or compiled around the beginning of the Common Era, roughly at the same time as the *Lotus Sūtra*. During their dialogue, the king asks why the Buddha said that there can only be one buddha in the universe at a time; if there were two, they might be able to share the labor of teaching the dharma. Nāgasena replies that the appearance of a buddha is such a rare and momentous event in the history of the universe that the cosmos is stretched to its limit by his majesty. The advent of a buddha is portrayed as an epochal moment that transforms the entire universe, requiring all its resources to sustain the brief presence of a single buddha. As Nāgasena says, "This ten-thousand world-system, sire, is the sustainer of one buddha, it sustains the special qualities of one tathāgatha only. If a second buddha were to arise, the ten-thousand world-system could not sustain him; it would tremble, shake, bend, bow down, twist, disperse, dissolve, scatter, it would disappear."[4]

Among the mainstream schools of Buddhism, the doctrine of a single buddha per world remained the orthodox position long after the *Lotus Sūtra* was composed. The *Abhidharmakośa* (and its auto-commentary) by the fourth-century monk Vasubandhu is one of the most influential compendia of "Hīnayāna" doctrine, widely read in India, East Asia, and Tibet. Its third chapter contains a long discussion of the question of whether two buddhas can appear in the same universe. However, the various opinions presented all accept that it is impossible. But what is meant by "universe"? Is it just one among the many world systems in the ten directions spoken of in Buddhist cosmology, or is the universe the whole of saṃsāra everywhere? Vasubandhu cites a sūtra that states, "It is impossible in the present, or in the future, for two tathāgatas, arhats, perfect buddhas to appear in the world without one preceding and the other following. It is impossible. It is the rule that there is only one." Vasubandhu offers four reasons why this is the case. First, there would be no utility in there being two buddhas in the same universe at the same time. Second, the bodhisattva who becomes a buddha vows to become a buddha "in a world blind and without a protector." If a buddha is already in that world, another protector is not needed. Third, a buddha receives greater respect in the world if he is the sole buddha. And fourth, sentient beings will feel the urgency of following a buddha's teachings if they know how rare it is for a buddha to appear in the world and realize that they will have no protector when he passes into nirvāṇa.[5] (We will see this same argument used for a different purpose in Chapter Sixteen of the *Lotus Sūtra*.)

And so the Buddhist mind is boggled by this scene. A huge stūpa appears, not flying down from another universe above, but breaking out from below the surface of our own world, coming up out of the earth like a fossil emerging from some prehistoric stratum, to then hover in the air. This is the stūpa of a buddha of the ancient past. And this stūpa does not contain a desiccated bit of bone; it contains a living, speaking buddha. Were this not enough, Śākyamuni, the buddha of the present, goes and sits down beside Prabhūtaratna, a buddha of the past, and both buddhas are alive in the present. The audience sees that the stūpa is not a reliquary, not a tomb. The buddhas are alive inside their stūpas. Thus, Śākyamuni will be alive within his stūpa. Indeed, the living Śākyamuni is now seated side by side with another living buddha.

All of this is happening in the air. The assembly cannot see well, so they ask the Buddha to elevate them so that they can see better. From here through the end of Chapter Twenty-Two, the action of the *Lotus Sūtra* takes place in the air above Vulture Peak. Having raised the entire assembly into open space, Śākyamuni declares, "Who in the Sahā world is able to extensively teach the *Lotus Sūtra*? It is now the right time! The Tathāgata will enter parinirvāṇa before long and the Buddha wants to transmit this *Lotus Sūtra* to you" (181). Here again, the *Lotus Sūtra* figures in its own narrative. It is at this point, in Chapter Eleven, with Prabhūtaratna having emerged from the earth and the other buddhas and bodhisattvas having arrived from across the universe, that the Buddha declares that the time is now right for him to teach the *Lotus Sūtra*.

The verse section that ends the chapter has a more somber tone, with the Buddha cautioning that it will be difficult to teach the *Lotus Sūtra* after he is gone. "It is not really difficult to enter into the conflagration at the time of the close of a kalpa carrying hay on your back and yet not be burned. It certainly will be difficult to preserve this sūtra and teach it even to a single person after my nirvāṇa" (184). But when the door of the stūpa opened, and the audience beheld the living body of Prabhūtaratna, they must have wondered what nirvāṇa really means.

What does this fantastic assembly, transcending the boundaries of time and space, represent? Throughout East Asia, the imagery of this chapter has inspired painting, sculpture, and exegesis. In Tiantai Buddhism, that imagery became part of a narrative of mythic origins: Zhiyi and his teacher Huisi, it was said, had together heard Śākyamuni Buddha's original preaching of the *Lotus Sūtra* in the Vulture Peak assembly and were later born together in China, where they became master and disciple. The Japanese Tendai founder Saichō incorporated this tradition into his account of his Tendai dharma lineage. Shortly after Saichō's death, when a new state-sponsored ordination platform was erected at the monastery that he had established on Mount Hiei, a representation of the jeweled stūpa of Prabhūtaratna, together with an image of Śākyamuni, was enshrined there. In medieval Japan, the Tendai esoteric "*Lotus* rite" or *Hokke hō*, conducted to realize buddhahood, eradicate sin, prolong life, quell disasters, and achieve other aims, employed a maṇḍala depicting the two buddhas Śākyamuni and Prabhūtaratna, seated side by side on a lotus, in its central court.

We have already touched on how, in part under the influence of the esoteric Buddhist teachings, medieval Tendai notions of practice and attainment shifted from a linear model of practice, in which one gradually cultivates merit and wisdom, striving for buddhahood as a future goal, to what one might call a timeless or "mandalic" model, in which buddhahood is revealed in the very act of faith and practice. Medieval Tendai texts sometimes express this conceptual shift with the phrase, "The assembly on Sacred Vulture Peak is still awesomely present and has not yet dispersed." Just as enlightenment was redefined as accessible in the present, so the assembly of the *Lotus Sūtra* where the two buddhas sat side by side in the jeweled stūpa came to be represented not as an event in the distant past, but as still ongoing. Some medieval Tendai writings identify this ever-present *Lotus* assembly with the liberating discernment of the three thousand realms in a single thought-moment, or more specifically, of the buddha realm within oneself.

Nichiren understood the emergence of the jeweled stūpa as the opening of the buddha realm in the act of chanting the daimoku. One of his followers, a lay monk known as Abutsu-bō, once asked him what the jeweled stūpa signified. Nichiren explained that, in essence, the stūpa's emergence meant that the śrāvaka disciples, on hearing the *Lotus Sūtra*, "beheld the jeweled stūpa of their own mind." The same was true, he said, of his own followers: "In the Final Dharma age, there is no jeweled stūpa apart from the figures of those men and women who uphold the *Lotus Sūtra*. . . . The daimoku of the *Lotus Sūtra* is the jeweled stūpa, and the jeweled stūpa is Namu Myōhō-renge-kyō. . . . You, Abutsu-bō, are yourself the jeweled stūpa, and the jeweled stūpa is none other than you, Abutsu-bō. . . . So believing, chant Namu Myōhō-renge-kyō, and wherever you chant will be the place where the jeweled stūpa dwells."[6]

Nichiren also drew on the imagery of the jeweled stūpa and the timeless *Lotus* assembly for the calligraphic maṇḍala that he devised as an object of worship for his followers. It is known as the great maṇḍala (*daimandara*) or "revered object of worship" (*gohonzon*). Where many Buddhist maṇḍalas represent pictorially the realms of buddhas and bodhisattvas, Nichiren's great maṇḍala is written entirely in Chinese characters, along with two Sanskrit glyphs. "Namu Myōhō-renge-kyō" is inscribed vertically down the center of the maṇḍala, flanked by the characters for the names of the two buddhas, Śākyamuni and Prabhūtaratna, just as they sat together in the jeweled stūpa. They in turn are surrounded by the names of representatives of the innumerable bodhisattvas, gods, humans, demons, and others present at the *Lotus* assembly. As an ensemble, the maṇḍala represents the realm of the primordial buddha, or the "three thousand realms in a single-thought moment in actuality." By chanting the title with faith in the *Lotus Sūtra,* Nichiren said, one is able to enter the assembly of the *Lotus* maṇḍala and participate in the enlightened reality that it depicts.

Nichiren wrote that the *gohonzon* represents the *Lotus* assembly "as accurately as the print matches the woodblock."[7] On it, all ten realms, even the lowest ones, are represented. We find the belligerent asura king; the dragon king, representing the animal realm; the demon Hārītī (J. Kishimojin); even the Buddha's malicious cousin Devadatta, who tried to kill him on multiple occasions; and Devadatta's patron, King Ajātaśatru, who murdered his father and supported Devadatta in his evil schemes. As Nichiren wrote, "Illuminated by the five characters of the *daimoku,* all ten realms assume their inherent enlightened aspect."[8] We might interpret this as reflecting Nichiren's message that, through the chanting of the daimoku, even life's harsh, ugly, and painful parts—the most adverse circumstances, or the darkest character flaws—can be transformed and yield something of value, becoming opportunities to further religious development.

In the concluding verse section of this chapter, now seated in midair within the jeweled stūpa beside Prabhūtaratna, Śākyamuni Buddha again stresses how difficult it will be to uphold the *Lotus Sūtra* after his passing, setting forth the analogy of what Nichiren summarized as the "nine easy and six difficult acts." There is some irony in this term; the "nine easy acts" are virtually impossible. They involve either extraordinary physical feats, such as placing the earth on one's toe and ascending with it to the heavens of Brahmā, or teaching incalculable numbers of sentient beings by means of provisional teachings, leading them to lesser attainments than buddhahood, such as arhatship or the six supernormal powers. In contrast, the "six difficult acts" all entail the practice of the true teaching, the *Lotus Sūtra*, in the troubled world after the Buddha's passing. The six acts are: (1) to teach the *Lotus Sūtra*; (2) to copy it, or cause others to copy it; (3) to recite it, even for a short while; (4) to teach it to even one other person; (5) to hear and accept it, and inquire about its meaning; and (6) to preserve it. The compilers of the *Lotus Sūtra* may have sought to ensure the *Lotus Sūtra*'s survival into the future by showing that the Buddha himself praised the heroism of those who would brave any adversity to uphold it after he was gone from the world.

Nichiren read this passage as directly addressing his own circumstances and those of his followers, and he stressed that the sūtra was in fact speaking to them. For example, to a lay nun who had asked him a question about the sūtra, he wrote that her query itself was "a root of great good." He continued: "Now in this Final Dharma age, those who ask about the meaning of even one phrase or verse of the *Lotus Sūtra* are rarer than those who can fling Mount Sumeru to the worlds of another quarter . . . or those who can uphold and preach countless other sūtras, causing the monastics and lay people who hear them to attain the six supernormal powers. The chapter called 'A Jeweled Stūpa' in the fourth fascicle of the *Lotus Sūtra* sets forth the important teaching of the six difficult and nine easy acts. Your posing a question about the *Lotus Sūtra* is among the six difficult acts. You should know thereby that, if you uphold the sūtra, you will become a buddha in your present body."[9]

Toward the end of the same verse passage, the Buddha declares that those who can uphold the *Lotus Sūtra* in a troubled age following his parinirvāṇa will be praised by all buddhas: they are courageous, persevering, and "are known as those who follow the rules of good conduct" (186). "The rules of good conduct" here refers to the precepts, the rules of moral discipline to be upheld by Buddhists. In Nichiren's time, the significance of the precepts was hotly disputed. Hōnen had taught that birth in the Pure Land depends solely upon entrusting oneself to the power of Amitābha Buddha's vow; whether one keeps or breaks the precepts has no bearing on one's salvation. Others, such as the monk Eison (1201–1290), held that, precisely because the times were degenerate and adverse, strict observance of the precepts was more essential than ever. Nichiren, following this sūtra passage, maintained that upholding the *Lotus Sūtra* is itself keeping the precepts. The five characters of the daimoku, the heart of the *Lotus Sūtra,* he said, form the "all-encompassing wonderful precept" by which all buddhas realize their enlightenment.[10] Nichiren generally endorsed the traditional Buddhist ethic of compassion and generosity, along with its moral principles that discourage such evils as killing, lying, theft, and sexual misconduct. However, he did not see following rules of conduct as a prerequisite to liberation in the age of the Final Dharma. Because the daimoku contains within itself all the countless practices and good acts of all past, present, and future buddhas, he taught, simply to chant it is to uphold the precepts. Nichiren also seems to have believed that this practice would foster upright conduct, for he claimed that "one who chants [the daimoku] as the *Lotus Sūtra* teaches will not have a crooked mind."[11]

CHAPTER TWELVE

Devadatta

The story of the Buddha has two villans—one divine, one human. The divine villain is Māra, mentioned by Śāriputra in Chapter Three. The human villain is Devadatta, the Buddha's cousin, often held up as the paradigmatic example of an *icchantika,* someone so profoundly and incorrigibly deluded as to have no prospect of liberation. Chapter Twelve is named after him. Accounts of Devadatta in the Buddhist canon vary. Devadatta became a monk when the Buddha returned to his home city of Kapilavastu one year after his enlightenment. Initially Devadatta seems to have been a dedicated monk and gained formidable meditative powers, winning a saintly reputation. At some point, however, he began to nurture a malign jealousy toward Śākyamuni Buddha and to plot against him. When the Buddha was past seventy, Devadatta stood up in the assembly of monks and suggested that, because of the Buddha's advanced age, leadership of the order of monks should be turned over to him. It was time for the Buddha to rest. But the Buddha refused, and in one of his harsher remarks as recorded in the canon demanded, "Why would I turn over the order to a clot of spittle like you?"[1]

Smarting from this public humiliation, Devadatta plotted to assassinate the Buddha. He first hired sixteen archers to kill him, but the Buddha ended up converting each of them. Next, Devadatta decided to kill the Buddha himself, pushing a large boulder down Vulture Peak as the Buddha was walking back and forth in its shade. Two large outcroppings miraculously rose out of the mountain to block its path, but a splinter of rock broke off and struck the Buddha's toe, causing it to bleed. Devadatta tried a third time to murder the Buddha, this time sending the great elephant Nāḷāgiri, made drunk on palm wine, to trample him. But when he reached the Buddha, the elephant kneeled, and the Buddha stroked his head.

Unable to kill the Buddha, Devadatta then resolved to win the allegiance of the order of monks by recommending that all monks follow five rules: (1) they should live in the forest and not in villages; (2) they should subsist on alms and not accept invitations to dine in the homes of the laity; (3) they should only wear robes made from discarded rags and not accept offerings of cloth from the laity; (4) they should dwell at the foot of a tree and not under a roof; (5) they should not eat fish or meat. In response, the Buddha declared that any monk who wished to obey these rules could do so, but he would not make these practices obligatory. Such practices, known as *dhutaguṇas*, represent extra austerities, beyond what is required by monastic rule. They are sometimes undertaken by monks of a strong ascetic bent. Devadatta's intent was clearly to present himself as more rigorous in monastic observance than even the Buddha; he then denounced Śākyamuni as being lax in ascetic practice. Devadatta apparently won over a substantial number of young monks, who departed with him to start a new saṃgha. But the Buddha sent Śāriputra and Maudgalyāyana to persuade them to return. At the news of their desertion, Devadatta vomited blood. Knowing that his end was near, he set off to see the Buddha one last time. Some accounts say that he was sincerely contrite; others relate that he smeared poison on his fingernails for one last assassination attempt. As he rested at the bank of a pond, he was slowly swallowed by the earth, first his feet, then his knees, then his chest, then his neck. He uttered a stanza of praise to the Buddha before he went under, descending to the Avīci hell, where he suffered a horrible fate.

As discussed earlier, five deeds, called "deeds of immediate retribution," cause one to be reborn in Avīci immediately after death. They are also known as the five heinous offenses. These five offenses are: (1) killing one's father, (2) killing one's mother, (3) killing an arhat, (4) wounding a buddha, and (5) causing dissension in the monastic community. Devadatta committed the fourth and fifth of these offenses. When the nun Utpalavarṇā had berated Devadatta for his evil conduct, he beat her to death. Because she was an arhat, he was also guilty of the third offense.

The story of Devadatta is quite famous, and the authors of the *Lotus Sūtra* would have known it well, making Chapter Twelve even more remarkable. The Buddha says that in a past life, a king tirelessly sought the Mahāyāna, renouncing the throne to find it. A sage came and told the king that he possessed a Mahāyāna teaching called the *Lotus Sūtra* and would expound it to him if the king would promise to obey him. The king joyfully accepted, becoming his servant. The king served the sage for a thousand years, gathering firewood and collecting water; he "never tired in either body or mind" (187). The Buddha explains that in that lifetime, he was the king and Devadatta was the sage; the Buddha declares that it is due to Devadatta's virtuous friendship that he eventually became a buddha. He then makes a prophecy of Devadatta's own future buddhahood, predicting the name he will bear and the length of his lifespan. (The sūtra makes no mention of Devadatta's crimes or of his punishment in the Avīci hell).[2] The Buddha concludes by saying that anyone in the future who hears the "Devadatta" chapter of the *Lotus Sūtra* and accepts it with a pure mind will never be reborn as an animal, as a ghost, or in the hells, but will be reborn in the presence of the buddhas.

That this chapter is mentioned in the text by name suggests that the chapter, or at least this part of it, is a later interpolation of a previously independent text. In fact, the "Devadatta" chapter was missing from Kumārajīva's original translation into Chinese. The Chinese pilgrim monk Faxian acquired a Sanskrit text of the chapter in his travels through Turfan and translated it together with an Indian monk named Dharmamati (Fayi) around 490. It was subsequently incorporated into Kumārajīva's version.[3] One might speculate that the "Devadatta" chapter was inserted into the *Lotus Sūtra* because it provides a powerful confirmation of the sūtra's claim that all beings will one day become buddhas. For here, two unlikely figures—one of the greatest sinners in the history of Buddhism, the other an eight-year-old princess—are exalted, one with a prophecy of buddhahood, the other by the achievement of buddhahood itself.

After Śākyamuni recounts his past relationship with Devadatta, the scene shifts abruptly back to Prabhūtaratna and his stūpa. A bodhisattva who was accompanying Prabhūtaratna suggests that they return home, but Śākyamuni asks him to wait because he wants this bodhisattva, whose name is Prajñākūṭa ("Wisdom Accumulation"), to meet Mañjuśrī. As we saw in Chapter One, Mañjuśrī had been in the assembly of the *Lotus Sūtra*, but here he is depicted as arriving from the depths of the ocean where he has been preaching the dharma in the palace of Sāgara, the *nāga* king. Nāgas, usually depicted with the head and torso of a human and the tail of a snake, are among the most important nonhuman creatures in Buddhism, said to abide in the depths of the waters and to possess great treasures. In China, *nāga* was translated as "dragon." The bodhisattva asks Mañjuśrī how many beings he instructed in the ocean. Countless beings, Mañjuśrī replies, and, as though to verify his words, innumerable bodhisattvas whom he has taught emerge from the ocean and arrive at the assembly seated on jeweled lotus blossoms. Mañjuśrī declares that in the ocean he taught only the *Lotus Sūtra*. Prajñākūṭa asks if sentient beings who practice the *Lotus Sūtra* will quickly become buddhas. Mañjuśrī says that they will. What follows is another of the famous scenes in the sūtra.

As an example of someone able to attain buddhahood immediately, Mañjuśrī mentions an eight-year-old nāga girl, the daughter of King Sāgara. Prajñākūṭa is skeptical, noting the many eons that the buddha Śākyamuni spent accumulating merit on the bodhisattva path. "It is hard to believe that this girl will instantly attain complete enlightenment" (192), he says. The nāga princess immediately appears and speaks verses of praise of the Buddha. At this point, Śāriputra joins the conversation, declaring that the female body is polluted and is not a fit vessel for the dharma. A woman has five obstructions that prevent her from becoming a universal monarch (*cakravartin*), the deities Brahmā, Śakra, and Māra, or a buddha.[4]

At that point, the nāga princess presents a priceless jewel to the Buddha, which he accepts. She then asks Prajñākūṭa and Śāriputra, "Was that done quickly, or not?" When they agree that it was done extremely quickly, she says, "Watch me become a buddha even more quickly than that" (193). She immediately turns into a male, fulfills the bodhisattva practices, goes to the *vimalā* ("stainless") world in the south, sits on a jeweled lotus flower, achieves buddhahood with a body endowed with the major and minor extraordinary marks, and then teaches the dharma, causing beings in both that world and the Sahā world to progress on the path, receiving predictions of buddhahood. Prajñākūṭa and Śāriputra look on in silence and believe.

This remarkable scene is often mentioned in discussions of the question of gender in Buddhism. The power of the nāga princess's transformation in the face of the misogyny of the monks and bodhisattvas is diluted, at least to some degree, by the fact that she first turns into a male before she becomes a buddha. Modern readers often find this element in the story disappointing and regard it as betraying the compilers' inability to conceive of buddhahood in female form. Undeniably, tensions have existed in the Buddhist tradition between doctrines that are soteriologically egalitarian (such as the emptiness of all constructed categories such as "male" and "female," or notions of a universal buddha nature) and entrenched social norms of female subordination.[5] Where gender hierarchy is now often understood as a human construct, susceptible to revision, a traditional Buddhist perspective would more likely have seen it as the fruit of past karma. Śāriputra's objection about the pollution of women's bodies and the "five obstructions" believed to constrain their potential reflected commonly held assumptions. Some contemporary exegetes accordingly argue that the nāga princess displayed her sex change as a compassionate "skillful means" designed to convince her (largely male) audience, who could not otherwise have recognized her buddhahood. From Mañjuśrī's description of her attainments, even before she appears at the assembly, it is obvious that the nāga girl's female form has not hindered her from achieving the highest levels of bodhisattva practice. No sooner had she "produced the thought of enlightenment" than she "attained the stage of non-retrogression," leaping over stages of cultivation ordinarily said to require many lifetimes (191). Indeed, for many monastic commentators on the sūtra in East Asia, what is remarkable about the story was not the sex of the nāga princess, but the speed with which she traversed the lengthy path to buddhahood.

As noted above, the "Devadatta" chapter underscores the *Lotus Sūtra*'s inclusivity by extending the possibility of buddhahood to categories of persons thought to labor under particularly heavy karmic burdens: evil men and all women. Nichiren took the Devadatta story as illustrating the unique power of the *Lotus Sūtra* to save even the most wicked and depraved.

According to conventional Buddhist thinking, moral conduct is the beginning and foundation of the path; persons can achieve liberation only by first renouncing evil and cultivating good. It is said that one cannot control one's mind until one first learns to control one's body and speech. The Buddhist ethical code seeks to provide such control. However, some Buddhist thinkers in Nichiren's time were concerned with the problem posed by evils that one cannot avoid. This concern had to do with a keen awareness of human limitations, heightened by a sense of living in an age of decline. It also spoke to the situation of warriors, who were gaining influence both as a social group and as an emergent body of religious consumers. From a Buddhist perspective, warriors were trapped in a hereditary profession that was inherently sinful, requiring them to kill animals as a form of war training and kill humans on the battlefield. Thus, they could not escape violating the basic Buddhist precept against taking life. Nichiren, who had a number of samurai among his followers, stressed that, as long as one chants the daimoku, one will not be dragged down into the hells or other evil paths by ordinary misdeeds or unavoidable wrongdoing. To one warrior, a certain Hakii (or Hakiri) Saburō, he wrote: "In all the earlier sūtras of the Buddha's lifetime, Devadatta was condemned as the foremost *icchantika* in all the world. But he encountered the *Lotus Sūtra* and received a prediction that he would become a tathāgata called Devarāja. . . . Whether or not evil persons of the last age can attain buddhahood does not depend upon whether their sins are light or heavy but rests solely upon whether or not they have faith in this sūtra."[6]

According to the "Devadatta" chapter, the relationship between Śākyamuni Buddha and his treacherous cousin was not purely a matter of this lifetime. The very fact that he has become the Buddha, Śākyamuni says, is due to Devadatta's past "good and virtuous friendship" (189). "Good and virtuous friendship" here translates *kalyāṇamitra* (J. *zenchishiki*, literally, "good friend"), one who teaches or encourages another on the Buddhist path. In view of the traditional accounts of his repeated betrayals, Devadatta would seem to have been no "friend" at all. Nichiren, however, took this passage as teaching not only the inevitability of meeting enemies in one's efforts to spread the dharma—"the Buddha and Devadatta are like a form and its shadow; in lifetime after lifetime, they are never separated"[7]—but also the importance of appreciating the opportunity for spiritual development that their hostility makes possible. "In this age as well, it is not one's allies but one's bitterest enemies who help one improve," he wrote. In this context, Nichiren expressed gratitude for the clerics and government officials who had persecuted him, adding that, without them, he could not have proven himself as a votary of the *Lotus Sutra*.[8]

The nāga girl's story was variously interpreted in premodern Japan.[9] Discourses of female karmic hindrances were widespread, especially among scholar-monks and other educated elites, but the *Lotus Sūtra* was believed to promise women full enlightenment; in the realm of religious practice, the nāga princess's transformation into a male seems often to have been ignored, or at least not belabored. The "Devadatta" chapter was sometimes recited as part of funerary and memorial rites for women, to ensure their future buddhahood.

Nichiren maintained that the *Lotus Sūtra* enables women to attain buddhahood as women, because it embodies the mutual encompassing of the ten dharma realms. He writes: "The other Mahāyāna sūtras would seem to permit women to attain either buddhahood or birth in the pure land [of Amitābha], but that is an attainment premised on changing their [female] form, not the direct manifestation of buddhahood grounded in the three thousand realms in a single thought-moment. Thus, it is an attainment of buddhahood or pure land birth in name but not reality. The nāga girl represents the 'one example that applies to all.' Her attainment of buddhahood opened the way for the attainment of buddhahood . . . by all women of the latter age."[10]

To be sure, Nichiren's assertions about women's realization of buddhahood tend to foreground the power of the *Lotus Sūtra,* rather than women's capacity for buddhahood in and of itself. Unless women place faith in the *Lotus,* buddhahood lies beyond their reach. But because he believed that no one, male or female, could attain buddhahood through provisional teachings, his stance is hardly discriminatory. Nichiren's core followers included several women whom, judging by his letters, he held in great respect. Unlike Śāriputra in the "Devadatta" chapter, and against notions of female pollution in his own time, Nichiren did not see the female body as filthy and on at least one occasion explicitly denied that menstrual blood is defiling.[11] He also suggested that faith in the *Lotus Sūtra* might even in some sense subvert conventional gender hierarchy: "A woman who embraces this sūtra," he wrote," not only surpasses all other women but also surpasses all men."[12]

Women's capacity for buddhahood was not the only message that East Asian exegetes drew from the nāga princess episode. Her story was also taken as evidence that some practitioners might "realize buddhahood with this very body" (*sokushin jōbutsu*). Within the Tiantai tradition, Zhanran may have been first to use this term for the nāga princess's enlightenment. One might question how her enlightenment could be termed realizing buddhahood "with this very body" when she transforms into a man: however, commentators did not necessarily see this sex change as a complete bodily transformation, such as one undergoes between successive lifetimes. The doctrine of *sokushin jōbutsu,* which developed especially in Japan, had two major implications: a drastic shortening of the length of time deemed necessary to achieve enlightenment, and the possibility of doing so without first eradicating the defilements of an ordinary person.

Saichō identified this doctrine as one of ten ways in which the *Lotus Sūtra* surpasses all others. In contrast to conventional Mahāyāna notions of the bodhisattva path as requiring three incalculable eons to fulfill—a position maintained by his chief rivals, the Hossō school—Saichō saw the *Lotus Sūtra* as the "direct path" or "great direct path" of rapid realization, requiring only one, two, or at the most three lifetimes. The nāga girl's story underscored this possibility. She had, Saichō noted, a threefold hindrance: as a nāga, she belonged to the animal realm; she was female and of poor faculties; and being only eight years old, she had not been able to devote much time to religious discipline. Nonetheless, through the wondrous power of the *Lotus Sūtra,* she had attained buddhahood.

In the development of Tendai Buddhism after Saichō, the implications of the nāga princess's achievement were analyzed and disputed from many angles. Was the enlightenment to be realized "with this body" full or partial? To which of the stages of bodhisattva practice did it correspond? Was this kind of immediate realization accessible to all, or only to those who had cultivated practice in prior lifetimes? With some exceptions, later Tendai thinking shifted away from Saichō's notion of attaining buddhahood within three lifetimes to an emphasis on direct realization of buddhahood in one's present body. By Nichiren's time, one strand of scholastic argument held that, at least in principle, even ordinary deluded persons might be able to access buddhahood at the beginning stages of faith and practice.[13] Nichiren taught that embracing the *Lotus Sūtra* would make this a reality: "The *Lotus Sūtra* is the Buddha's teaching and the Buddha's wisdom. When one puts faith in even a single character or brushstroke, one immediately becomes a buddha in one's present body. . . . Just as poison can be turned into medicine, so [the *Lotus Sūtra*] transforms ordinary beings into buddhas. That is why it is called the wonderful dharma."[14]

CHAPTER THIRTEEN

Perseverance

This chapter begins with two bodhisattvas, Bhaiṣajyarāja ("Medicine King") and Mahāpratibhāna ("Great Eloquence"), pledging to preserve, recite, and teach the *Lotus Sūtra* "in the troubled world to come" after the Buddha passes into nirvāṇa. We have already encountered these two bodhisattvas in Chapters Ten and Eleven, respectively. They are joined by two thousand other bodhisattvas in making this vow. Then the five hundred arhats who had received prophecies of their future buddhahood in Chapter Eight pledge to teach the *Lotus Sūtra* extensively in other worlds. The eight thousand persons who had received predictions of their future buddhahood in Chapter Nine, both those who had more to learn and those who did not, similarly vow to teach the *Lotus Sūtra* in lands other than this Sahā world after the Buddha passes into nirvāṇa, because this world has "many erring people . . . who are quick to anger, deceitful and untrue" (195).

At that point, the Buddha's aunt and foster mother, the eminent nun Mahāprajāpatī, along with six thousand other nuns, stands up with her palms joined and gazes intently at the Buddha. The Buddha says to her, "Why are you anxiously staring at the Tathāgata? Are you thinking that I have not given you your prediction of highest, complete enlightenment?" (196). There is a hint of annoyance in his question, reminiscent of his annoyance at Ānanda, suggested in a traditional account, for badgering him into establishing an order of nuns in the first place. He then gives rather perfunctory predictions for both Mahāprajāpatī as well as his former wife, Yaśodharā, who is also a nun. They too vow to propagate the *Lotus Sūtra* "in other lands" (197).

This marks an important moment in the sūtra, for here, with the Buddha's prediction that his foster mother and his former wife will become buddhas in the future, all the members of the assembly enumerated in the first paragraph of Chapter One have received predictions of their future buddhahood. In other words, all the major figures of the earlier tradition have now become passengers on the single vehicle, the buddha vehicle. They are not depicted as having been kidnapped or coerced; having heard the good news that there is but one vehicle, they have clambered on board. This is yet another brilliant device of the sūtra's self-promotion, that shortly before the Buddha passed into nirvāṇa, he revealed a teaching that all the famous monks and nuns of the tradition joyfully accepted.

At that point, billions of bodhisattvas come forward, pledging to enable sentient beings throughout the worlds of the ten directions to copy, preserve, recite, explain, and practice the *Lotus Sūtra* after the Buddha has passed into nirvāṇa. In the verse portion that follows, they predict a sad state of future affairs, where followers of the sūtra will be disparaged with harsh words and attacked with sticks and swords. The monks at that time will be arrogant and deceitful. About the followers of the *Lotus Sūtra,* such evil monks will say, "All of these monks here teach heretical doctrines because they are greedy for profit! They have fabricated this sūtra to deceive the people of the world, and they explain this sūtra out of desire for fame!" "They will mockingly address us, saying: 'All you buddhas!'"

"They will utter evil words with angry countenances, and they will repeatedly expel us, and keep us away from the monasteries and stūpas" (198–99).

Though purporting to foretell the future, prophecies—especially ominous ones—often describe the present. The grim predictions in this passage may in fact reflect experiences of ostracism and insult endured by the early *Lotus* community at the hands of the mainstream Buddhist establishment; whether the specifics refer to events that actually happened or simply reflect the beleaguered sensibilities of a small and marginalized community is hard to know. In either event, this passage describes the harsh trials accompanying the *Lotus Sūtra*'s propagation in the form of prophecy. This is how it was received a millennium later in Japan.

In Nichiren's reading, the predictions of future buddhahood that Śākyamuni Buddha confers at the beginning of this chapter on the remaining śrāvaka disciples—Mahāprajāpatī, his aunt and foster mother, and Yaśodharā, his former wife and the mother of Rāhula—were further evidence that the *Lotus*, unlike other Mahāyāna sūtras, guaranteed buddhahood to women, a point he stressed to his female followers. To one woman he wrote that she, practicing as she did in the present, troubled world, far surpassed Mahāprajāpatī, who had vowed in this chapter only to "extensively expound this sūtra in other lands" (197).[1]

What particularly drew Nichiren's attention in Chapter Thirteen, however, was the verse section just discussed, comprising twenty lines in Kumārajīva's Chinese version, in which eighty myriad *koṭis* of *nayutas* of advanced bodhisattvas who have gathered from other worlds all vow to Śākyamuni Buddha to preach the *Lotus Sutra* throughout the worlds of the ten directions, going on to enumerate the trials they are willing to undergo in order to disseminate the sūtra in an evil age after his final nirvāṇa. Based on this passage, in his commentary on Zhiyi's *Lotus Sutra* lectures, Zhanran formulated the concept of "three kinds of powerful enemies" who will obstruct *Lotus Sūtra* devotees: ignorant lay people, who will speak ill of them or attack them with staves and swords; deceitful monks of false wisdom who in their conceit "think they have attained what they have not" (198); and prominent monks who make a show of holiness, acting like forest-dwelling saints, but are actually greedy and arrogant and who slander *Lotus* devotees to persons in authority, including kings, ministers, and members of the priestly caste, as well as to other monks and lay householders. Sentenced to exile for the second time, Nichiren wrote that while the three types of enemies predicted in the "Perseverance" chapter were much in evidence in his day, not one of the eighty myriad *koṭis* of *nayutas* of bodhisattvas who had pledged themselves to the *Lotus Sūtra*'s propagation was to be seen. There was only himself. Accordingly, he resolved, "I will propagate this sūtra on behalf of those eighty myriad *koṭis* of *nayutas* of bodhisattvas. May they extend to me their aid and protection."[2]

Indeed, the passage in the "Perseverance" chapter coincided eerily with Nichiren's own ordeals. He himself had been "disparaged with evil words" and "attacked with sticks and swords" (198). He had been slandered to the high officials of the shogunate by monks revered as holy by the people at large and been "repeatedly expelled" (199). Especially during the ordeals of his Sado Island exile, Nichiren wrestled with self-doubts. Had the protective deities abandoned him? Was he, after all, not correctly practicing the *Lotus Sūtra*? By his own account, however, on recalling the verse section of the "Perseverance" chapter, he realized that he was living out the sūtra's prophecies in a way unlike any other *Lotus* devotee. "Without me," he concluded, "the predictions in these verses would all be lies."[3] One modern interpreter of Nichiren has termed this a "circular hermeneutic" in which text and reader simultaneously mirror and bear witness to one another. Nichiren validated the truth of the *Lotus Sūtra*'s words by undergoing in his own person the very trials that it predicted. Yet at the same time, the *Lotus Sūtra* now validated Nichiren's practice, as the persecutions he encountered were predicted in the *Lotus* itself.[4]

Nichiren termed his practice "bodily reading" of the *Lotus Sūtra*, meaning that he had fulfilled its predictions in his own person and was "not attached to body or life" (199) in his efforts to propagate it. The same applied, he said, to those disciples who shared his commitment. On the eve of his banishment to Sado Island, he wrote to his disciple Nichirō who had also been seized and imprisoned, praising his dedication. "Others read the *Lotus Sūtra* with their mouths alone, reading only the words, but they do not read it with their mind. And even if they read it with their mind, they do not read it with their body. To read the sūtra as you are doing with both body and mind is truly admirable."[5]

In Nichiren's time, those who devoted themselves to reciting or copying the *Lotus Sūtra* as their primary practice were known as *jikyōsha*, "one who holds the sūtra." Nichiren instead used the term *gyōja* (literally, "one who practices"; translated in this volume as "practitioner" or "votary"). *Gyōja* was often used to mean an adept or ascetic, denoting those who performed harsh austerities, such as going without sleep, fasting, and practicing in isolation in the mountains, with the aim of acquiring spiritual powers. Though Nichiren did not endorse ascetic practice for its own sake, his use of the word *gyōja*, like that of "bodily reading," suggests both that he was "living" the *Lotus Sūtra,* personally encountering the hardships it predicts, and also that he had committed his life to its propagation. The term reflects his self-understanding as one entrusted with the task of spreading the *Lotus* in the Final Dharma age. He wrote, "None of the *jikyōsha* of Japan have encountered the trials predicted in these passages. I alone have read them. This is what is meant by the statement [in the "Perseverance" chapter], 'We will not be attached to our bodies or lives. We only desire the highest path' (199). This being the case, I am the foremost votary of the *Lotus Sūtra* in Japan."[6]

Willingness to give even one's life if need be took on deep soteriological meaning for Nichiren over the course of his career. By persevering for the *Lotus Sūtra*'s sake, he taught, one could expiate in a single lifetime one's evil karma from countless past lifetimes; repay one's obligations to the Buddha and to all living beings; fulfill the bodhisattva path; and be assured of fully realizing buddhahood in this lifetime. On this theme, he wrote to his followers: "Life flashes by in but a moment. No matter how many powerful enemies may oppose us, never think of retreating or give way to fear. Even if they should cut off our heads with a saw, impale our bodies with lances, or bind our feet and bore them through with a gimlet, so long as we have life, we must chant Namu Myōhō-renge-kyō, Namu Myōhō-renge-kyō. And if we chant up until the very moment of death, Śākyamuni, Prabhūtaratna, and the buddhas of the ten directions will come to us instantly . . . and surely escort us to the jeweled land of Tranquil Light."[7]

CHAPTER FOURTEEN

Ease in Practice

This chapter continues the theme of practice "in the troubled world to come" after the Buddha's nirvāṇa (201). It begins with Mañjuśrī asking the Buddha how bodhisattvas who teach the *Lotus Sūtra* should comport themselves in the difficult time ahead (again, likely reflecting the experience of devotees at the time of the sūtra's compilation). The main body of the chapter explains in detail four kinds of practices that Mahāyāna bodhisattvas should follow in teaching the *Lotus Sūtra* in that troubled age, consisting of bodily actions, speech, thoughts, and vows. In China, they would be summarized as the "four practices of ease and bliss" (*si anle xing*). The phrase "ease in practice" (J. *anrakugyō*) in the chapter title, sometimes translated as "peaceful (or blissful) practice," can mean tranquil stability of mind in the midst of all activities. Huisi (515–577), Zhiyi's teacher, termed this "practice without characteristics," meaning a meditation that is not defined by a specific posture or ritual setting, but that can be carried out in the course of whatever one may be doing. Many of the Buddha's instructions for "peaceful practice" in this chapter suggest actions that do not give offense. For example, the bodhisattva (who here is evidently assumed to be a monk) should "stay away from kings, princes, ministers, [and] chief officials" (203), connections that might draw the saṃgha into political entanglements. He should not associate with outcastes, wrestlers, clowns, jugglers, courtesans, butchers, or others on the margins of society whose company might arouse social criticism. He should avoid situations that might seem compromising, for example, close association with women or with persons of ambiguous gender. In fact, he should not talk to women; if he teaches the dharma to them, he should not show his teeth when he smiles, and he should not bare his chest. A bodhisattva should avoid monks and nuns who follow the śrāvaka vehicle. He should not have young boys as disciples. Nor should he arouse others' enmity by harsh criticism of their views; instead, he should always be gentle and forbearing. Other instructions speak to the bodhisattva's mental comportment and attitude in preaching. He should always draw his explanations from the Mahāyāna and not from the teachings of the śrāvaka vehicle. He should not expect offerings of clothing, bedding, food, or medicine but think single-mindedly of teaching the dharma. He should not get caught up in doctrinal disputes but always be motivated by compassion, freeing himself from jealousy, anger, pride, and falsity. These are just a few of the many instructions given in this chapter.

The Buddha goes on to explain that the bodhisattva who has mastered these injunctions will be faultless in teaching the dharma and will be respected by all members of society, including kings, ministers, monks, nuns, commoners, and householders. Gods will accompany him and will protect him when people come to ask him questions. Sticks and stones cannot hurt him, poison cannot harm him, and the mouths of those who slander him will be sealed.

Conveying once again the rarity of hearing the *Lotus Sūtra*, the Buddha declares, "O Mañjuśrī! Even the title of this *Lotus Sūtra* cannot be heard in incalculable lands. How much more it is unable to be seen, accepted, preserved, and recited!" (211).

The chapter concludes with the sixth of the seven parables of the *Lotus Sūtra,* one of the more enigmatic, the parable of the jewel in the topknot. When an emperor decides to go to war, he gathers his army; afterward, he bestows all manner of gifts on the soldiers who have acquitted themselves bravely in battle. But he does not give them his most priceless treasure, the jewel in his topknot. Were he to do so, his attendants would be dismayed. Finally, however, he does bestow it. In the same way, the Buddha teaches many doctrines, but he does not initially teach the *Lotus Sūtra.* Yet in the end, "he now teaches the *Lotus Sūtra,* which is treated with hostility by the entire world and is difficult to believe in, and which he has never taught before, and enables sentient beings to attain omniscience." Indeed, the *Lotus Sūtra* is taught by all the buddhas, but it is "conferred at the very end" (212).

Nichiren knew the *Lotus Sūtra* thoroughly, and, as he did with other chapters, drew occasionally on phrases and passages from the "Ease in Practice" chapter to support his teaching. For example, he cited the statement following the parable of the jewel in the topknot—"This *Lotus Sūtra* is the secret treasure house of all the buddha tathāgatas, and the foremost among all the sūtras" (212)—to argue against claims that the secret or esoteric teachings surpassed the *Lotus Sūtra.* He quoted the passage, "Even the title of this sūtra cannot be heard in incalculable lands" (211), to stress the immense good fortune of being born in a country where, although far from Buddhism's birthplace in India, one could encounter the *Lotus Sūtra* and chant its daimoku. He also cited the "Ease in Practice" chapter's reference to "the troubled world to come," which his predecessor

Saichō had identified specifically with the age of the Final Dharma, and frequently invoked the statement that the *Lotus* is "treated with hostility by the entire world and is difficult to believe in." Nonetheless, he explicitly rejected the "four kinds of practice" set forth in the chapter as unsuited to the present era. Those practices had been appropriate, he said, in the preceding eras, the ages of the True Dharma and the Semblance Dharma, but they were not suited to the Final Dharma age. "The four peaceful practices [in the "Ease in Practice" chapter] correspond to *shōju*," he wrote. To carry them out now in the mappō era would be as misguided as sowing seeds in winter and expecting to reap the harvest in spring. Rather, Nichiren saw the situation in Japan in his day as demanding the *shakubuku* approach: "The present era is defined in the sūtras as an age of quarrels and disputes, when the pure dharma will be obscured and lost. At this point, the provisional and true teachings have become utterly confused. . . . When the time has come for the one vehicle to spread, the provisional teachings become enemies. If they generate confusion, they must be refuted from the standpoint of the true teaching. Of the two propagation methods, *shōjū* and *shakubuku*, this is *shakubuku* as it pertains to the *Lotus Sūtra*."[1]

CHAPTER FIFTEEN

Bodhisattvas Emerging from the Earth

The dramatic tension that has been building since the "Jeweled Stūpa" chapter continues to build here. At the end of that chapter, the Buddha calls for those who are willing to step forward and, in the presence of the assembled buddhas, vow to spread the *Lotus Sūtra* after his parinirvāṇa. In the "Perseverance" chapter, billions of great bodhisattvas who have arrived from other worlds vow to spread the *Lotus Sūtra* throughout the ten directions. The theme of volunteers vowing to preserve the *Lotus Sūtra* after the Buddha is gone continues in this chapter, which opens with the bodhisattvas who have arrived from other lands to witness the opening of the stūpa now offering to preserve, recite, copy, and pay homage to the *Lotus Sūtra* in this Sahā world after the Buddha has passed into final nirvāṇa. However, the Buddha replies that there are sufficient bodhisattvas in his own world, the Sahā world, a statement that would be imbued with great meaning by Nichiren. The Buddha's polite refusal of the offer of assistance from the foreign bodhisattvas, that is, the bodhisattvas who have arrived from other worlds, sets the scene for yet another dramatic event.

In Book Three of the third-century BCE Greek poem, the *Argonautica*, Jason is made to sow a field with dragon's teeth. Armed soldiers rise out of the earth and attack, but Jason defeats them with a stratagem. (With certain artistic license, the soldiers were turned into skeletons by the legendary stop-motion animator Ray Harryhausen for the 1963 film *Jason and the Argonauts.*) Here in the *Lotus Sūtra,* billions of golden bodhisattvas emerge out of the earth. They approach the floating stūpa where Śākyamuni and Prabhūtaratna still sit, bow to them, and then withdraw to one side, offering eulogies to the assembled buddhas for fifty intermediate eons, although it seems to the assembly that only half a day has passed. Even in the fantastic world of a Mahāyāna sūtra, bodhisattvas emerging out of the earth is apparently a rare event; Maitreya, himself a bodhisattva and just one lifetime away from attaining buddhahood, asks Śākyamuni Buddha who they are and where they came from. Here, as in Chapter One, even Maitreya, the future buddha, is shown to be ignorant of the reasons behind the extraordinary events that precede the Buddha's preaching.

After praising Maitreya's question, the Buddha admonishes the assembly to listen attentively, as he will now reveal a most profound teaching. These noble bodhisattvas, he says, are his own disciples, instructed by him since the time he achieved enlightenment. Thus, unlike the bodhisattvas who have arrived from other universes, they are bodhisattvas of our world, yet bodhisattvas whose existence has been previously unknown because they have been living underground, where they have been reciting, studying, and contemplating the sūtras. Some scholars see in this description evidence that the Mahāyāna, or at least the cult of the *Lotus Sūtra,* began among monks living in the forest, away from the cities and the seats of Buddhist institutional authority.[1] The Mahāyāna, they suggest, was an underground movement.

Maitreya is nonetheless bewildered by the Buddha's answer. He knows well that the Buddha had been born as Prince Siddhārtha, how at age twenty-nine he had left the palace in search of enlightenment, and how after six years of ascetic practice he achieved buddhahood at the age of thirty-five. Or, if we follow the traditional East Asian chronology, the Buddha left the palace at age nineteen and achieved buddhahood at age thirty. In either case, the same doubt arises. Maitreya asks: "Since then more than forty years have passed. How is it possible, O Bhagavat, for you to have done such great buddha acts in such a short period of time?" (226). Maitreya is justifiably puzzled by two things. First, how could the Buddha teach so many billions of bodhisattvas in a mere forty years without anyone knowing about it? Second, these are highly advanced bodhisattvas, who have proceeded far along the path to buddhahood, a path that takes billions of lifetimes to complete. How could they have made such progress in a mere forty-odd years? As Maitreya says, Śākyamuni's claim that these countless noble beings are his disciples is like a twenty-five-year-old man pointing to a hundred-year-old man and saying, "This is my son." Maitreya is quick to note that he himself does not doubt the Buddha's word; the Buddha always speaks the truth. It is simply that what the Buddha has said is so implausible that in the future, after he has passed into final nirvāṇa, his statement might arouse doubt in the minds of beginning bodhisattvas. Maitreya thus implores the Buddha to explain.

As we have seen, passages earlier in the *Lotus Sūtra* indicate that the Buddha will soon enter final nirvāṅa, pointing to the sūtra's status as his final teaching. Maitreya's statement that more than forty years have passed since the Buddha's enlightenment reaffirms the place of the *Lotus* within the scheme of his traditional biography. With Maitreya's statement, we know that the Buddha is now past seventy. He would die when he was eighty, as traditional sources tell us. Or, at least this is what we would conclude, until we read the next chapter.

In Zhiyi's parsing of the *Lotus Sūtra,* Chapter Fifteen begins the "origin teaching" (J. *honmon*) or second fourteen chapters of the sūtra, so called because in this latter section of the *Lotus* the Buddha casts off his transient guise as someone who first gained enlightenment in the present lifetime, and he reveals his true identity as the primordial buddha awakened immeasurable eons ago. As he had with the preceding "trace teaching" (*shakumon*), or first fourteen chapters, Zhiyi divided this section of the sūtra into three parts. The "introduction" corresponds to the first part of Chapter Fifteen, up to the Buddha's response to Maitreya's question about the identity of the bodhisattvas who have emerged from the earth (223). The "main exposition" consists of the remainder of Chapter Fifteen, the whole of Chapter Sixteen, and the first part of Chapter Seventeen (up to the end of Maitreya's verses on 245). The remaining chapters then correspond to the "dissemination" portion. Though quite short—"one chapter and two halves," as Nichiren termed it—the main exposition section of the origin teaching was revered by many Japanese Tendai teachers as the very heart of the sūtra and inspired great doctrinal innovation, especially in Nichiren's own teaching.

According to the sūtra text, the vast throng of bodhisattvas who appear suddenly in Chapter Fifteen "had all previously been living in the space under the earth of the Sahā world" (217). Zhiyi identified this "space" as the mysterious depth that is the dharma nature and as the middle way; he also equated it with the "land of ever-tranquil light," a metaphor for the Buddha's enlightened realm. One modern *Lotus* commentator interpreted "living in the space under the earth of the Sahā world" to mean having insight into the empty and constructed nature of all things, which permits one "to be in the midst of the swirl of the world of desire, without being dragged down by it, constantly maintaining a stance of unattached freedom."[2] This interpretation echoes the description of these bodhisattvas later in the chapter as being "as undefiled by worldly affairs as the lotus blossom in the [muddy] water" (228).

Zhiyi proposed several reasons why the Buddha ultimately rejected the offer of the bodhisattvas from other worlds to propagate the *Lotus Sūtra* in the present, Sahā world and instead summoned the bodhisattvas from beneath the earth. The bodhisattvas from other worlds, he said, had responsibilities to benefit the beings of their own lands that they could not neglect. Furthermore, their ties to this world were only superficial, and so their efforts at spreading the dharma would have been ineffective. Had the Buddha accepted their offer, he would have had no reason to summon the bodhisattvas from beneath the earth. These bodhisattvas were Śākyamuni's original disciples, taught by him since the inconceivably distant past. Their ties to the Sahā world were profound, and they could also travel to other realms and benefit the beings there. And, without their presence, Śākyamuni could not have revealed his true identity as the Buddha awakened since the inconceivably distant past.

Who are these bodhisattvas who emerge from beneath the earth? One interpretative move, current in medieval Japanese Tendai circles in Nichiren's day, was to associate their four leaders—Viśiṣṭacāritra (J. Jōgyō, "Superior Conduct"), Anantacāritra (Muhengyō, "Boundless Conduct"), Viśuddhacāritra (Jyōgyō, "Pure Conduct"), and Supratiṣṭhitacāritra (Anryūgyo, "Firm Conduct")—with the four universal elements of fire, wind, water, and earth, which were believed to constitute and benefit all beings. In a sense, Nichiren also understood these bodhisattvas as innate, for example, when he writes that they represent the bodhisattva realm within us; they are "the followers of the Śākyamuni Buddha who dwells within ourselves."[3] However, he also took them to be historical agents, entrusted by the Buddha with the mission of propagating the *Lotus Sūtra* specifically in the Final Dharma age, that is, his own time. "And what is this dharma that was entrusted to them?" he asked. "From within the *Lotus Sūtra*, it discards the broad to take up the condensed and discards the condensed to take up the essence, that is, the five characters Myōhō-renge-kyō."[4]

Nichiren observed that these four bodhisattvas were not present at the Buddha's first sermon nor at the last. They appear in no sūtra other than the *Lotus*, and even there, they are present only to receive the Buddha's transmission of the sūtra and his charge to propagate it after his parinirvāṇa. Based on his understanding of the Buddha's teaching process, Nichiren argued that these bodhisattvas could only appear in the Final Dharma age. During the two thousand years following the Buddha's passing, that is, the True Dharma and Semblance Dharma ages, persons who had received the seed of buddhahood from Śakyamuni Buddha were led to the stages of maturation and harvesting through provisional teachings. Had the bodhisattvas from beneath the earth appeared and spread the daimoku during that time, many of those people would have reviled it, thereby destroying the merit gained through the maturing of the seeds that they had already received. During those two thousand years, Nichiren said, some of the bodhisattvas from other worlds remained to teach the *Lotus Sūtra* in this world. Specifically, Zhiyi and his teacher Huisi, long revered as manifestations of the bodhisattvas Bhaiṣajyarāja (J. Yakuō) and Avalokiteśvara (Kannon), respectively, had taught the three thousand realms in a single thought-moment from the abstract perspective of the trace teaching. But by the beginning of the Final Dharma age, those able to achieve liberation through the provisional teachings had vanished, and the bodhisattvas from other worlds had all returned to their original lands. Now, in the present, mappō era, "Hīnayāna is employed to attack Mahāyāna, and the provisional used to destroy the true. East and west are confused, and heaven and earth turned upside down. . . . At this time, the bodhisattvas who emerged from the earth will make their first appearance in the world, solely to have the children drink the medicine of the five characters Myōhō-renge-kyō."[5]

While chronologies differed, in Japan, widespread opinion held that the Final Dharma had begun in 1052. Thus, the bodhisattvas who emerged from underground could be expected to appear at any time. Indeed, were they not overdue? "Should they fail to appear in the Final Dharma age, they would be great liars, and the prophecies made by Śākyamuni, Prabhūtaratna, and the buddhas of the ten directions would prove as empty as foam on the waters," Nichiren wrote.[6] In observing that no one other than himself was enduring the great trials predicted in the *Lotus Sūtra*, Nichiren concluded that he himself must be the representative of the bodhisattvas of the earth, or might even be one of them, a conviction that sustained him through years of danger and privation. Usually he referred to himself only in modest terms as a forerunner or emissary of their leader, the bodhisattva Viśiṣṭacāritra, but there is little doubt that he identified his efforts with the work of this bodhisattva. Much of the later Nichiren tradition identifies him as a manifestation of Viśiṣṭacāritra in this world.

Nichiren maintained that those who shared his practice and commitment were also to be counted among the bodhisattvas who emerged from the earth: "If you are of the same mind as me, then are you not a bodhisattva of the earth? And if you are a bodhisattva of the earth, then without doubt you have been a disciple of Śākyamuni Buddha since the remotest past. . . . There should be no discrimination as to men or women among those who spread the five characters Myōhō-renge-kyō in the Final Dharma age, for unless they were bodhisattvas of the earth, they could not chant the daimoku. At first, I alone chanted Namu Myōhō-renge-kyō, but then gradually two, three, and a hundred began to chant and transmit it. This will happen in the future as well. Isn't this what it means to 'emerge from the earth'?"[7]

The claim that those who chant the daimoku are Śākyamuni Buddha's disciples from the remotest past might initially seem at odds with Nichiren's idea that people in the Final Dharma age have never before received the seed of buddhahood. The apparent contradiction resolves, however, when we recall that for Nichiren and other Buddhist thinkers of the time, the term "remotest past" (*kuon*) signified not merely an immensely long time ago in linear, historical terms, but also carried the meaning of timelessness, and thus, of the Buddha's constant presence. The practice and propagation of the *Lotus Sūtra* in the mappō era is the juncture where the linear time of ordinary experience and the timeless realm of the Buddha intersect. In embracing the daimoku with the "same mind" as Nichiren, one immediately becomes a disciple of the ever-present primordial Śākyamuni Buddha and is encompassed in his enlightened realm.

One can imagine how identification with the task of the bodhisattvas of the earth must have inspired and sustained those followers of Nichiren, in his own lifetime and later, who upheld their faith in the face of opposition. Its implication, that one has been born into this world to aid in a vast salvific task, could invest even the most ordinary life with immense meaning. This dimension of Nichiren's teaching helps explain its ongoing attraction in the contemporary world. However humble one's place in society or how limited one's personal resources or abilities, to be a follower of Nichiren was to stand in the vanguard of history as someone who, having embraced the sole teaching leading to buddhahood in the present age, shoulders the responsibility to preserve and transmit it.

CHAPTER SIXTEEN

The Lifespan of the Tathāgata

In a sūtra filled with fireworks, Chapter Sixteen is the bombshell, intimated by the Buddha saying, not once, but three times, "You should believe the true words of the Tathāgata" (231). When the great assembly agrees to do so, he comes right to the point: although all gods and humans think that he left his father's palace and later achieved enlightenment near the city of Gayā, in fact, incalculable eons have passed since he attained buddhahood. The Buddha reiterates that he teaches what is suitable based on his understanding of the capacity of his audience. To those who take pleasure in inferior teachings, he told the standard story of his life: his rejection of life in the palace, his pursuit of the truth, and his eventual enlightenment. "However, it has been a very long time indeed since I attained buddhahood" (233). To be somewhat more precise, he goes on to describe a number so vast that it can only be indicated by reducing entire world systems to dust and using each dust particle to represent an eon: "The period of time since I became a buddha would exceed this by hundreds of thousands of myriads of *koṭis* of *nayutas* of incalculable *kalpas*" (232). This is a staggering length of time, incalculably longer ago than even his past life as the son of the buddha Mahābhijñājñānābhibhū described in Chapter Seven.

In the early chapters of the *Lotus Sūtra,* Śākyamuni Buddha's teaching about the goal of nirvāṇa was shown to have been not ultimately a true goal but a pedagogical expedient; here, the major events of his traditional life story are recast in the same way. Prince Siddhārtha's deep anxiety at being confronted with the reality of aging, sickness, and death; his difficult decision to abandon his wife and newborn child and go forth into the forest in search of a state beyond sorrow; his ardent practice of meditation and asceticism for six years; and his triumphant attainment of liberation under the Bodhi Tree were all a performance. He was enlightened all the time, yet feigned these deeds to inspire the world. All this serves to legitimate the *Lotus Sūtra* by having the Buddha preempt the particularity of the earlier teaching; everything that the Buddha did was but a magical display created by a being who was enlightened many eons ago. The events that once seemed so momentous and unique are, so to speak, devalued as stock scenes from a long running play. In this new time scale in which the Buddha reveals the *Lotus Sūtra,* not forty years, but countless eons have passed since his enlightenment. Here again, the *Lotus Sūtra* acknowledges its own belatedness, not by conceding that it is teaching something new, but by asserting the Buddha's enlightenment to be very old.

By declaring the historical Śākyamuni to be a mere emanation of this primordially awakened buddha, the *Lotus Sūtra* diminished his standing as he faded, like all buddhas before him, further and further into the past. By the time of the *Lotus Sūtra*'s compilation, the historical Buddha was already a distant memory, known only through rather formulaic stories of his last lifetime, and, often more importantly, through the even more formulaic stories of his previous lives, the *jātaka* tales. The *Lotus Sūtra* here replaces that buddha with a new buddha, a buddha enlightened eons ago, a buddha who is all buddhas, a buddha to whom teachings unknown to the earlier tradition can be ascribed. Thus, in an important sense, the question of the identity of the historical Buddha, a question that we identify with European scholarship of the nineteenth century (and which continues to haunt scholarship in the twenty-first), is a question that the *Lotus Sūtra* asked, and that the *Lotus Sūtra* answered, centuries ago: the historical Buddha was a magical manifestation.

We thus encounter what some scholars have called Buddhist docetism, after the patristic heresy which asserted that it was impossible for God, in the person of Jesus Christ, to have experienced suffering during the passion. Hence, it was not Christ on the cross, but a representation of him who seemed to suffer and die. Yet the motivation in the Buddhist case exceeds a repugnance at the notion of a divine being suffering physical pain (although something similar may be at play here). Instead, this is another claim to authority, a case of revisionist myth presented as revisionist history. The early story of Gautama Buddha and his disciples, found preserved, for example, in the Pāli canon and already accepted as an historical account by the mainstream tradition, is here radically rewritten in such a way as to glorify the *Lotus Sūtra* as the unique record of what really happened.

Were this not enough to absorb, the Buddha now goes on to say that his lifespan is immeasurable. "I abide forever without entering parinirvāṇa. . . . The lifespan that I first attained through practicing the bodhisattva path has not yet expired. It is twice as great as the number previously mentioned. Although I do not actually enter parinirvāṇa, I proclaim that I do. It is through this skillful means that the Tathāgata leads and inspires sentient beings" (233). The "lifespan" of the Buddha, that is, the length of time that has elapsed since he became the Buddha, as described in this chapter might be expressed as 10^{23} eons. Thus, he will live twice that long. The Buddha explains that although his disciples believe that he achieved enlightenment under the Bodhi Tree a mere forty-some years ago, he in fact achieved enlightenment eons ago. And the time that he has left is not just a few years but double the number of incalculable eons that have already passed since he achieved enlightenment.

The authors of the *Lotus Sūtra* were well versed in the Buddhist scriptures, as their language here reflects. Two scenes from the *Mahāparinibbana Sutta,* the traditional account of the Buddha's final days, are evoked here. The first, and most obvious, is that of the Buddha's final illness and death at the age of eighty. As we have noted, in Chapter Fifteen, Maitreya alludes to the fact that slightly more than forty years have passed since the Buddha achieved enlightenment (generally said to have occurred when he was thirty-five—or thirty, by the chronology widely adopted in East Asia). Thus, the authors of the sūtra knew that their readers would understand that the Buddha's end was near. And yet the Buddha declares that he will abide for countless eons to come.

The less obvious allusion is to a scene that occurs earlier in the *Mahāparinibbana Sutta* when the Buddha informs Ānanda that, if asked to do so, a buddha can live "for an eon or until the end of an eon." That is, a buddha's lifespan is not that of an ordinary human and can be extended, albeit not indefinitely, upon request. Although the Buddha tells Ānanda this three times, Ānanda is too distracted to make the request, and so the Buddha "abandons his life force" and an earthquake portends that his end is near. Here in the *Lotus Sūtra,* the Buddha is not asked to live until the end of the eon. Yet he does not abandon his life force and instead declares that he will live, not for an eon, but for billions of eons. What is the reason for this dissimulation, for saying that he will enter final nirvāṇa when in fact he will not? In answer, the Buddha provides the seventh and final parable of the *Lotus Sūtra*, the parable of the physician.

A wise physician has many sons. When he is away on a journey, they take poison, which drives some of them mad. When the father returns home, he prepares the antidote. Some of the children take it and are immediately cured. But with others, the poison has entered their system so deeply that they have lost their minds and refuse to take the medicine, although it is fragrant and attractive. To impel them to do so, the father departs from the city, telling the children that he is old and feeble; he leaves the medicine behind, assuring them that it cannot fail to cure them. He then has a messenger return to his home to inform his children that their father has died. Those who had been driven mad are so shocked and saddened by the news that they come to their senses and take the antidote. The father then returns home.

In the same way, Śākyamuni explains, if sentient beings knew that the Buddha's lifespan was immeasurable, they would not be inspired to practice the dharma, not understanding how rare it is to encounter the Buddha. The Buddha and his teachings would always be available, removing all urgency to take advantage of his presence in the world. Believing that the Buddha has passed forever into nirvāṇa, sentient beings are able to see the world as beset with distress, bereft of the Buddha. And so he pretends to enter nirvāṇa.

Here again, in a manner reminiscent of the parable of the burning house in Chapter Three, the Buddha demands: Would anyone say that this good doctor is guilty of lying? And, as Śāriputra did in the earlier chapter, the bodhisattvas vehemently deny it. Here again, the *Lotus Sūtra* turns the tables on the charge so often leveled by the Buddhist mainstream, that the Mahāyāna is not the Buddha's teaching. It is not the Buddha of the *Lotus Sūtra* who is false. Rather, the Buddha of the mainstream tradition—and the goal of nirvāṇa that he taught—is proclaimed to be a mirage.

We now learn that the Buddha is ever present, and this land, this Sahā world that is supposed to be incinerated by the fire of seven suns at the end of the eon, is in fact a buddha field, a pure land. As the Buddha says at the end of the chapter, this world "is in fact my tranquil land, always full of devas and humans. All the gardens and palaces are adorned with various gems. The jeweled trees abound with flowers and fruits, and the sentient beings are joyful among them. . . . Although my pure land never decays, the sentient beings see it as ravaged by fire and torn with anxiety and distress. . . . To the deluded and unenlightened I say that I have entered nirvāṇa, although, in fact, I am really here" (238, 239).

What is the significance of the revelation of the Buddha's immeasurable "lifespan," that is, the time that has elapsed since his original attainment of supreme enlightenment? English-language scholarship on *Lotus Sūtra* often speaks of the primordial Śākyamuni of the "Lifespan" chapter as the "eternal buddha." This term is easy to understand but carries Western philosophical overtones of abstract metaphysical truth; the sūtra's emphasis lies rather in the Buddha's "constant residing" (232) here in the world. For the sūtra's compilers, this claim refigured the Buddha in accordance with the Mahāyāna bodhisattva ideal: No longer was he a teacher of the past, forever departed into final nirvāṇa, but an awakened being perpetually active in this and other worlds for living beings' sake. Chinese exegetes debated how this primordially awakened buddha should be understood. Was he a finite being who had attained enlightenment an incalculably long time ago? Or was he without beginning or end? Zhiyi argued that the Buddha of the "Lifespan" chapter unites in one all three kinds of buddha "body" set forth in Mahāyāna teachings: the dharma body (*dharmakāya*), or timeless truth conceived as a "body"; the reward or enjoyment body (*saṃbhogakāya*), a subtle body endowed with transcendent powers resulting from a buddha's countless eons of practice; and the manifest or emanation body (*nirmāṇakāya*), the historical person who appears in the world. While the dharma body was understood as having neither beginning or end, conventionally, the reward body was said to have a beginning, and the manifested body, both a beginning and end. For Zhiyi, however, the buddha of the perfect teaching possesses all three bodies in one, interfused and interpenetrating. This concept inflects, in terms of the buddha, the nondual logic of "one in many, many in one" that we have already encountered with the threefold truth and the three thousand realms in a single thought-moment. Through this integration, the reward and manifested bodies participate in the timelessness of the dharma body, which does not exist apart from the other two.[1] Notions of the primordial buddha's constant presence in the phenomenal world were further developed by esoteric Buddhist thinkers, both in China and Japan, who equated the primordial Śākyamuni of the "Lifespan" chapter with the omnipresent cosmic buddha Mahāvairocana (J. Dainichi) who manifests as all phenomena.

Nichiren understood the revelation of Buddha's inconceivable "lifespan" as the very heart of the sūtra. The sūtra text makes clear that, even after realizing buddhahood, Śākyamuni has remained in the world, and will continue to do so, for countless eons, "teaching the dharma and inspiring sentient beings"

(232). For Nichiren, this signaled a seismic shift in the entire concept of buddhahood as a realm apart from the nine realms of ordinary experience. Conventional understanding holds that the cause of buddhahood and its effect, that is, practice and attainment, are separated in time. To become a buddha, one must carry out the practices of the bodhisattva for three immeasurable eons, a staggering length of time spanning countless lifetimes. The "trace teaching" or *shakumon* portion of the *Lotus Sūtra,* even while extending the promise of buddhahood to all beings, still preserves this perspective on realizing buddhahood as a linear process in which one moves from practice (nine realms) toward attainment (buddhahood). We see this in Śākyamuni Buddha's predictions in the sūtra's early chapters that his individual śrāvaka disciples such as Śāriputra, Mahākāśyapa, and others will become buddhas in the remote future, after many eons of bodhisattva practice. From this perspective, buddhahood remains a distant goal, abstracted from one's present experience.

But with the origin teaching, Nichiren wrote, the cause and effect of the pre–*Lotus Sūtra* teachings and of the trace teaching are "demolished" and "original cause and original effect" are revealed: "The nine realms are inherent in the beginningless buddha realm, and the buddha realm inheres in the beginningless nine realms. This represents the true mutual inclusion of the ten realms . . . and three thousand realms in a single thought-moment."[2] That is, he saw the origin teaching as overturning linear views of practice and attainment, in which one first makes efforts and then realizes buddhahood as a later result, and revealing that cause (the nine realms) and effect (the buddha realm) are present simultaneously; buddhahood is manifested in the very act of practice.

"In terms of realizing buddhahood with this very body," Nichiren wrote, "the trace teaching is the gate that affords entry, while the origin teaching holds its true meaning, that is, its actualization."[3] Where the trace teaching presents buddhahood as a potential inherent in the nine realms of unenlightened beings, the origin teaching shows the buddha realm revealed through the Buddha's conduct in the nine realms, represented in particular by the bodhisattva realm. The buddha realm has no separate existence or mode of expression apart from the nine realms. Rather, the nine realms, without losing their individual character, are purified, elevated, and positively redirected in the light of the realized buddha realm. This is the awakened reality of the Buddha, which Nichiren termed "the single thought-moment comprising three thousand realms in actuality" (*ji no ichinen sanzen*). For him, this revelation had one sole scriptural locus: it was "hidden in the depths" of the "Lifespan" chapter of the origin teaching of the *Lotus Sūtra*.[4]

Medieval Japanese Tendai thinkers of various teaching lineages shared a loose consensus that the enlightenment of the primordial Śākyamuni Buddha was "hidden in the depths" of the "Lifespan" chapter and could be accessed through the practitioner's "mind contemplation" or "mind discernment" (J. *kanjin*). *Kanjin* in the Tiantai/Tendai tradition was originally a broad term for practice, in contrast to doctrinal study. Though interpretations varied, by Nichiren's time, *kanjin* had come to mean the essence of the Tendai *Lotus* teachings and was often associated specifically with the "Lifespan" chapter. For Nichiren, now in the mappō era, the "mind discernment" that opens the primordial buddha's awakening to all people is the chanting of Namu Myōho-renge-kyō. He took the daimoku to be the "good medicine" that the excellent doctor leaves for his children in the "Lifespan" chapter's narrative. In his reading, this chapter's revelation of the primordial buddha's constant presence in this world immediately collapses all temporal and spatial separation between the Buddha and the devotee. "Two thousand years and more have passed since the Buddha entered nirvāṇa," he wrote. "But for those who embrace the *Lotus Sūtra*, at each day, each hour, each moment, the Buddha's voice reaches them, conveying to them the message, 'I do not die.'"[5] Through chanting the daimoku, the timeless realm of the Buddha's original enlightenment is retrieved in the present moment; ordinary people manifest buddhahood just as they are, and their world becomes the buddha land.

Another important implication that this chapter held for Nichiren was indeed this very possibility of realizing the buddha land in the present world. In the "Parable" chapter of the *Lotus Sūtra*, Śākyamuni describes the world as a "burning house" in which there is no safe place (72). But now in the "Lifespan" chapter, having revealed his true identity as the primordially awakened buddha, Śākyamuni declares that, even in the fire that destroys the world at the end of the cosmic cycle, his land—the present world—is "tranquil" and "never decays"; it is a place where sentient beings are "joyful" (238). This is the realm depicted on Nichiren's maṇḍala. Alluding to this sūtra passage, Nichiren writes, "Now the Sahā world of original time is the constantly abiding pure land, liberated from the three disasters and beyond the [cycle of the] four kalpas [eons]. Its buddha has not already entered nirvāṇa in the past, nor is he yet to be born in the future. And his disciples are of the same essence. This [reality] . . . is the three thousand realms of one's own mind."[6]

"Original time" here is Zhiyi's expression for the time of the Buddha's original enlightenment in the remotest past, which medieval Japanese exegetes often took to mean "original," not in the diachronic, historical sense of "at the beginning," but ontologically, meaning that it is fundamental, timeless, and ever present. By devotion to the *Lotus Sūtra* and to its daimoku practice, Nichiren taught, one manifests the reality of *ichinen sanzen*—or more simply stated, the Buddha's enlightened state—within oneself, opening a ground of experience that is joyful and meaningful, independent of whether one's immediate circumstances are favorable or not. Nichiren called this the "joy of the dharma." In the *Lotus Sūtra*'s language, even in a world "ravaged by fire and torn with anxiety and distress" (238) one can, so to speak, experience the gardens, palaces, and heavenly music of the buddha realm.

"The originally enlightened buddha of the perfect teaching abides in this world," Nichiren wrote. "If one abandons this land, to what other land should one aspire? Wherever the practitioner of the *Lotus Sūtra* dwells should be considered the pure land."[7] Based on such thinking, Nichiren opposed the idea, extremely common in his time, of shunning this world as wicked and impure and aspiring to birth in the pure land of a buddha or bodhisattva after death. Because the various sūtras preached before the *Lotus* do not teach the perfect interpenetration of the buddha realm and the nine deluded realms, Nichiren asserted, the superior realms of buddhas and bodhisattvas that they mention, such as Amitābha's Sukhāvatī realm or Maitreya's Tuṣita heaven, are merely provisional names; the "Lifespan" chapter of the *Lotus* reveals that the true pure land is to be realized here in the present, Sahā world.

The idea that the Buddha's pure land is immanent in our deluded world by no means originated with Nichiren. The concept of the nonduality or inseparability of person and land, or of the living subject and their objective world (J. *eshō funi*), is integral to Zhiyi's concept of three thousand realms in a single thought-moment. Because the environment mirrors the life-condition of the persons inhabiting it, the world of hell dwellers would be hellish, while the world of a fully awakened person would be a buddha land. In light of the *ichinen sanzen* principle, to break through the narrow confines of the small self and to "see" or access the realm in which oneself (person) and everything else (environment) are mutually inclusive and inseparable is to realize enlightenment. As Zhanran expressed it, "You should know that one's person and land are [both] the single thought-moment comprising three thousand realms. Therefore, when one attains the way, in accordance with this principle, one's body and one's mind in that moment pervade the dharma realm."[8] To manifest buddhahood is thus to experience this present world as the buddha land.

But for Nichiren, the immanence of the buddha land was not merely a truth to be realized subjectively, in the practice of individuals; it would actually become manifest in the outer world as faith in the *Lotus Sūtra* spread.[9] We have already seen how he saw the disasters of his age as stemming fundamentally from rejection of the *Lotus Sūtra* in favor of inferior, provisional teachings no longer suited to the age. Conversely, he taught that—because people and their environments are inseparable—spreading faith in the *Lotus Sūtra* would transform this world into an ideal buddha realm. He famously argued this claim in his treatise *Risshō anokoku ron*, written early in his career, and maintained it throughout life. This was the conviction that underlay his aggressive proselytizing and that prompted him to risk his life in repeated confrontations with the authorities.

A marginal, often persecuted figure with only a small following, Nichiren himself had to abandon expectations that this goal would be achieved soon. Nonetheless, he introduced into the tradition of *Lotus Sūtra* interpretation what might be called a millennial element, a prophecy or vision of an ideal world based on the spread of exclusive faith in the *Lotus Sūtra*. Especially since the modern period, that vision has undergone multiple reinterpretations from a range of social and political perspectives.[10] Nichiren's ideal of manifesting the buddha land in the present world gives his doctrine an explicitly social dimension that sets it apart from other Buddhist teachings of his day. It is also the aspect of his teaching that speaks most powerfully to the "this-worldly" orientation of today's Buddhist modernism.

CHAPTERS SEVENTEEN AND EIGHTEEN

Description of Merits *and* The Merits of Joyful Acceptance

Chapter Seventeen

Nothing of consequence in terms of plot occurs in the next five chapters. Each is devoted in one way or another to enumerating (often tediously, at least to the modern reader) the benefits of honoring the *Lotus Sūtra* and the dangers of disparaging it. In Chapter Seventeen, appropriately entitled "Description of Merits," the Buddha lists the various benefits of having heard him proclaim, in the previous chapter, that his lifespan is immeasurable. Some auditors gained liberating insight into the nonorigination of all things (dharmas); others acquired the power to recollect everything that they hear; and still others gained the power of unhindered eloquence. Some will attain buddhahood in eight lifetimes, some in four, some in three, some in two, and some in a single lifetime. The aspiration for buddhahood has been awakened in countless more. In addition, Śākyamuni declares, anyone who hears about the great length of the Buddha's lifespan and believes it even for a moment will gain immeasurable merit. Such persons need not build stūpas (an act extolled in previous chapters) because the fact that they have accepted the *Lotus Sūtra* is proof that they performed countless meritorious deeds of this kind in past lives. Yet, wherever a preacher of the dharma recites a single verse of the sūtra, there a stūpa should be built.

Benefits are also enumerated for those who hear the *Lotus Sūtra* after the Buddha has passed into parinirvāṇa and do not disparage it. This may seem strange, given that in the previous chapter the Buddha has declared that he will not pass into parinirvāṇa, a declaration that he reiterates here in a famous passage, saying that he always resides on Vulture Peak, "together with the great bodhisattvas and śrāvakas, teaching the dharma to the assembly" (248). One could say that the *Lotus Sūtra* works here on two levels, referring both to the historical buddha celebrated in the early Buddhist tradition, who has passed beyond reach into final nirvāṇa, and the primordially awakened buddha, who is always here for those who embrace the *Lotus Sūtra*.

Chapter Eighteen

More benefits for the faithful are described here, again, benefits for those who rejoice in the *Lotus Sūtra* and teach it to others after the Buddha has passed into parinirvāṇa. A standard literary device in Buddhist sūtras is to reference some great traditional act of merit making, such as a vast gift to the saṃgha or the building of a stūpa, and then explain that in fact the merit of such deeds is a mere fraction of that accruing to one who performs the deed favored in that particular sūtra. In this case, all traditional meritorious deeds pale compared to hearing a single verse of the *Lotus Sūtra* and receiving it with joy, or inviting another person to sit down and listen to the *Lotus Sūtra*. Here, the Buddha offers another, rather more material, incentive for teaching the *Lotus*. Should the person do so and the other person then respond with joy, the person who offered the invitation will be free from all manner of physical defects in billions of future lives, including bad breath; dirty, black, yellow, gapped, missing, or crooked teeth; drooping lips; a flat, thin, or crooked nose; and hollow cheeks. Furthermore, "wherever they may be born, life after life, they will meet a buddha, hear the dharma, and accept the teaching" (256).

The first part of Chapter Seventeen is counted as part of the "one chapter and two halves" that constitute the "main exposition" section of the origin teaching. The remainder of the chapter (from "At that time the Buddha addressed bodhisattva mahāsattva Maitreya . . . ," 245) speaks of the merits to be gained after the Buddha's parinirvāṇa and thus begins the "dissemination" section of the origin teaching. Nichiren drew on this chapter and the next to support his fundamental assertion that chanting Namu Myōhō-renge-kyō is the practice appropriate to the Final Dharma age and contains all possible merit—indeed, the whole of the Buddhist path—within itself.

Buddhist thinkers over the centuries have elaborated various models of the path as guidelines for practice. Early Buddhism set forth the "three disciplines" of moral conduct, meditative concentration, and wisdom as comprising the entirety of the path. Mahāyāna scriptures set forth a list of six perfections (*pāramitās*), discussed below, that bodhisattvas must master, which add to the original three disciplines the virtues of giving, perseverance, and effort. Specific texts enumerate ten stages, forty-one stages, or fifty-two stages of bodhisattva practice. Some models entail sequential stages; in others, elements of the path are cultivated simultaneously.

Based on the "Description of Merits" chapter (245–250), Zhiyi enumerated "four stages of faith" and "five stages of practice" of the *Lotus Sūtra*. The four stages of faith are (1) to arouse even a single thought of willing acceptance (also translated as "a single moment's faith and understanding"); (2) to understand the intent of the sūtra's words; (3) to place deep faith in the sūtra and expound it widely for others; and (4) to perfect one's own faith and insight. The "five stages of practice" are (1) to rejoice on hearing the *Lotus Sūtra*; (2) to read and recite it; (3) to explain it to others; (4) to practice it while cultivating the six perfections; and (5) to master the six perfections. The "four stages of faith" apply to those living in Śākyamuni Buddha's lifetime, while the "five stages of practice" are intended for persons living after his nirvāṇa; however, the spirit behind them is the same.

Within these two models of the path, Nichiren focused on the first stage of faith, arousing a single moment's faith and understanding, and the first stage of practice, rejoicing on hearing the *Lotus Sūtra*. But to what level of practice did these stages correspond? Nichiren noted that the works of Zhiyi and Zhanran give three interpretations. Two of these equate these stages with advanced levels, either the third or fourth of the "six stages of identity" (J. *rokusoku*) into which Zhiyi had divided the practice of the perfect teaching. The third interpretation, however, identifies them with only the second of the six levels, "verbal identity" (J. *myōji-soku*), the stage of a beginning practitioner, at which one first encounters the words of the dharma and has faith in them. Nichiren thought that this third interpretation accorded most closely with the sūtra passage; for him, the stage of "verbal identity" meant embracing faith in the *Lotus Sūtra* and chanting its daimoku.[1] In the Final Dharma age, he taught, advancing to later stages becomes irrelevant, because the merits of all stages are fully encompassed in the beginning stage.

For Nichiren, significantly, those merits included wisdom. Traditionally, wisdom was deemed necessary for liberation; it is the last of the three disciplines and the six perfections. In its claims for the salvific powers of the *Lotus Sūtra,* the "Description of Merits" chapter says that the merit accruing to those who generate even a single thought of willing acceptance—that is, faith—in the *Lotus Sūtra* immeasurably surpasses that gained by men and women who cultivate the first five perfections of a bodhisattva for eighty myriads of *koṭi*s of *nayuta*s of eons (245). The sixth perfection, wisdom, is not included. But Nichiren held that wisdom, too, is inherent in, and emerges from, faith in the *Lotus Sūtra.* Scholars of his day, he notes, all agree that those who would practice the *Lotus Sūtra* must devote themselves to the three disciplines of moral conduct, meditative concentration, and wisdom; lacking any of these, one cannot attain the way. Nichiren adds, "I too once thought the same." But over time, he became convinced that this was not the case. Citing the "Description of Merits" chapter to support his argument, Nichiren asserts that the Buddha had restrained persons at the first, second, and third of the five stages of practice from focusing on the cultivation of moral conduct and meditative concentration and directed them solely to cultivate some degree of wisdom. "And because our wisdom is inadequate, he teaches us to substitute faith, making this single word 'faith' the basis. . . . Faith is the cause for wisdom and corresponds to the stage of verbal identity."[2]

Nichiren grounded his reasoning in his understanding that the *Lotus Sūtra,* and specifically its title, is all-encompassing. In a famous passage, he explained that simply by upholding the daimoku, one can gain the merit of the entire bodhisattva path: "The *Sūtra of Immeasurable Meanings* states: 'Even if one is not able to practice the six perfections, they will spontaneously be fulfilled.' The *Lotus Sūtra* states, 'They wish to hear the all-encompassing way. . . .' The heart of these passages is that

Śākyamuni's causal practices and their resulting merits are inherent in the five characters *myō-hō-ren-ge-kyō*. When we embrace these five characters, he will spontaneously transfer to us the merits of his causes and effects."[3]

The "six perfections" systematize the practices required of Mahāyāna bodhisattvas to achieve buddhahood: giving, good conduct, perseverance, effort, meditation, and wisdom, in the Kubo and Yuyama translation (341). Traditionally, each perfection was said to require a hundred eons to complete, one eon being explained, for example, as the time required for a heavenly goddess to wear away great Mount Sumeru, the axis mundi, if she brushes it lightly with her sleeve once every hundred years. Such was the vast effort that Śākyamuni was said to have expended over staggering lengths of time in order to become the Buddha; the perfections represent his "causes" or "causal practices" and form the model for bodhisattva practice more generally. The wisdom, virtue, and power that he attained in consequence are his "resulting merits" or "effects." Nichiren's claim here is that all the practices and meritorious acts performed by Śākyamuni over countless lifetimes to become the Buddha, as well as the enlightenment and virtuous attributes he attained in consequence, are wholly contained within the daimoku and are spontaneously transferred to the practitioner in the act of chanting it.

A similar logic of total inclusivity underlies Nichiren's explanation of the merits of the first stage of practice: rejoicing on hearing the *Lotus Sūtra*. "Since life does not extend beyond the moment," he wrote, "the Buddha expounded the merits of a single moment of rejoicing [on hearing the *Lotus Sūtra*]. If two or three moments were required, this could no longer be called the original vow expressing his impartial great wisdom, the single vehicle of the sudden teaching that enables all beings to realize buddhahood."[4] In Nichiren's reading, both the "first stage of faith" and the "first stage of practice" enumerated by Zhiyi on the basis of the "Description of Merits" chapter comprise "the treasure chest of the three thousand realms in a single thought-moment" and the gate from which all buddhas throughout time and space emerge.[5]

Nichiren's assertion that, for *Lotus* practitioners of the mappō era, the daimoku replaces cultivation of the traditional three disciplines in effect opened the merits of the sūtra to persons without learning or insight. Here he used the analogies of a patient who is cured by medicine without understanding its properties, or of plants that, without awareness, bloom when they receive rainfall. In like manner, he said, beginning practitioners may not understand the meaning of the daimoku, but by chanting it, "they will naturally accord with the sūtra's intent."[6] In making such claims, Nichiren was not taking an anti-intellectual stance that would deny the importance of Buddhist study. Nor was he negating the need for continuing effort in practice or the value of the qualities that the six perfections describe: generosity, self-discipline, forbearance, diligence, and so forth, even though he rejected the need to cultivate them formally as prerequisites for enlightenment. It is important to recall that Nichiren often framed his teaching in opposition to Pure Land teachers who insisted that the *Lotus Sūtra* should be set aside as too profound for ignorant persons of the Final Dharma age. As we have seen, this assertion appalled Nichiren, who saw it as blocking the sole path by which the people of this age could realize liberation. In response, he argued passionately that the *Lotus Sūtra*'s salvific scope embraces even the most ignorant persons; in chanting the daimoku, all have full access to the merits of buddhahood, without practicing over countless lifetimes or seeking liberation in a separate realm after death.

Nichiren makes a similar point with respect to Chapter Eighteen, "The Merits of the Joyful Acceptance," with its teaching of "transmission to the fiftieth person." Here, in another extravagant illustration of the *Lotus Sūtra*'s inconceivable liberative powers, the Buddha asks his hearers to imagine that one person, hearing the *Lotus Sūtra,* rejoices and teaches it to another, who similarly rejoices and teaches it to another, and so on. The merit gained by the fiftieth person in succession on merely hearing the sūtra and rejoicing in its message, Śākyamuni says, is incalculably, inconceivably greater than that of someone who over an eighty-year period first gives immeasurable gifts to beings in billions of worlds and then leads them to the liberation of an arhat.

Today we are inclined to read these statements with attention to their rhetorical function in "constructing" the *Lotus Sūtra* as inconceivably wonderful. Nichiren and his contemporaries, however, would not have seen this as a rhetorical device. For them, the sūtras faithfully recorded the words of the Buddha, who is by definition both omniscient and free from falsehood. In short, they were statements of literal truth. "What other sūtra," Nichiren asks, "teaches that incalculable merit accrues to one who arouses even a single thought of willing acceptance, or to the fiftieth person who rejoices upon hearing it? Other sūtras do not claim such merit for even the first, second, third, or tenth hearer, let alone the fiftieth!"[7]

As he had with the notions of the first stage of faith and the first stage of practice that are based on the "Description of Merits" chapter, Nichiren employed the analogy of "transmission to the fiftieth person" from the "Merits of Joyful Acceptance" chapter to counter claims from Pure Land devotees that the *Lotus Sūtra,* being extremely profound, was too difficult to practice for deluded persons of the Final Dharma age. If ease of practice were to be a criterion, he said, no practice could be easier than spontaneously rejoicing on hearing the *Lotus Sūtra*. Nichiren argued that, far from excluding the ignorant, it is precisely because the *Lotus Sūtra* is so profound that it can save beings of any capacity whatsoever. In this connection, he often cited Zhanran's remark: "The more true the teaching, the lower the capacity [of the persons it can bring to liberation.]"[8] However limited one's capacity might be, that person is ennobled by their *Lotus Sūtra* practice. Therefore, Nichiren wrote, his followers were not to be despised: "If one looks into their past, they are great bodhisattvas who have made offerings for eight billion eons to buddhas numerous as the sands of the Hiraṇyavatī and Ganges rivers. And in terms of the future, they will be endowed with the merit of the fiftieth person [to hear the sūtra], which surpasses that of one who gives gifts to incalculable sentient beings for a period of eighty years. They are like a crown prince wrapped in swaddling clothes or a newborn dragon. Do not look down on them. Do not hold them in contempt!"[9]

CHAPTER NINETEEN

The Benefits Obtained by an Expounder of the Dharma

Where the previous two chapters stress the merit of those who accept the *Lotus Sūtra* and rejoice in hearing it, even for a moment, this chapter emphasizes the merit accruing to those who teach the sūtra to others. In the body "given by their parents"—that is, in this lifetime, without rebirth in a higher state and without relinquishing their status as ordinary people—they will achieve the "purification of the six sense faculties" (J. *rokkon shōjō*). The six sense faculties are the eyes, ears, nose, tongue, and body—the physical bases for sight, hearing, smell, taste, and touch—along with the mind, which grasps mental objects and also interprets the experience of the other five senses, unifying their perceptions into a coherent picture.

From a Buddhist perspective, the "picture" of the world perceived by the unenlightened is incomplete or distorted, prompting unwholesome, ego-based actions that result in frustration and suffering both for ourselves and others, now and in the future. Thus, a chief goal of Buddhist practice is to "purify the six sense faculties," that is, to perceive things, not through the filter of a deluded consciousness, but as they truly are.

Because Buddhism is renowned for its skepticism of sense experience—with numerous texts warning against the pleasures of the senses and disparaging the objects of the senses as sources of suffering—it is noteworthy that in this chapter, the Buddha discusses eight hundred qualities of the eye, twelve hundred qualities of the ear, eight hundred qualities of the nose, twelve hundred qualities of the tongue, eight hundred qualities of the body, and twelve hundred qualities of the mind that will adorn and purify those who preserve, recite, explain, and copy the *Lotus Sūtra*. Although these hundreds of qualities are not enumerated individually, the chapter is nonetheless a fascinating fantasy of the senses. For example, such devotees can see the entire cosmos from the lowest hell to the summit of the universe and perceive the causes and effects of the deeds of all the beings born there. They can hear the sounds and voices of all beings in the universe. They can smell all fragrances and identify the scent of all humans, animals, and plants, even from a great distance. They can smell treasure buried underground. They can smell whether a woman is pregnant or not, and if so, the sex of the child, and whether she will give birth easily to a happy child. Everything their tongue touches will taste like divine nectar, and they will speak with great eloquence. Their body will be as pure as clear lapis lazuli, and all beings in the cosmos, as well as their states, will be reflected there. Their minds will be such that they will derive immeasurable meaning from a single verse; all that they teach will be marked by truth; and they will know the minds of all beings in the universe.

Nichiren does not comment extensively on the six forms of sensory purification. But in one letter, he addresses at some length a passage from the "Benefits Obtained" chapter in the section discussing the purification of the mental faculty: "If they [expounders of the *Lotus*] teach the works on worldly affairs, treatises on political science or enterprise, all these will be in harmony with the true dharma" (271). This means, Nichiren says, that the *Lotus* takes worldly dharmas, or phenomena, as "immediately comprising the whole of the buddha-dharma," a feature that he saw as distinguishing it from other sūtras: "The sūtras preached before the *Lotus Sūtra* hold in essence that all dharmas are produced from the mind. To illustrate, they say that the mind is like the great earth, while the grasses and trees [that grow from it] are like the dharmas. Not so with the *Lotus Sūtra*. [It teaches that] the mind is itself the great earth, and the great earth is precisely the grasses and trees. The sūtras preached before it say that clarity of mind is like the moon and that purity of mind is like a flower. Not so with the *Lotus Sūtra*. It teaches that the moon *is* the mind, the flower *is* the mind."[1] But what is the difference between the two perspectives?

When Buddhism was transmitted to China, the Mahāyāna concept of all things as empty of fixed, independent existence and therefore mutually interpenetrating and nondual seemed to echo indigenous Chinese notions of a holistic cosmos in which all things are interrelated. This stance proved congenial to early Chinese Buddhist thinkers. But how exactly was the ultimate principle (Ch. *li*, J. *ri*)—whether conceptualized as emptiness, mind, or suchness—related to the concrete phenomena or actualities (*shi*, *ji*) of our experience? Some teachers conceived of principle in terms of an originally pure and undifferentiated "one mind" that, refracted through deluded perception, gives rise to the phenomenal world, with its distinctions of self and other, true and false, subject and object, good and evil, and so forth. To use a famous metaphor, the mind is originally like still water that accurately mirrors all things. When stirred by the wind of ignorance, waves appear, and the water begins to reflect things in a distorted way, producing the notion of self and other as substantially real entities and thus giving rise to attachment, suffering, and continued rebirth in saṃsāra.

Liberation lies in discerning that the differentiated phenomena of the world are in their essence no different from the one mind and thus originally pure. From this perspective, the purpose of Buddhist practice is to dispel delusion and return the mind to its original clarity. This idea developed especially within the Huayan (J. Kegon) and Chan (Zen) traditions.

This model explains principle and phenomena as nondual, but it does not value them equally. The one mind is original, pure, and true, while concrete phenomena are ultimately unreal, arising only as the one mind is filtered through human ignorance. From that perspective, the ordinary elements of daily experience remain at a second-tier level as the epiphenomena of a defiled consciousness. Zhiyi termed this perspective the "realm of the conceivable"—understandable, but not yet adequately expressing the true state of affairs. He himself expressed a different, more subtle view. In a passage already cited in Chapter Two of this volume, he states: "Were the mind to give rise to all phenomena, that would be a vertical [relationship]. Were all phenomena to be simultaneously contained within the mind, that would be a horizontal [relationship]. Neither horizontal nor vertical will do. It is simply that the mind is all phenomena and all phenomena are the mind. . . . [This relationship] is subtle and profound in the extreme; it can neither be grasped conceptually nor expressed in words. Therefore, it is called the realm of the inconceivable."[2]

In Zhiyi's understanding, phenomena do not arise from a pure mind or abstract prior principle. "Principle" means that the material and the mental, subject and object, good and evil, delusion and enlightenment are always nondual and mutually inclusive; this is the "real aspect of all dharmas" that only buddhas can completely know, referred to in the "Skillful Means" chapter (24). This perspective revalorizes the world, not as a realm of delusion, but as the very locus of enlightenment. The aim of practice, then, is not to recover a primal purity, but to manifest the buddha wisdom even amid ignorance and delusion.

In referring in the letter just mentioned to the passage on the purification of the mind indicated in the "Benefits Obtained" chapter, Nichiren writes that "the true path lies in the realities of this world."[3] Like Zhiyi, he denied any notion of a two-tiered hierarchy between the realm of deluded beings and the realm of the Buddha's enlightenment: one entails the experience of suffering, and the other, the experience of inner stability and joy, but the distinction between them lies solely in whether or not one embraces the the *Lotus Sūtra*. Elsewhere, as we have seen, Nichiren draws on the mutual inclusion of mind and all phenomena to assert that our own actions are what make this world a hell or a buddha land. Here, however, he draws a slightly different inference: there is no buddha-dharma to be achieved apart from one's everyday reality. One's ordinary affairs, whatever they may be, form the arena of practice, and by faith in the *Lotus Sūtra*, one can bring to bear the wisdom and compassion of the dharma to negotiate all worldly matters.

CHAPTER TWENTY

Bodhisattva Sadāparibhūta

Here the Buddha tells of another buddha, Bhīṣmagarjitasvararāja ("King of Imposing Sound"), of the far distant past. After that buddha had passed into parinirvāṇa, the period of his true dharma had ended, and the period of his Semblance Dharma had begun, there were many conceited and overbearing monks. At that time, there was a bodhisattva named Sadāparibhūta ("Never Disparaging"), so named because he never disparaged anyone, saying to all he met: "I deeply respect you. I dare not belittle you. Why is this? Because all of you practice the bodhisattva path, and will become buddhas" (276). This statement, which comprises twenty-four characters in Kumārajīva's translation, was often considered as encapsulating the spirit of the *Lotus Sūtra*. Some Japanese exegetes even called it the "*Lotus Sūtra* abbreviated in twenty-four characters."

Yet in the story, many who were so addressed became annoyed and threw rocks at the bodhisattva, but he never disparaged them. People thus came to refer to him, rather sarcastically, as "Never Despising." When he was about to die, billions of verses of the *Lotus Sūtra* resounded through space, purifying his senses and extending his lifespan. He upheld the *Lotus Sūtra*, teaching it far and wide. Consequently, he met and practiced under countless buddhas and eventually became a buddha himself. Śākyamuni reveals that he himself was

Sadāparibhūta in a previous life. He also reveals that those who had mocked him were reborn in the Avīci hell for a thousand eons. When they had expiated their offense and were subsequently reborn as humans, they again met and became followers of Sadāparibhūta, who led them to supreme enlightenment.

We cannot know for certain, but the story of Sadāparibhūta may reflect the experience of the *Lotus Sūtra*'s compilers in encountering anger and contempt from mainstream Buddhist monastics. The Sanskrit name Sadāparibhūta actually means "Always Despised." As an ordinary monk without any particular accomplishments, Sadāparibhūta had no obvious authority for delivering predictions of future buddhahood, and monastics who looked askance at the nascent Mahāyāna movement may have found his words presumptuous and offensive. Hence, he was "always despised." Dharmarakṣa, who first rendered the *Lotus Sūtra* into Chinese, translated the bodhisattva's name in this way. But Kumārajīva instead adopted "Never Despising," shifting emphasis to the bodhisattva's attitude of reverence for all. As Nichiren expresses it: "In the past, the bodhisattva Sadāparibhūta carried out the practice of veneration, saying that all beings have the buddha nature; that if they embrace the *Lotus Sūtra,* they are certain to attain buddhahood; and that to slight another is to slight the Buddha himself. He bowed even to those who did not embrace the *Lotus Sūtra,* because they too had the buddha nature and might someday accept the sūtra."[1]

As already noted in this volume's discussion of Chapter Eight, the *Lotus Sūtra* itself does not contain the words "buddha nature," a concept developed in later Mahāyāna sūtras, such as the *Nirvāṇa Sūtra*. For that reason, some early Chinese exegetes argued that the *Nirvāṇa Sūtra,* and not the *Lotus,* represented the Buddha's highest teaching. In contrast, the "three great masters of the Sui dynasty"—Huiyuan, Zhiyi, and Jizang—drew on the Sadāparibhūta chapter to argue that the idea of innate buddha nature is fully present in the *Lotus Sūtra,* even though that specific phrase does not occur there.[2]

Chinese commentators also stressed the bodhisattva Sadāparibhūta's attitude as a model for practice. Huisi, Zhiyi's teacher, commented on this sūtra chapter as follows: "Looking upon each and every being as though it were a buddha, you should join your palms and venerate it as though paying reverence to the Lord [Buddha himself]. You should also regard each and every being as a great bodhisattva and good spiritual friend."[3] Fragmentary evidence suggests that East Asian Buddhists sometimes literally attempted to imitate the bodhisattva Sadāparibhūta's practice of bowing to all. One example can be found in the "Three Stages" movement, founded by the Chinese master Xinxing (540–594) as a form of Buddhism suited to the degenerate Final Dharma age. Xinxing incorporated Sadāparibhūta's practice of bowing into a set of interrelated practices combining the attitudes of universally venerating others and recognizing one's own shortcomings.[4] The practice of bowing to others was also sometimes conducted in Japan. The monk Shōnyo (781–867), to repay his debt to his parents, is said to have carried out Sadāparibhūta's practice by bowing at the homes of more than 167,600 people.[5] In aristocratic circles, this practice was carried out on the fourteenth day of the seventh month. Entries for that date in the diary of the poet and courtier Fujiwara no Teika (1162–1241) record that he himself performed this practice in the streets or had others do it on his behalf.[6]

Nichiren took Sadāparibhūta as a personal model and strongly identified with him. First, there were obvious parallels in their practice. "Sadāparibhūta was a practitioner at the initial stage of rejoicing," Nichiren wrote, "while I am an ordinary person at the level of verbal identity. He sowed the seeds of buddhahood with twenty-four characters, while I do so with just five characters [Myōhō-renge-kyō]. The age differs, but the buddhahood realized is exactly the same."[7] This passage suggests that Nichiren saw Sadāparibhūta, like himself, as someone at the initial stages of practice who was carrying out *shakubuku*, planting the seeds of buddhahood in the minds of people who had never before received them. He saw other similarities as well. Both Nichiren and Sadāparibhūta lived long after the passing of the respective buddhas of their age, in an era of decline when there was much hostility. And both persevered in the face of emnity, enabling their persecutors to form a "reverse connection" (J. *gyakuen*) with the *Lotus Sūtra*. In short, Sadāparibhūta was for Nichiren an exemplar of practice for the latter age, and in this sense, he wrote, "The heart of the practice of the *Lotus Sūtra* is found in the 'Sadāparibhūta' chapter."[8]

Nichiren also read the story of Sadāparibhūta in a way that reflected—and perhaps inspired—his understanding of his own ordeals as a form of redemptive suffering. The prose portion of the "Sadāparibhūta" chapter says that those who mocked the bodhisattva suffered for a thousand eons in the Avīci hell, but after expiating this offense, they were again able to meet him and were led by him to attain "the highest, complete enlightenment" (278). The verse section, however, suggests that the bodhisattva himself had "expiated his past errors" (279) by patiently bearing the insults and mistreatment he received in the course of his practice. Nichiren focused on this second reading, encouraging his followers, and himself as well, by explaining that hardship encountered for the *Lotus Sūtra*'s sake would eradicate one's past slanders against the dharma. "The bodhisattva Sadāparibhūta was not reviled and disparaged, and assailed with sticks and stones, for no reason," Nichiren suggested. "It would appear that he had probably slandered the true dharma in the past. The phrase 'having expiated his past errors' seems to mean that because he met persecution, he was able to eradicate his sins from prior lifetimes."[9]

During the hardships of his exile to Sado Island, Nichiren became convinced that his own trials were not retributions for ordinary misdeeds. Rather, in previous lives, he himself must have slandered the dharma, the offense that he now so implacably opposed. He reflected: "From time without beginning I must have been born countless times as an evil ruler who robbed practitioners of the *Lotus Sūtra* of their clothing and food, paddies and fields . . . countless times I must have beheaded *Lotus Sūtra* practitioners."[10] Ordinarily, he explained, the karmic retribution for such horrific offenses would torment a person over the course of innumerable lifetimes. But by asserting the unique truth of the *Lotus Sūtra* and meeting persecution as a result, he had in effect summoned the consequences of those misdeeds into the present lifetime to be eradicated once and for all. "By being pounded in the fire, iron is forged into swords," he said. "Worthies and sages are tested by abuse. My present sentence of exile is not because of even the slightest worldly wrongdoing. It has come about solely that I may expiate my past grave offenses in this lifetime and escape [rebirth in] the three evils paths in the next."[11]

In seeing himself as charged by the Buddha with the mission of disseminating the *Lotus Sūtra* in the evil, Final Dharma age, Nichiren identified with the noble and heroic figure of the bodhisattva Viśiṣṭacāritra, leader of the bodhisattvas of the earth. But at the same time, in seeing his trials as opportunities to rid himself of the consequences of past errors, he identified with the humbler figure of the bodhisattva Sadāparibhūta. In so doing, Nichiren placed himself on the same level as the people he was attempting to save and identified a karmic bond between them.

Both perspectives come together in Nichiren's understanding that practice, propagation, and attainment were unfolding in his own time just as in Sadāparibhūta's. Noting that the all buddhas throughout time preach the *Lotus Sūtra* as the culmination of their teaching, he observed that the hostility encountered by Sadāparibhūta in the age of a past buddha corresponded to the predictions of persecution made in Chapter Thirteen of the *Lotus Sūtra* as preached by the present buddha (Śākyamuni). One chapter tells of the past, the other foretells the future, but their content accords perfectly. When the *Lotus Sūtra* will be preached by buddhas in ages to come, he asserted, the present, "Perseverance," chapter would become the "Sadāparibhūta" chapter of the future," suggesting that its predictions would come true through his own actions, "and at that time I, Nichiren, will be its bodhisattva Sadāparibhūta."[12]

Based on his reading of these two chapters, Nichiren saw himself and his opponents as linked via the *Lotus Sūtra* in a vast soteriological drama of error, expiation, and the realization of buddhahood. Those who malign a practitioner of the *Lotus Sūtra* must undergo repeated rebirth in the Avīci hell for countless eons. But because they have formed a "reverse connection" to the *Lotus* by slandering its votary, after expiating this error, they will eventually encounter the sūtra again and be able to become buddhas. By a similar logic, practitioners who suffer harassment must encounter this ordeal precisely because they maligned the *Lotus Sūtra* in the past, just as their tormenters do in the present. But because of those practitioners' efforts to protect the *Lotus* by opposing slander of the dharma in the present, their own past offenses will be eradicated, and they will not only attain buddhahood themselves in the future, but also enable their persecutors to do the same. The *Lotus* practitioners and those who oppose them are thus inseparably connected through the sūtra in the same web of karmic causes that will ultimately lead both to buddhahood.

CHAPTERS TWENTY-ONE AND TWENTY-TWO

The Transcendent Powers of the Tathāgata *and* Entrustment

Chapter Twenty-One

Here Śākyamuni Buddha and all the buddhas in attendance perform various feats, such as extending their tongues up to the heavens of Brahmā and emitting multicolored rays of light from each pore in their bodies. They then withdraw their tongues, cough, and snap their fingers in unison, causing the earth to quake. This is a rare scene in a Buddhist sūtra.

The Buddha explains that the *Lotus Sūtra* that he has just taught (again, it is unclear exactly where it began and where it ended) reveals all the teachings and powers of the Tathāgata. For this reason, after he has passed into parinirvāṇa, it should be preserved, recited, explained, copied, and practiced. Wherever it is taught, that place should become a shrine, because such a place becomes a "terrace of enlightenment," the *bodhimaṇḍa,* the place where the Buddha (and all buddhas) sit when they achieve buddhahood and hence the most sacred place in the world.

Chapter Twenty-Two

Many Mahāyāna scriptures, such as the *Greater Perfection of Wisdom* and *Mahāvairocana* sūtras, conclude with a chapter by this title, in which the Buddha enjoins the assembly to spread and uphold the sūtra, and his listeners vow to do so. In the case of the *Lotus*, however, as we have seen, exhortations to preach and propagate the sūtra, along with related stories about the past and prophecies of the future, are not confined to the "Entrustment" chapter or even to the final, "dissemination" section of the sūtra, but constitute a recurring theme throughout the text: the theme of the *Lotus* votary committed to the sūtra's propagation. In this way, even while legitimating itself by references to events in the inconceivably remote past, the *Lotus* also writes itself into the limitless future—a sūtra that never ends, an assembly that never disperses, and a mission that is ongoing.

Nonetheless, at one point in the compilation process, this was probably the final chapter of the *Lotus Sūtra,* and scholars tend to regard it as such, with the remaining six chapters thought to be later interpolations. Caressing the heads of the assembled bodhisattvas, the Buddha once again exhorts them to spread the teaching, and the bodhisattvas promise to do so. The Buddha then causes all the buddhas who had arrived from the ten directions to return to their own abodes. In a concluding sentence common to many sūtras, all the members of the audience rejoice.

Yet the *Lotus Sūtra* does not end here. We do not find in the Mahāyāna sūtras anything akin to Revelation 22:18–19 of the Bible, which states: "I warn everyone who hears the words of the prophecy of this book: if any one adds to them, God will add to him the plagues described in this book, and if any one takes away from the words of the book of this prophecy, God will take away his share in the tree of life and in the holy city, which are described in this book." Whole chapters would be added to this Buddhist book.

In these two chapters, Śākyamuni Buddha entrusts the teachings of the *Lotus Sūtra* for propagation in the future. To make clear the momentousness of the occasion, he first displays his awe-inspiring transcendent powers. According to Zhanran, of the ten powers described, the first five—from Śākyamuni and all other buddhas extending their tongues to the heavens of Brahmā to the buddha worlds of the ten directions quaking in six ways (283)—were intended for beings in his lifetime. The remaining supernatural events—from all beings in those worlds beholding the buddhas present on their lion thrones at the *Lotus* assembly to the worlds of the ten directions becoming pellucid, as though they were one buddha land (284)—were intended for beings of the future.[1]

Though he acknowledged this reading, Nichiren concluded that ultimately the entire display was directed to the future, when the four leaders of the bodhisattvas of the earth would appear in order to spread the five characters Myōhō-renge-kyō. He also assimilated these extraordinary happenings to contemporary portents: "The quaking of the earth in the 'Introduction' chapter was limited to a single world system, but in the 'Transcendent Powers' chapter the lands of the various buddhas all shook violently, quaking in six different ways. The [earthquakes and other] omens of our own time are just like this. The great omens of the 'Transcendent Powers' chapter portend that the essence of the *Lotus Sūtra* will spread widely after the Buddha's nirvāṇa, when the two thousand years of the True Dharma and Semblance Dharma ages have passed and the Final Dharma age has begun."[2]

The first of the ten signs, the buddhas extending their tongues to the heavens of Brahmā, is culturally bound and may not resonate with modern readers. In the context of the sūtra's compilation, a long and wide tongue was considered one of a buddha's distinguishing physical marks, a sign that he never lies, and the buddhas' act of extending their tongues was intended to verify the *Lotus Sūtra*'s truth. Nichiren often mentioned this act as underscoring the significance of the transmission that Śākyamuni was now about to make: "Having summoned these people [i.e., the four bodhisattvas who lead the bodhisattvas of the earth], Śākyamuni Buddha entrusted to them the five characters Myōhō-renge-kyō. This was no ordinary transmission, for the Buddha first manifested ten transcendent powers. When Śākyamuni extended his wide and long tongue to the upper limit of the world of form, all the other buddhas did likewise, their tongues reaching into the air above four million *nayuta*s of worlds and filling the sky like billions of crimson rainbows arched together—an altogether awesome display."[3] Elsewhere, Nichiren would note that the Buddha sitting side by side with another buddha (in Chapter Eleven) and buddhas extending their tongues to the heavens of Brahmā appear in no other Buddhist sūtra, Hīnayāna or Mahāyāna, further proof of the unique truth of the *Lotus Sūtra*.[4]

Nichiren's name derives in part from his understanding of the "Transcendent Powers" chapter as foretelling that the bodhisattvas of the earth would appear at the beginning of the Final Dharma age. In premodern Japan, as in other cultures, it was common to change one's name on entering a new stage of life or undergoing some transformative experience. Nichiren's childhood name is said to have been Yakuō-maro. When he was first ordained, he assumed the monastic name Renchō. After reaching the insight that the daimoku of the *Lotus Sūtra* is the sole path of liberation in the Final Dharma age, he changed his name to Nichiren ("Sun Lotus"). The concluding verse section of this chapter reads in part, "As the light of the sun and moon eliminates the darkness, these people practicing in the world will extinguish the blindness of sentient beings" (287). In the Chinese text, "these people," the subject of this sentence, can be read either in the plural, as Kubo and Yuyama translate it, or in the singular, as Nichiren took it, that is, as referring to anyone—particularly himself, but also his followers—who took upon themselves the task of the Buddha's original disciples to propagate the *Lotus Sūtra* in the Final Dharma age. As he comments:

> Calling myself Nichiren (Sun Lotus) means that I awakened by myself to the buddha vehicle. That may sound as though I am boasting of my wisdom, but I say so for a reason. The sūtra reads, "As the light of the sun and moon eliminates the darkness. . . ." Think well about what this passage means. "These people practicing in the world" means that in the first five hundred years of the Final Dharma age, the bodhisattva Viśiṣṭacāritra will appear and illuminate the darkness of ignorance and defilements with the light of the five characters of Namu Myōhō-renge-kyō. As the bodhisattva Viśiṣṭacāritra's envoy, I have urged all people of Japan to accept and uphold the *Lotus Sūtra*; that is what this passage refers to. The sūtra then goes on to say, "The wise . . . should preserve this sūtra after my nirvāṇa. Those people will be resolute and will unwaveringly follow the buddha path" (287). Those who become my disciples and lay followers should understand that we share a profound karmic relationship and spread the *Lotus Sūtra* as I do.[5]

Among Chinese exegetes, Zhiyi was the first to identifiy both Chapters Twenty-One and Twenty-Two as describing Śākyamuni's transmission to the future. Nichiren built upon

Zhiyi's reading to claim that there had been two transmissions: a specific transmission to Viśiṣṭacāritra and the other bodhisattvas who had emerged from beneath the earth, which occurs in the "Transcendent Powers" chapter (284–285, beginning from "Thereupon the Buddha addressed the great assembly of bodhisattvas, beginning with Viśiṣṭacāritra . . ."), and a general transmission, which occurs in the "Entrustment" chapter, to all the bodhisattvas, including those from other worlds and those instructed by Śākyamuni when he was still in his provisional guise as the historical Buddha, as he is represented in the trace teaching, as well as to persons of the two vehicles and others in the *Lotus* assembly.[6]

Let us review the process of the Buddha's entrustment of the *Lotus Sūtra* from this twofold perspective. In the "Jeweled Stūpa" chapter, Śākyamuni Buddha calls for persons willing to spread the sūtra in an evil age after his nirvāṇa. Right before the concluding verse section, Śākyamuni announces: "The Tathāgata will enter parinirvāṇa before long and the Buddha wants to transmit this *Lotus Sūtra* to you" (181). Zhiyi says that this implies both a "near" transmission, to those bodhisattvas who have already assembled, and a "distant" transmission, to the bodhisattvas who will emerge from the earth several chapters later and to whom the Buddha will transfer the essence of the sūtra.[7] In the "Perseverance" chapter, a great throng of bodhisattvas from other worlds vow to spread the *Lotus Sūtra* throughout the ten directions. But in the "Bodhisattvas Emerging from the Earth" chapter, Śākyamuni rejects their offer and instead summons his original disciples, the bodhisattvas from beneath the earth led by Viśiṣṭacāritra. Their appearance at the assembly in open space provides the occasion for Śākyamuni, in the "Lifespan" chapter, to cast off his provisional guise as someone who first realized enlightenment in the present lifetime and reveal his true identity as the primordially awakened buddha who "constantly resides" here in this world. Now in the "Transcendent Powers" chapter, he formally transfers the *Lotus Sūtra* to the bodhisattvas of the earth, who in the next chapter solemnly vow to uphold and disseminate it as the Buddha directs.

But what was transferred to the bodhisattvas of the earth? Śākyamuni declares that in the *Lotus Sūtra* he has "clearly revealed and taught all the teachings of the Tathāgata, all the transcendent powers of the Tathāgata, all the treasure houses of the hidden essence of the Tathāgata, and all the profound aspects of the Tathāgata" (285). Based on this passage, Zhiyi formulated five major principles of the *Lotus Sūtra*—its name, essence, purport, function, and position among all teachings—principles that he also understood as inherent in the five characters that comprise the sūtra's title. Nichiren too spoke of "Namu Myōhō-renge-kyō endowed with the five profound principles," drawing on the Tiantai commentarial tradition to assert that what Śākyamuni Buddha transferred to the bodhisattvas of the earth was none other than the daimoku, the heart or intent, of the *Lotus Sūtra*:

> As for the five characters Myōhō-renge-kyō: Śākyamuni Buddha not only kept them secret during his first forty-some years of teaching, but also refrained from speaking of them even in the trace teaching, the first fourteen chapters of the *Lotus Sūtra*. Not until the "Lifespan" chapter did he reveal the two characters *renge*, which [represent the five characters and] indicate the original effect and original cause [of the Buddha's enlightenment]. The Buddha did not entrust these five characters to Mañjuśrī, Samantabhadra, Maitreya, Bhaiṣajyarāja, or any other such bodhisattvas. Instead he summoned forth from the great earth

of Tranquil Light the bodhisattvas Viśiṣṭacāritra, Anantacāritra, Viśuddhacāritra, and Supratiṣṭhitacāritra along with their followers and transmitted the five characters to them.[8]

In short, in Nichiren's reading, in the "Transcendent Powers" chapter, the Buddha first transmitted the daimoku, Namu Myōhō-renge-kyō, to the bodhisattvas who had emerged from the earth, for them to propagate in the Final Dharma age. To presage this momentous event, the Buddha displayed his ten transcendent powers and, extracting the essence of the *Lotus Sūtra,* entrusted it to the four bodhisattvas. Then, in the "Entrustment" chapter, he made a more general transmission of the *Lotus* and all his other teachings to the bodhisattvas from other worlds, the bodhisattvas of the trace teaching who had been his followers in his provisional guise as the buddha who first attained awakening in this lifetime, and persons of the two vehicles. This general transmission was intended for the more limited period of the True Dharma and Semblance Dharma ages.

Nichiren's idea of the transmission of the *Lotus Sūtra* is also twofold in another sense. On the one hand, the transmission unfolds through a line of teachers in historical time. Nichiren saw himself as heir to a lineage that passed from Śākyamuni Buddha, to Zhiyi, to Saichō, and then to himself—the "four teachers in three countries," as he put it.[9] The Nichiren tradition terms this the "outer transmission," passing over the centuries from Śākyamuni Buddha down to Nichiren and his followers. At the same time, however, it speaks of an "inner transmission" received directly from the primordial buddha, namely, the daimoku itself. Nichiren said that teachers such as Zhiyi and Saichō had known inwardly of Namu Myōhō-renge-kyō but had not spoken of it openly because the time for its dissemination had not yet come.

Nichiren alludes to this direct transmission in a personal letter connecting his retreat in the depths of Mount Minobu in Kai province, where he spent the last years of his life, to the "Transcendent Powers" chapter, where it says that wherever the *Lotus Sūtra* is practiced—"in a garden, a forest, under a tree, in a monk's chamber, in a layman's house, in a palace, on a mountain, in a valley, or in the wilderness" (285)—is a sacred place of the Buddha's activity. Nichiren elaborates: "This place is deep in the mountains, far from human habitation. East, west, north, or south, not a single village is to be found. Although I dwell in this forlorn retreat, hidden in the fleshly heart within my breast I hold the secret dharma of the 'one great purpose' (31) transmitted from Śākyamuni Buddha, the lord of teachings, at Vulture Peak. Within my breast the buddhas enter nirvāṇa; on my tongue, they turn the wheel of the dharma; from my throat, they are born; and in my mouth, they attain supreme awakening. Because this the wondrous votary of the *Lotus Sūtra* dwells in this mountain, how could it be inferior to the pure land of Vulture Peak?"[10]

In other words, the daimoku of the *Lotus Sūtra* is the source of all buddhas. One who chants it directly receives its transmission from the primordial buddha on Vulture Peak, and the place where one chants it is that buddha's pure land. This claim is in keeping with the logic that "the assembly on Vulture Peak is awesomely present and has not yet dispersed" or of the primordial buddha's realm of "original time" depicted on Nichiren's maṇḍala that can be entered through faith. Another of Nichiren's personal letters explains the inner transmission in this way: "To chant Myōhō-renge-kyō with the understanding that these three—Śākyamuni Buddha who realized enlightenment in the remotest past, the *Lotus Sūtra* that enables all to attain the buddha way, and we ourselves, living beings—are altogether inseparable and without distinction is to receive the transmission of the one great purpose of birth and death."[11] "Transmission" in this sense does not pass through a single historical lineage of teachers but is immediately accessible to any practitioner who chants the daimoku.

CHAPTER TWENTY-THREE

Ancient Accounts of Bodhisattva Bhaiṣajyarāja

Several of the final chapters of the *Lotus Sūtra* seem intended to promote the cults of specific bodhisattvas. One of these is Bhaiṣajyarāja ("Medicine King"), who has already appeared in Chapter Ten. Chapter Twenty-Three begins with a bodhisattva asking the Buddha to explain why the bodhisattva Bhaiṣajyarāja wanders through the world performing difficult deeds. The Buddha explains that in the distant past, in the time of a buddha named Candrasūryavimalaprabhāsaśrī ("Pure and Bright Excellence of Sun and Moon"), there was a bodhisattva named Sarvarūpasaṃdarśana ("Manifesting All Forms"), so called because after hearing the *Lotus Sūtra* he had mastered a meditation that enabled him to display any appearance at will. In some versions of the sūtra he is called Sarvasattvapriyadarśana, or "Seen with Joy by All Sentient Beings," which is how Kumārajīva renders his name. Despite this difference in the two names, the idea behind them is the same: this bodhisattva can delight all sentient beings precisely because he can display himself to them in the form, whatever it may be, that they will find most pleasing. This ability suggests his profound realization of the emptiness of all phenomena, which enables him both to manifest freely in any form and to relinquish his own body as an offering. The ability of accomplished bodhisattvas to display themselves in any form is a theme linking chapters Twenty-Three through Twenty-Five. Here, this accomplishment is represented as a product of devotion to the *Lotus Sūtra* (292).

The sūtra describes Sarvarūpasaṃdarśana as "devoted entirely to severe practices" (292), that is, to asceticism. Ascetic practices were well established in ancient India across religious traditions. Although the Buddha is said to have advocated a "middle way" between the extremes of self-indulgence and self-mortification, Buddhism historically has had its own strand of ascetic practice, rooted in the idea that subjecting the body to severe disciplines would yield spiritual powers. In order to pay homage to the buddha Candrasūryavimalaprabhāsaśrī and to the *Lotus Sūtra*, Sarvarūpasaṃdarśana decided to make an offering of his body. He ingested all manner of fragrant oils, covered his body with a scented ointment, and donned a jeweled garment soaked in oil. He then set his body alight. It burned for twelve hundred years, illuminating billions of worlds. All the buddhas in those worlds praised his act as the supreme offering to the dharma.

Sarvarūpasaṃdarśana was then reborn spontaneously, sitting cross-legged in the palace of his father the king. Because the buddha Candrasūryavimalaprabhāsaśrī was still in the world, the bodhisattva went immediately to pay homage to him. The buddha informed him that he would pass into parinirvāṇa that very night and entrusted the bodhisattva with the distribution of his relics. Sarvarūpasaṃdarśana duly cremated the buddha's body, gathered the relics, and erected eighty-four thousand stūpas. Feeling that this was not enough, he paid homage to the stūpas by burning off his arms. The gruesome sight of an armless teacher was distressing to his students.

In Buddhist literature, cases of self-mutilation for the sake of the dharma are relatively common, and the person who is mutilated is almost always healed, typically by what is called an asseveration of truth (*satyavacana*), a kind of oath that, if true, has magical powers. In this case, the bodhisattva declared, "I have abandoned both my arms, and I shall definitely attain the golden body of the Buddha. If this is true and not false, may both arms be restored as before" (296). His arms were immediately restored and jeweled flowers fell from the sky.

Śākyamuni explains that this bodhisattva Sarvarūpasaṃdarśana of the past is in fact the present Bhaiṣajyarāja. The Buddha goes on to say, "If there is anyone who sets forth and wishes to attain highest, complete enlightenment, he should pay homage to the stūpas of the Buddha by burning either a finger or a toe" (296). Over the next two thousand years, many in this Sahā world would do so, recreating the bodhisattva's self-immolation in real world tableaux.

The chapter ends with the Buddha praising the "Bhaiṣajyarāja" chapter and extolling the benefits for those who hear it and hold it (a statement providing additional evidence that the chapter was an independent work that had been inserted at the end of the *Lotus Sūtra*). For example, those who do so will always have breath with the scent of lotus flowers and skin with the scent of sandalwood; the sick who hear the chapter will be cured; and women who hear and hold the chapter will never again be reborn in a female body.

The *Lotus Sūtra* would be far more influential in China than in India, both as a whole and in terms of its specific themes and chapters. There is little evidence to suggest that the bodhisattva Sarvarūpasaṃdarśana's offering of a lamp made from his own body was emulated in India, although this may be due solely to a lack of historical records. In China, however, stories beginning as early as the late fourth century CE tell of monks and nuns who wrap themselves in waxed cloth and then set themselves alight, chanting the twenty-third chapter of the *Lotus Sūtra* until their voices fall silent. Thus, the grisliest story in the *Lotus Sūtra* was not read as a parable. In a sūtra famous for proclaiming that the Buddha does not always mean what he says, the story of the self-immolation of Bhaiṣajyarāja was taken quite literally. Self-immolation has been carried out for a range of recorded motives: as a dharma offering (as in the present case), to save or benefit other beings, to achieve birth in a pure land, or as an act of protest when Buddhism was persecuted by secular authorities.[1]

A Tang-dynasty anthology entitled *Accounts in Dissemination and Praise of the Lotus* (*Hongzan fahua zhuan*) tells of a monk named Huiyi who performed the deed in 463: "Huiyi climbed into the cauldron and seated himself on a small bench. First he wrapped his upper body in bark cloth from the *karpāsa* tree. Over this he wound a single long [strip of cloth] in the form of a turban, which he then sprinkled with oil. . . . Thereupon, taking candle in hand, Huiyi set the turban alight. As the turban caught fire he tossed the candle aside, joined his palms and began to recite the Medicine King (Bhaiṣajyarāja) Chapter [of the *Lotus*]. The flame began to creep down over his brow, but the sound of his chanting was still clear and distinct. When it reached his eyes, all was silent. Noblemen and commoners everywhere set up a loud wail, the echo of which reverberated throughout the valley. There wasn't one among them who didn't snap his fingers and praise the name of the Buddha [in admiration], as tears of grief streamed down their sobbing faces."[2]

A less extreme and far more common practice was the burning of fingers or the joints of fingers. The finger (or joint) would be anesthetized by tying a string very tightly below the portion to be burned to cut off the circulation. The finger would then be wrapped in pine resin and sandalwood and set ablaze, as the monk (and those who attended him) chanted the twenty-third chapter of the *Lotus Sūtra*. This practice continued into the twentieth century. An influential abbot in early twentieth-century China and one of the teachers of the famous Chinese reformer monk Taixu was Bazhi Toutuo or "Eight Fingers Ascetic," so named because he had burned off a finger of each hand in reverence to the *Lotus Sūtra*.

Acts of "relinquishing the body" have been highly controversial, even within the Buddhist tradition. One recurrent criticism was that examples in the Buddhist scriptures, such as that of Bhaiṣajyarāja, were carried out by bodhisattvas highly advanced in practice who had already discarded all attachments. Ordinary people could not possibly emulate them. The monk and scholar Yijing, who traveled to India and Sumatra in the seventh century, included a lengthy condemnation of the practice in the account of his travels, under such headings as "The Burning of the Body is Unlawful," "The Bystanders Become Guilty," and "Such Actions Were Not Practiced by the Virtuous of Old." It is noteworthy, however, that his condemnation extends only to monks; he argues that for a monk to perform self-immolation is suicide, which the Buddha specifically proscribed in the *vinaya*, the code of monastic conduct. Yijing seems to have had no objection to self-immolation by lay people.[3]

Yet the *Lotus Sūtra* seems to urge giving one's life in its service. Bodhisattvas in the "Perseverance" chapter vow that they "will not be attached to our bodies or lives" (199), and the "Lifespan" chapter says that the primordial Śākyamuni Buddha will appear before those beings who "are willing to give unsparingly of their bodies and their lives" (237). How should such passages be understood?

Nichiren addresses this issue in a letter to a disciple, the lay nun Myōichi-ama, expressing sympathy on the death of her husband, who had held fast to his faith despite great difficulties: "Your late husband gave his life for the *Lotus Sūtra*. His small landholding that barely sustained him was confiscated on account of [his faith in] the *Lotus Sūtra*. Surely that equaled 'giving his life.' The youth of the Snow Mountains [described in the *Nirvāṇa Sūtra*] offered his body in exchange for half a verse [of a Buddhist teaching], and the bodhisattva Medicine King [Bhaiṣajyarāja] burned his arms [in offering to the Buddha]. They were saints, [and for them, such acts were] like water poured on fire. But your husband was an ordinary man, [and so for him, this sacrifice was] like paper placed in fire. When we take this into consideration, his merit must surely be the same as theirs."[4]

In short, Nichiren emphasized, not the literal performance of self-sacrifice in offering to the sūtra as exemplified by Bhaiṣajyarāja's self-immolation, but the willingness to face abuse, ostracism, verbal and physical attacks, or indeed, any sort of hardship in order to uphold and spread the sūtra's teachings. In his reading, the offering that ordinary people can make, done with firm resolve, is the moral equivalent of the advanced bodhisattva's sacrifice of his body, and it yields identical merit.

From another perspective, Nichiren concluded that the acts of Bhaiṣajyarāja and other bodhisattvas in the sūtras who relinquished eyes, limbs, and life itself for the dharma's sake were no longer appropriate to his own era. As a young man, he wrote, he had taken the statement in the "Perseverance" chapter, "We will not be attached to our bodies or our lives," to mean heroic undertakings on the order of making the perilous sea crossing to China to study the dharma, as pioneering Japanese monks like Saichō and Kūkai had done, or offering up one's body in self-sacrifice like the bodhisattva Bhaiṣajyarāja. But over time, he concluded that this was not the sūtra's true intent: "At a time when the country is filled with respected persons who declare that there are other sūtras that surpass the *Lotus Sūtra* and join in attacking its votary, and when such persons are revered by the ruler and his ministers while the votary of the *Lotus Sūtra*, being poor and humble, is despised by the entire country, if he persists in his assertions as did [the bodhisattva] Sadāparibhūta or the scholar-monk Bhadraruci, it may well cost his life. [To maintain one's resolve at such at time] is the most important thing of all."[5] What counts, in short, is upholding the *Lotus*, no matter what.

The "Bhaiṣajyarāja" chapter next offers ten analogies illustrating the supreme status of the *Lotus Sūtra* among all the Buddha's teachings. It surpasses them just as the ocean is greater than all streams, rivers, and other bodies of water; as Mount Sumeru towers over all other mountains; and so forth. Then follow ten vivid similies illustrating the powers and blessings of the sūtra. Nichiren was deeply struck by these passages and often cited or elaborated on them to stress the merits of upholding the *Lotus*. Here, for example, in a personal letter to a follower called Shiiji Shirō, he expands on the statement that the *Lotus Sūtra* is "like a boat for a traveler" (297). This boat, he says, might be described as follows. Note how he weaves together Buddhist technical terms and phrases from different portions of the *Lotus Sūtra*:

> The Lord Buddha, a shipbuilder of infinitely profound wisdom, gathered the lumber of the four flavors and eight teachings, planed it by "openly setting aside skillful means" (45), cut and assembled the planks, using both right and wrong in their nonduality, and completed the craft by driving home the spikes of

> the single truth that is like the supreme flavor of ghee. Then he launched it upon the sea of birth and death. Unfurling its sails of the three thousand realms on the mast of the single truth of the middle way, driven by the fair wind that is the "real aspect of the dharmas" (24), the vessel surges ahead, carrying aboard all sentient beings, who can "understand through faith" (76). The tathāgatha Śākyamuni takes the helm, the tathāgatha Prabhūtaratna mans the sails, and the four bodhisattvas led by Viśiṣṭacāritra strain in unison at the creaking oars. This is the vessel in "a boat for the traveler." Those who can board it are the disciples and lay followers of Nichiren.[6]

After the ten analogies and ten similies, the *Lotus* goes on to extol the merits of embracing the "Bhaiṣajyarāja" chapter specifically, suggesting that it may have been composed by a group of *Lotus* practitioners particularly devoted to this bodhisattva. Nichiren, however, read the passage as applying to his own time and to the *Lotus* as a whole. For example, a statement near the end of this chapter reads, "During the period of five hundred years after my parinirvāṇa, you must spread it far and wide in Jambudvīpa [i.e., this world] and not allow it to be destroyed" (299). The "five hundred years after my parinirvāṇa" here probably indicates the time in which the *Lotus Sūtra*'s compilers understood themselves to be living, that is, within five centuries of the historical Buddha's death. But in Kumārajīva's Chinese translation, "the period of five hundred years after" can also be read as "the last five hundred years." Nichiren, like other later East Asian interpreters, took this phrase to mean the last of five consecutive five-hundred-year periods following the parinirvāṇa as described in the *Great Collection Sūtra* (Skt. *Mahāsaṃnipāta Sūtra*; Ch. *Daji jing*, *T* 397); the "last five hundred years" is predicted to be a time of dissension among the

Buddha's followers, corresponding to the beginning of the mappō era, when the true dharma will be obscured.[7] In other words, Nichiren took this passage as referring to his own, present time. Repudiating the idea that mappō is necessarily an age of Buddhism's decline, he drew on the third analogy of the "Bhaiṣajyarāja" chapter, which compares the *Lotus Sūtra* to the moon that outshines all stars. "The blessings of the *Lotus Sūtra* surpass those of other sūtras even during the two thousand years of the True and Semblance Dharma ages," he wrote. "But when the spring and summer of the two thousand years of the True Dharma and Semblance Dharma ages are over and the autumn and winter of the Final Dharma age have arrived, then the light of this moon [i.e., the *Lotus*] will shine even more brightly."[8] In the sūtra text, the "it" which is to be "spread far and wide" (J. *kōsen-rufu*) refers specifically to the "Bhaiṣajyarāja" chapter. Nichiren, however, took it as referring to the sūtra itself, and more specifically, to its title or daimoku, Namu Myōhō-renge-kyō.

As noted above, the blessings promised in this chapter run the gamut from fragrant breath and skin—highly desirable, one imagines, in a hot climate where frequent bathing may have been difficult—to transcending the sufferings of birth and death. It is a very modern viewpoint, and a privileged one at that, to see spiritual insight as the only true aim of religion and dismiss a concern with practical benefits as a corruption or a concession to the uneducated. For the sūtra's compilers in India, as for Nichiren's followers more than a millenium later in Japan, the benefits of faith and practice encompassed the entire spectrum of the mundane and the transcendent.

Several points in this section merit comment. One is the promise that any woman who upholds the present "Bhaiṣajyarāja" chapter will never again be born female but will go after death to the realm of the buddha Amitābha (J. Amida), to be freed forever from the three poisons of greed, anger, and ignorance (298). This passage reflects the idea, already well established at the time of the *Lotus Sūtra*'s compilation, that there are no women in Amitābha's pure land; presumably, women are reborn there as men (Kubo and Yuyama signal this in their translation by a switch of pronouns, which Chinese does not employ).[9] This passage, like similar ones in other sūtras, is subject to multiple, not necessarily mutually exclusive, readings. One reading would see it as reflecting the gender hierarchy, if not outright misogyny, of the larger culture. At the same time, those who composed sūtras about Amitābha and his realm may have seen the promise of an end to female rebirths as offering release from the biological and social constraints that bound women in premodern societies, limitations understood at the time as karmically "inherent" in the fact of having a female body. Such statements could also reflect the idea that, in Amitābha's pure land, one is said to quickly achieve the highest level of bodhisattva practice, in which one is not karmically bound to any particular physical form, male or female, but can assume any appearance needed to benefit others. Whatever the case, we know that many women in medieval Japan who were devoted to Amitābha, as well as the men around them, simply assumed that they would be born in the Pure Land as women—an example of how, on the ground, devotees may ignore uncongenial elements of scripture. Nichiren, however, was quick to point out the rejection of women as a problem in the sūtras praising Amitābha's pure land. Women who chant the nenbutsu, he warned, are relying upon sūtras that can never lead women to buddhahood and therefore, in effect, are but "vainly counting other people's riches."[10]

In addressing the present passage, Nichiren first reminds his reader that the *Lotus Sūtra,* the Buddha's ultimate teaching, supersedes the Pure Land sūtras dealing with Amitābha, which are all provisional. Invoking the first of the ten analogies given in the "Bhaiṣajyarāja" chapter, he says that the *Lotus Sūtra* is like the great ocean, while the *Amitābha Sūtra,* the *Visualization Sūtra,* and other sūtras dealing with Amitābha are like small streams.[11] Moreover, the "Amitābha" mentioned in the "Bhaiṣajyarāja" chapter is not the Amitābha Buddha of the Pure Land sūtras but an emanation of the primordial Śākyamuni Buddha.[12] In this way, Nichiren was able to dissociate this passage from the Pure Land devotion that he saw as no longer valid in his age. At the same time, he continued to maintain that the *Lotus Sūtra* enables all women who embrace it to attain buddhahood.

The Mahāyāna imagination populated the cosmos with worlds presided over by buddhas or bodhisattvas. Such realms were considered "pure" in the sense that these worlds did not contain animals, ghosts, or denizens of hell. Some acquired mythic narratives, and their buddhas became the objects of devotional and contemplative practices. Thought to be attainable through accomplishments in meditation or by acquisition of sufficient merit, birth after death in such a realm was considered an opportunity for rapid advancement in practice and, thus, a shortcut on the long bodhisattva path. In East Asia, the pure land most commonly sought was the buddha Amitābha's "Land of Bliss" (Skt. Sukhāvatī; Ch. Jile; J. Gokuraku). Birth in Amitābha's pure land had widely come to be equated with achieving the stage of nonretrogression; once born there, it was said, one would not fall back into the samsaric realms but was assured of attaining buddhahood. In a more immediate sense, people also thought of Amitābha's land as a place where they could be reunited with deceased loved ones, transcending the pain of separation that characterizes the Sahā world. Another focus of postmortem aspirations was the Tuṣita heaven, whose inner court, where the future buddha Maitreya dwells, was also regarded as a pure land. Birth in the Tuṣita heaven is one of the many benefits promised to devotees in Chapter Twenty-Eight of the *Lotus Sūtra* (333).

Nichiren was adamant that the *Lotus Sūtra* enables the realization of buddhahood here in this world, not in a pure land after death. And, being implacably opposed to the Pure Land teachings, he could not accept the common idea that the worthy dead go to Amitābha's realm. Yet, especially in his later years, he was confronted with the need to explain what happens to *Lotus Sūtra* practitioners after they die. He taught that they join the constantly abiding Śākyamuni Buddha in the "pure land of Vulture Peak." "Vulture Peak" (Skt. Gṛdhrakūṭa; J. Ryōjusen, also translated as "Eagle Peak") in Rājagṛha in India was where Śākyamuni is said to have preached the *Lotus Sūtra*, and the term "pure land of Vulture Peak" had been used long before Nichiren's time to designate the realm of the primordial buddha described in the "Lifespan" chapter. Nichiren was not the first to conceptualize this realm as a postmortem destination. It seems to have entered Japan by at least the ninth century, as the courtier Sugawara no Michizane (845–903) once composed a poem of parting expressing the hope of reunion after death at Vulture Peak.[13] After Nichiren's time, "Vulture Peak" became virtually the proprietary pure land, so to speak, of his followers. But it was not merely a *Lotus*-inflected substitute for Amitābha's Land of Bliss. For Nichiren, the pure land of Vulture Peak is not a distinct realm posited in contrast to the present world; unlike Amitābha's pure land in the west or the tathāgata Bhaiṣajyaguru's (J. Yakushi Nyorai) *vaidūrya* world in the east, it has no specific cosmological location. Rather, it exists wherever one embraces the *Lotus Sūtra*. This pure land is the realm of the constantly abiding primordial buddha, a land that "never decays," even in the fire at the kalpa's end (238); it is the ever-present *Lotus* assembly and the three thousand realms in a single thought-moment depicted on Nichiren's maṇḍala. Accessible in the present, it also extends to encompass the faithful dead, a realm transcending life and death. The "pure land of Vulture Peak" thus also offered devotees the promise of reunion. To a young man who had just lost his father, Nichiren wrote: "Even strangers, if they embrace this [*Lotus*] sūtra, will meet at the same Vulture Peak. How much more so, in the case of you and your father! Both believing in the *Lotus Sūtra*, you will be born together in the same place."[14] And some years later, he wrote to the young man's mother, who had lost not only her husband, but also another son, "Now he [your son] is with his father in the same pure land of Vulture Peak; how happy they must be to hold one another's hands and place their heads together!"[15]

Chapter Twenty-Three goes on to state: "This sūtra is good medicine for the ills of the people of Jambudvīpa. If there is any sick person who hears this sūtra, his illness will disappear, and he will neither die nor grow old" (299). Nichiren, who understood Namu Myōhō-renge-kyō to be the "good medicine" in the parable of the excellent doctor in the "Lifespan" chapter, often cited this passage. On one level, he did so to encourage followers to rouse the power of faith in order to battle actual physical sickness. "Life is the most precious of treasures. . . ." he wrote to a sick follower. "Moreover, you have encountered the *Lotus Sūtra*. If you can live even one day longer, you can accumulate that much more merit."[16] But on another level, he understood this matter metaphorically: The people of Japan were "sick" with the illnesses of attachment to provisional teachings and slander of the dharma, which could only be cured by the "medicine" that is the daimoku. The daimoku, Nichiren taught, can also cure sufferings of an existential nature. Of course, it is not the case that *Lotus* devotees invariably recover from sickness, or "neither die nor grow old" in a literal sense. What the sūtra, and Nichiren, promise here is that the *Lotus* can, in this chapter's words, "free sentient beings from every suffering, all the pains and bonds of sickness and of birth and death" (298) and ferry them "across the ocean of old age, illness, and death" (299). Where there is birth, then old age, illness, and death are inevitable. But through faith and the insight that accompanies it, the sufferings associated with them can be transcended.

Chapters Twenty-Three, Twenty-Four, and Twenty-Five describe how specific bodhisattvas display their powers in the world to benefit sentient beings. As noted earlier, at one point in its compilation history, the *Lotus Sūtra* probably concluded with Chapter Twenty-Two, "Entrustment." These three subsequent chapters represent a later stratum of the text, added as devotion to the bodhisattvas in question was gradually assimilated to the *Lotus*. From Nichiren's standpoint, the bodhisattvas appearing in these chapters had received only the general transmission described in the "Entrustment" chapter. Either they had come from other worlds, or they were followers of Śākyamuni in his provisional guise as the Buddha of the trace teaching or *shakumon* portion of the sūtra. Thus, their work was chiefly confined to the True and Semblance Dharma ages. Yet, as we see, Nichiren drew on these chapters to make points about the *Lotus Sūtra* and its practice in the Final Dharma age.

CHAPTERS TWENTY-FOUR AND TWENTY-FIVE

Bodhisattva Gadgadasvara *and* The Gateway to Every Direction

Chapter Twenty-Four

In this chapter, a bodhisattva named Gadgadasvara ("Stammering Utterance" in Sanskrit, although rendered as "Fine Sound" or "Wonderful Sound" in Chinese) in a distant universe travels to the Sahā world with a large retinue to pay homage to Śākyamuni. Before he departs, he is warned by his buddha not to despise the irregular and rocky terrain of the Sahā world or to disparage the tiny buddha and bodhisattvas there; Gadgadasvara is forty-two thousand *yojanas* tall. Upon his arrival, the Buddha explains that this bodhisattva has taught the *Lotus Sūtra* in many places and has the power to appear in any form for the sake of sentient beings, including various gods and *asuras*, householders, brahmans, monks, nuns, laymen, and laywomen.

Chapter Twenty-Five

Among the twenty-eight chapters of the *Lotus Sūtra,* this one is perhaps the most popular. Like the other later chapters, it is almost certainly an interpolation; unlike those chapters, it circulated widely as an independent text even after its incorporation into the *Lotus*. Its verse section (314–316), in particular, was (and still is) often recited. The chapter is devoted to the most famous of the bodhisattvas of Mahāyāna Buddhism, Avalokiteśvara (Ch. Guanyin or Guanshiyin; J. Kannon or Kanzeon; "Lord Who Looks Down" in Sanskrit, rendered as "He Who Observes the Sounds of the World" in Chinese).[1]

The chapter begins with the bodhisattva Akṣayamati ("Inexhaustible Mind") asking why Avalokiteśvara is called by that name. The Buddha explains that if sentient beings in distress call his name, Avalokiteśvara will appear and rescue them. The Buddha goes on to describe some of the desperate situations from which the bodhisattva will save those in trouble. These include fires, drowning, being beaten with sticks, being attacked by demons, being thrown into prison, being robbed by bandits, and being overcome by desire, hatred, or ignorance. If a woman who wants to have a baby pays homage to Avalokiteśvara, she will do so, either a boy or girl depending on her wish. The bodhisattva has the power to turn himself into whatever form is most helpful in teaching the dharma in any given situation, including the forms of a buddha, or a pratyekabuddha, or a śrāvaka, or of various gods (given by name), *asuras*, men, women, and even boys and girls. Many stories in East Asian and Tibetan Buddhism tell of the bodhisattva appearing in these forms.

In Buddhist iconography, one of the typical accoutrements of a Mahāyāna bodhisattva is a jeweled necklace, and in this chapter the bodhisattva Akṣayamati presents Avalokiteśvara with such a necklace. At the Buddha's urging, he accepts it but gives half to the Buddha and half to the stūpa of Prabhūtaratna (313).

This chapter and the preceding, "Bhaiṣajyarāja" chapter feature bodhisattvas who manifest themselves in a variety of forms in order to meet the needs of sentient beings. Chapter Twenty-Four enumerates thirty-four appearances assumed by the bodhisattva Gadgadasvara through his mastery of the samādhi of manifesting all physical forms, the same samādhi attributed to the bodhisattva Sarvarūpasaṃdarśana in Chapter Twenty-Three. Chapter Twenty-Five similarly lists thirty-three forms assumed by the bodhisattva Avalokiteśvara. The phrase "gateway to everywhere" (J. *fumon*), sometimes translated as "universal gate," in the title of Chapter Twenty-Five refers to precisely this activity by which buddhas and bodhisattvas assume various forms to aid suffering beings. An eleventh-century poem based on this chapter celebrates the universal compassion of Avalokiteśvara:

> the world is saved
> because no one can shut
> the gate to everywhere: O who
> will not enter?[2]

For Nichiren, these two bodhisattvas, Gadgadasvara and Avalokiteśvara, fell into the category of bodhisattvas who were followers of the provisional teachings and the trace teaching of the *Lotus Sūtra* and who had been active in the True and Semblance Dharma ages, but whose time had now passed. Neither figures prominently in his writings. Gadgadasvara finds brief mention in a personal letter Nichiren wrote to a woman who had made offerings to each of the *Lotus Sūtra*'s twenty-eight chapters. "The 'Gadgadasvara' chapter," he wrote to her, "tells of a bodhisattva called Gadgadasvara ("Fine Sound") who dwells in the land of the buddha Kamaladalavimalanakṣatrarājasaṃkusumitābhijña ("Knowledge [Conferred by] the King of Constellations [Named] Pure Flower") in the east. In the past, in the age of the buddha Jaladharagarjitaghoṣasusvaranakṣatrarājasaṃkusumitābhijña ("Flowering Wisdom of the King of Constellations [Named] Thunder-Sound of Clouds"), he was Lady Vimaladattā (Pure Virtue), the consort of King Śubhavyūha (Fine Adornment). At that time, Lady Vimaladattā made offerings to the *Lotus Sūtra* and was reborn as the present bodhisattva Gadgadasvara. When the tathāgata Śākyamuni expounded the *Lotus Sūtra* in the Sahā world, this bodhisattva arrived and promised to protect those women who would embrace the *Lotus Sūtra* in a latter age."[3]

Here Nichiren draws on the interpretive tradition that Gadgadasvara had in a past life been the consort of King Śubhavyūha, who appears in Chapter Twenty-Seven of the *Lotus,* to assert that this bodhisattva will watch over the sūtra's female devotees. But this is an isolated reference in his writings.

Unlike Gadgadasvara, who would seem to appear only in the *Lotus Sūtra,* the bodhisattva Avalokiteśvara features in numerous texts and has been revered throughout Asia, down to and including the present time. Avalokiteśvara has been worshipped in many guises. The Dalai Lama is regarded as an incarnation of Avalokiteśvara. In China, this bodhisattva was often represented in female form.[4] In Japan one finds pilgrimage routes dedicated to the bodhisattva comprising thirty-three sites, one for each of his manifestations listed in this chapter of the *Lotus Sūtra*. He also figures prominently in the Pure Land tradition as the right-hand attendant of the buddha Amitābha, accompanying him when he descends to welcome his devotees at the moment of death and escort them to his pure land.

It was possibly because of these Pure Land connections that Nichiren makes so little mention of Avalokiteśvara, despite the pervasiveness in medieval Japan of devotion to this bodhisattva. On the maṇḍalas he inscribed for his followers, Nichiren wrote the names of representative bodhisattvas of the trace teaching below the names of the leaders of the bodhisattvas of the earth. Usually he chose Mañjuśrī and Samantabhadra as these representatives; no extant maṇḍala in his hand bears the name of Avalokiteśvara.

Nichiren acknowledged the tradition that held Zhiyi's teacher Huisi to have been an embodiment of Avalokiteśvara in this world. However, Huisi had lived during the Semblance Dharma age, and Nichiren represents him as spreading only the trace teaching of the *Lotus Sūtra*. He saw Avalokiteśvara, like Mañjuśrī, Bhaiṣajyarāja, and Samantabhadra, as bodhisattvas of the pre–*Lotus Sūtra* and trace teachings. "Since they were not bearers of the original dharma [of Namu Myōhō-renge-kyō], they were perhaps unequal to propagating it in the Final Dharma age," he suggested.[5]

Nonetheless, given the bodhisattva's popularity, Nichiren occasionally sought to disengage Avalokiteśvara from a Pure Land context and assimilate him to the *Lotus Sūtra*. In one rather humorous passage, he depicts Avalokiteśvara and Mahāsthāmaprāpta, another bodhisattva attendant of Amitābha, as being utterly dismayed on hearing the *Lotus Sūtra* preached directly by Śākyamuni Buddha himself and learning that the teachings associated with Amitābha's pure land were merely provisional. When Amitābha himself confirms this (since all buddhas assemble to testify to the *Lotus Sūtra*'s truth), Avalokiteśvara reflects that it would be pointless now to return to Amitābha's land and instead joins the other eighty thousand bodhisattvas who are attending the *Lotus* assembly, "vowing in all sincerity to protect practitioners of the *Lotus Sūtra* as he, in the words of the 'Avalokiteśvara' chapter, 'wanders throughout the Sahā world' (313)."[6]

Some temples within the Nichiren tradition have incorporated Avalokiteśvara among the various protectors enshrined on their premises. In such cases, the bodhisattva is understood as representing the compassionate workings inherent in the daimoku of the *Lotus Sūtra*, Namu Myōhō-renge-kyō, and protecting its propagation.

CHAPTER TWENTY-SIX

Dhāraṇī

In this chapter, in the presence of the Buddha, persons in the assembly offer *dhāraṇīs*—spells or incantations—for the protection of those who expound the *Lotus Sūtra*. A *dhāraṇī* is a kind of magic spell, often claimed to have apotropaic powers. Dhāraṇīs occur throughout Buddhist literature and are often found among the later chapters of a Mahāyāna sūtra, as is the case here. In the *Lotus Sūtra*, two bodhisattvas, including Bhaiṣajyarāja, two of the gods of the four directions, and a group of female demons (*rākṣasī*), including the famous stealer of children Hārītī, each offers a dhāraṇī to protect those who preserve and recite the *Lotus Sūtra* from various forms of human and demonic enemies.[1]

Dhāraṇīs are often said to encapsulate the meaning of a larger text; those who are able to memorize a dhāraṇi are said to gain the power to retain the full meaning of that larger text. They are also said to contain special powers to achieve enlightened states and to bring worldly benefits such as protection and healing. The word derives from the Sanskrit root *dhṛ* (to hold) and is linguistically related to the idea of upholding or preserving a sūtra that is fundamental to *Lotus Sūtra* practice.[2] Dhāraṇīs often consist of strings of opaque sounds without discernible semantic meaning; their power is said to reside not in their discursive content, but in their sound. In Chinese texts, they were usually simply transliterated, being written in characters whose pronunciation gave the closest approximate sound to the Indic original. It is difficult to draw a firm distinction between dhāraṇīs and mantras, although invocations identified as mantras are often shorter. The Shingon monk Kūkai (774–835) distinguished mantras as a special class of dhāraṇī restricted to esoteric Buddhist ritual, while dhāraṇī, he said, were found in both esoteric and exoteric practice.[3] However, this distinction was not universal.

In this chapter dhāraṇīs are presented, first by two bodhisattvas: Bhaiṣajyarāja, who was the subject of Chapter Twenty-Three, and another bodhisattva called Pradānaśūra ("Brave Donor"); then, by two of the four "world protectors" or heavenly kings (*devarāja*) who guard the four quarters: Vaiśravaṇa (J. Tamonten) in the north and Dhṛtarāṣṭra (Jikokten) in the east; and lastly, by ten *rākṣasīs*, or female demons, who are in attendance at the assembly together with Hārītī (J. Kishimojin), the most famous demoness in Buddhist literature. In some readings, Hārītī is said to be the mother of the ten *rākṣasīs*. According to tradition, as the result of a misguided vow made in a past life, Hārītī would capture and devour human children, terrorizing the people of Rājagṛha. Intending to lead her to reform her conduct, the Buddha hid one of her five hundred children in his begging bowl. She was grief-stricken by its disappearance, and the Buddha asked her to imagine, when she suffered so greatly over the loss of just one child out of so many, how terrible a sorrow she was inflicting on the human parents whose children she consumed. Hārītī repented and became a guardian of children and monasteries.

In Japan, Hārītī is known as Kishimojin. Nichiren clearly regarded her as a protector of the *Lotus Sūtra*. She appears on most of the maṇḍalas that he inscribed, as do the ten rākṣasīs. The half-dozen references to Kishimojin in his writings all mention her together with these ten demon women, an association drawn from the "*Dhāraṇī*" chapter. In one instance, he refers to the ten rākṣasīs as "the mothers of all demons in the four continents," and Kishimojin as "the mother of the ten rākṣasīs," thus suggesting her power.[4] In the larger religious culture, Kishimojin was often worshipped independently of the *Lotus Sūtra*, for example, in esoteric prayer rites to quell disasters and increase good fortune. After Nichiren's time, as his tradition spread during Japan's later medieval period and drew followers from a range of social groups, its protector deities diversified, and statues and paintings of Kishimojin began to be enshrined as independent images at some Nichiren temples. Represented in both fierce and gentle forms, Kishimojin was revered as a guardian of *Lotus* devotees, a destroyer of false views, and a grantor of prayers for this-worldly benefits, such as healing, safe childbirth, and the protection of children. Devotion to Kishimojin within the Nichiren tradition reached its height in Japan's early modern period (roughly, seventeenth through nineteenth centuries) and drew both on her specific associations with the *Lotus Sūtra* as well as broader traditions of Kishimojin worship.[5]

Nichiren's own writings, however, give less attention to Kishimojin than to the ten rākṣasīs, whom he mentions more than fifty times. Unlike such bodhisattvas as Bhaiṣajyarāja, Gadgadasvara, and Avalokiteśvara of the immediately preceding chapters, whom he understood to have been active chiefly in the True Dharma and Semblance Dharma ages, the ten demon women were, in Nichiren's understanding, presently active on behalf of *Lotus* devotees and devising plans to facilitate the sūtra's spread. Toward the end of the present chapter, the Buddha praises them, saying, "Splendid, splendid! You protect *those who preserve the name* of the *Lotus Sūtra*! Your merit is immeasurable"

(322, emphasis added). In the sūtra, the Buddha goes on to say that the merit of protecting those who serve the sūtra in various other ways is greater still. For Nichiren, however, the passage just quoted underscored the overriding importance of the daimoku:

> QUESTION: What proof is there that one should embrace the name of the *Lotus Sūtra,* in particular, in the same way that people embrace the name of a buddha?
>
> ANSWER: The sūtra states, "The Buddha said to the rākṣasīs, 'Splendid, splendid! You protect those who preserve the name of the *Lotus Sūtra*! Your merit is immeasurable' (322). This passage means that, when the ten rākṣasīs vowed to protect those who embrace the title of the *Lotus Sūtra,* the world-honored one of great enlightenment praised them, saying, "Splendid! Splendid! The merit you will receive for protecting those who accept and uphold Namu Myōhō-renge-kyō will be incalculable and marvellous!" This passage implies that, whether walking, standing, sitting, or lying down, we living beings should chant Namu Myōhō-renge-kyō. [6]

Elsewhere, Nichiren interprets the same sūtra passage to stress the unfathomable benefits of the chanting the daimoku: "This merit [deriving from the vow of the ten rākṣasīs] to protect those who embrace the daimoku of the *Lotus Sūtra* is beyond even the reach of the buddha wisdom, which perfectly comprehends the past, present, and future. One might think that nothing could exceed the grasp of the buddha wisdom, but the Buddha here declares that the merit accruing from accepting and upholding the daimoku of the *Lotus Sūtra* is the one thing alone that it cannot fathom."[7]

Nichiren saw the workings of the ten rākṣasīs in the events surrounding him, both great and small. He saw their roles as protecting *Lotus* devotees, occasionally testing their faith, aiding their practice, relieving their sufferings, and chastising those who obstruct their devotion. To a follower, the lay monk Myōmitsu, he wrote: "The ten rākṣasīs in particular have vowed to protect those who embrace the daimoku of the *Lotus Sūtra.* Therefore they must think of you and your wife as a mother does her only child . . . and safeguard you day and night."[8] To two new parents, the samurai Shijō Kingo and his wife, Nichiren wrote that the ten rākṣasīs would watch over their infant daughter, so that "wherever she may frolic or play, no harm will come to her; she will 'travel fearlessly, like a lion king' (214)."[9] He saw the protection of the ten rākṣasīs in the kindness of an elderly lay monk on Sado Island who had come to his aid, helping him to survive in exile, and in the devotion of a woman who had made him a robe to shield him from the cold in the recesses of Mount Minobu. Their protection was further evident to him in the fact that he had been able to escape unscathed from an attack on his dwelling in Kamakura and survived other threats as well. To two brothers whose father had threatened to disinherit them on account of their faith in the *Lotus Sūtra,* he suggested: "Perhaps the ten rākṣasīs have possessed your parents and are tormenting you in order to test your resolve."[10] He also asserted that the ten rākṣasīs, along with other deities, had induced the Mongol ruler to attack Japan to chastise its people for abandoning the *Lotus Sūtra.*

Nichiren was struck by the words in the vow made by the ten rākṣasīs that if anyone troubles those who expound the *Lotus Sūtra,* "his head will be split into seven pieces just like a branch of the *arjaka* tree" (322). Zhanran, in summarizing the powers of the *Lotus* referred to in the sūtra text, had written, "Those who trouble [*Lotus* devotees] will have their heads split into seven pieces; those who make offerings to them will enjoy good fortune surpassing [that represented by the Buddha's] ten titles."[11] The two parts of this sentence are inscribed as "passages of praise" on either side of a number of Nichiren's maṇḍalas. We can think of them as illustrating the principle of karmic causality as applied to the *Lotus Sūtra*.

CHAPTER TWENTY-SEVEN

Ancient Accounts of King Śubhavyūha

Here, the Buddha relates another story from the distant past and a distant land, during the time of a buddha named Jaladharagarjitaghoṣasusvaranakṣatrarājasaṃkusumitābhijña, the longest of the many long names in the sūtra (meaning "Flowering Wisdom of the King of the Constellations [Named] Thunder-Sound of the Clouds"). At that time, there was a king named Śubhavyūha who was a follower of the brahmans. He had two sons, Vimalagarbha and Vimalanetra, who wished to convert him to Buddhism by having him attend the Buddha's exposition of the *Lotus Sūtra*. On the advice of their mother, they performed all manner of miraculous feats for their father, including shooting fire out of the upper part of their bodies and water out of the lower part, and then vice versa, expanding the size of their bodies, disappearing and reappearing, and walking on water. The father was duly impressed and asked to meet their teacher. After the boys received permission from their parents to become monks, the king and queen and their huge retinue went to see the Buddha, who predicted the king's future buddhahood. The king renounced the throne and became a monk.

The scene then returns to the present, where the Buddha identifies the figures in the story of the past with members of his present assembly. King Śubhavyūha is the bodhisattva Padmaśrī. His two sons are the bodhisattvas Bhaiṣajyarāja and

Bhaiṣajyamudgata. And his queen consort Vimladattā is the bodhisattva Vairocanaraśmipratimaṇḍitādhvajarāja ("King with Marks of Adornment by Rays of Light").

In his *Words and Phrases of the Lotus Sūtra* (*Fahua wenju*), Zhiyi provided a backstory about the past-life relationship of these four persons: the king, the queen, and their two sons. In the remote past, four monks were practicing austerities in pursuit of enlightenment. However, the struggle to obtain sufficient food and other necessities seriously hindered their practice. At length, one of them abandoned his efforts in order to support the other three. With his aid, they attained the way, while he, thanks to the merit gained by assisting them, was born repeatedly as a king in the human or heavenly realms. Eventually he became King Śubhavyūha. By that point, however, he was exhausting his merit. Perceiving that his downward trajectory would soon lead him to rebirth in the hells, the other three whom he had once assisted resolved to repay their debt to him, choosing to be reborn as his consort and sons in order to lead him to the dharma.[1]

In the *Lotus Sūtra* chapter, Śubhavyūha, being steeped in wrong views, is by implication initially opposed to Buddhism. At their mother's urging, his two sons then demonstrate the supernormal powers they have gained through their Buddhist practice. Convinced by their extraordinary display, the king goes with them to see the Buddha, hears from him the *Lotus Sūtra*, and receives a prediction of his future buddhahood.

Śākyamuni reveals that one of the princes is now Bhaiṣajyarāja, marking the fourth time that this bodhisattva appears in *the Lotus Sūtra*. The Buddha addresses him as a representative of the assembly in the "Expounder of the Dharma" chapter; the "Ancient Accounts of Bodhisattva Bhaiṣajyarāja" chapter recounts his past acts of ascetic self-sacrifice; in the

"Dhāraṇī" chapter, he offers an incantation for the protection of *Lotus* devotees; and here he is revealed in a former role as a son of King Śubhavyūha.

Nichiren regarded King Śubhavyūha as an example of an "evil man" attaining buddhahood through the power of the *Lotus Sūtra*. He often referenced this chapter in letters to his followers to stress the importance of family relations in promoting faith and to assuage the anxieties they sometimes felt about the postmortem fate of their deceased parents or children. One example occurs in a letter to his follower Jōren-bō, whose father had been a follower of Hōnen's Pure Land teaching. Jōren-bō was presumably anxious about what karmic retribution his father would incur in his next life. Indeed, Nichiren says, those who support teachers who slander the dharma, such as Hōnen and other Pure Land teachers, must fall into the Avicī hell. In this case, however, the father will surely be saved by the son's devotion. He writes: "A ruler's mind is broadened by his minister, and parents' pain is eased by their children. Maudgalyāyana saved his mother from the sufferings of the realm of hungry ghosts, and the sons Vimalagarbha and Vimalanetra persuaded their father to rectify his false views. . . . The merit that you have acquired by embracing the *Lotus Sūtra* will become your father's strength."[2]

In another case, Nichiren referred to the two princes from the "Śubhavyūha" chapter in encouraging an unidentified couple, possibly Lord Matsuno of Suruga and his wife, who were mourning their deceased son and had apparently become more earnest in their Buddhist practice following his death. Nichiren's disciple Nichiji, who was related to Matsuno and had reported the matter to Nichiren, informed him that the young man had not only been unusually handsome, but also straightforward and wise. According to Nichiren, Nichiji had told him that he had initially been struck with pity that so remarkable an individual should die young. "But on reflection, I realized that, because of this boy's death, his mother aroused the aspiration for the way and his father began to take thought for his next life. This is far from ordinary, I thought. And the fact that they have placed faith in the *Lotus Sūtra,* which everyone opposes, must mean that their deceased son has been at their side, encouraging them to do so."[3] Nichiren told the parents that he fully concurred with Nichiji's reading of events, adding, "The king Śubhavyūha was an evil monarch. But when guided by their two sons, the princes [Vimalagarbha and Vimalanetra], father and mother were both able to place their trust in the *Lotus Sūtra* and become buddhas. The same must be true in your case as well!"[4]

Cases of family discord inevitably arose among Nichiren's followers when their relatives opposed his teaching. Nichiren often cited this chapter to stress that, when faced with the choice between following one's parents' wishes or being faithful to the *Lotus Sūtra,* the *Lotus Sūtra* must take precedence. Such a stance flew in the face of common understandings of filial piety, an important cultural value of Nichiren's time. A writing attributed to him, possibly authored by a close disciple with his approval, states:

"King Śubhavyūha, the father of Vimalagarbha and Vimalanetra, adhered to heretical teachings and turned his back on the buddha-dharma. The two princes disobeyed their father's orders and became disciples of the buddha Jaladharagaritaghoṣasusvaranakṣatrarājasaṃkusumitābhijña, but in the end they were able to guide their father so that he became a buddha called Śālendrarāja ["King of the Śāla Trees"]. Are they to be called unfilial? A sūtra passage explains: 'To renounce one's obligations and enter the unconditioned is truly to repay those obligations.' Thus, we see that those who cast aside the bonds of love and indebtedness in this life and enter the true path of the buddha-dharma are persons who truly understand their obligations."[5]

The logic here is that abandoning the *Lotus Sūtra* to satisfy one's parents might please them in the short run, but by so doing, one severs both them and oneself from the sole path of liberation in the present age. Because such an act constitutes "slander of the dharma," it can only lead to suffering for all concerned in this and future lifetimes. By upholding faith in the *Lotus Sūtra,* however, one can realize buddhahood oneself and eventually lead one's parents to do the same.

Some of Nichiren's followers actually found themselves in such a situation. Among them were two brothers, samurai of the Ikegami family living in Kamakura. They may have been direct vassals of the Hōjō family who ruled the Bakufu or military government. The elder was called Munenaka, and the younger, Munenaga. Their father, Yasumitsu, was a supporter of the eminent monk Ryōkan-bō Ninshō, widely acclaimed as a holy man for his acts of public charity and scrupulous adherence to the precepts. By Nichiren's account, however, Ninshō's machinations had brought about his second arrest and exile to Sado Island; Nichiren and his followers had learned to regard Ninshō as an enemy. Because their father revered this cleric, the two brothers, like Śubhavyūha's two sons, must have felt that they had been born into a "house of wrong views" (324). Yasumitsu demanded that Munenaka, whose faith was the stronger, renounce his commitment to the *Lotus Sūtra* and to Nichiren. When Munenaka refused, his father disowned him. At this point, the younger brother began to waver, swayed perhaps by a more conventional understanding of the obedience owed to one's father and by the unexpected opportunity to replace Munenaka as his father's heir. Nichiren admonished him, "If you obey your father who is an enemy of the *Lotus Sūtra* and abandon your brother who is a votary of the one vehicle, are you really being filial? In the end, you should resolve single-mindedly to pursue the buddha way like your brother. Your father is like King Śubhavyūha, and you brothers are like the princes Vimalagarbha and Vimalanetra. Their situation occurred in the past while yours is happening in the present, but the principle of the *Lotus Sūtra* remains unchanged."[6]

In the end, perhaps strengthened by Nichiren's admonishment, the younger brother stood firmly by his elder brother and refused to abandon his faith. Eventually the two were even able to convert their father, and Nichiren praised them as Vimalagarbha and Vimalanetra reborn.[7]

Let us look now at two passages from this chapter that are frequently cited in Japanese Buddhist sources and at how Nichiren interpreted them. First, in asking their parents' permission—a requirement of the monastic rule—to renounce household life and become Buddhist monks, the two princes state that it is "difficult to meet a buddha, just as it is to see *uḍumbara* flowers or for a one-eyed turtle to find the hole in a floating piece of wood" (326). The *uḍumbara* tree was said to bloom once every three thousand years and thus stands as a symbol for an extremely rare opportunity. The same analogy occurs in the "Skillful Means" chapter (30) to illustrate the rarity of hearing the *Lotus Sūtra*.

The analogy of the turtle and the floating piece of wood appears in a number of sūtras and commentaries, where it is used to illustrate the rarity of being born human and encountering the Buddha's teaching. In a letter to a follower, the wife of the same Matsuno Rokurōzaemon mentioned above, Nichiren develops the analogy in great detail and applies it specifically to the *Lotus Sūtra*. To summarize his expanded version: A large turtle with only one eye and lacking limbs or flippers dwells on the ocean floor. His belly is burning hot, but the shell on his back is freezing cold. Only the rare red sandalwood has the power to cool the turtle's belly. The turtle yearns to cool his belly on a piece of floating red sandalwood and at the same time to warm his back in the sun. However, he can rise to the ocean's surface only once in a thousand years, and even then, he can rarely find a piece of floating red sandalwood. When he does so, it may not contain a hollow, or at least not one of the proper size to hold him. Even when he finds a floating sandalwood log with an appropriate hollow place, without limbs, he cannot easily approach it, and having only one eye, he mistakes east for west; thus, he cannot accurately judge the direction of the log's drift and winds up moving in the wrong direction. Nichiren interprets: "The ocean represents the sea of the sufferings of birth and death, and the turtle is ourselves, living beings. His limbless state indicates our lack of good roots. The heat of his belly represents the eight hot hells of anger, and the cold of the shell on his back, the eight cold hells of greed. His remaining for a thousand years on the ocean floor means that we fall into the three evil paths and are unable to emerge. His surfacing only once every thousand years illustrates how difficult it is to emerge from the three evil paths and be born as a human even once in immeasurable eons, at a time when Śākyamuni Buddha has appeared in the world."[8]

The turtle mistaking east for west, Nichiren continues, means that ordinary people in their ignorance confuse inferior and superior among the Buddha's teachings, clinging to provisional teachings that have lost their efficacy and rejecting the one teaching that can lead to enlightenment. And the rarity of the turtle finding a floating sandalwood log with a hollow in it just big enough to hold him means that "even if one should meet the *Lotus Sūtra*, it is rarer and more difficult still to encounter the daimoku, which is its heart, and chant Namu Myōhō-renge-kyō."[9] In this way, Nichiren stressed the inconceivable good fortune of his followers, who had not only been born as humans and met the *Lotus Sūtra* but, although living in a degenerate age in a remote country far from the Buddha's birthplace, were able to chant the wonderful dharma of the daimoku.

As to the second passage: In this chapter of the *Lotus*, the Buddha recounts that, once awakened to the dharma, King Śubhavyūha said that his two sons were his "good friends," because they had enabled him to meet the Buddha (327). The Buddha underscores the point, saying: "You should know that a good friend is indeed the great spur [literally, "the great cause and condition"] that brings inspiration to others, causing . . . the thought of highest, complete enlightenment to awaken in them" (328). This passage has often been quoted to stress the importance of a "good friend" on the Buddhist path. This expression (Skt. *kalyāṇamitra*; J. *zenchishiki*), also translated as "teacher" or "spiritual advisor," broadly refers to one who assists another on the Buddhist path. Zhiyi, for example, divides "good friends" into the three categories of patrons, fellow practitioners, and teachers.[10] The term has been variously interpreted. For example, in premodern Japan, in addition to its broader meaning of one who assists another's practice, a "good friend" meant the ritual attendant who assisted someone at the time of death, helping that person to focus his or her thoughts on a buddha—usually Amitābha—in order to achieve birth in his pure land.

Nichiren gave considerable thought to the concept of a "good friend" and interpreted it in light of his understanding of the Final Dharma age. In an early but important essay called

"On Protecting the Country," he poses the question: In this deluded age, the Buddha has departed, and great teachers such as Nāgārjuna or Zhiyi no longer make an appearance. How then can one escape samsaric suffering? Because there are no worthy human teachers, Nichiren concluded that, in this age, the *Lotus* and *Nirvāṇa* sūtras are to be accounted "good friends," in accord with Zhiyi's statement: "At times following a good friend, and at times following the sūtra scrolls, one hears . . . the single truth of enlightened wisdom."[11] Nichiren's insistence that the *Lotus Sūtra* is the "good friend" for the present age is perfectly in line with his frequent admonition, drawn from the *Nirvāṇa Sūtra,* to "rely on the dharma and not on the person."[12]

What one should most avoid, Nichiren asserted, were "evil friends," teachers such as Kūkai, who had said that the *Lotus Sūtra* was inferior to the esoteric teachings, or Hōnen, who had insisted that the *Lotus* should be set aside as beyond human capacity to practice in the latter age. When Nichiren spoke of such people as "evil friends," he meant, not that they were morally corrupt or insincere, but that they were promoting incomplete teachings that, in his understanding, no longer led to buddhahood in the Final Dharma age. Occasionally he cited a passage from the *Nirvāṇa Sūtra,* which says that "evil friends" are more to feared than mad elephants. It states, "Even if you are killed by a mad elephant, you will not fall into the three evil paths. But if you are killed by an evil friend, you are certain to fall into them. A mad elephant is merely an enemy of one's person, but an evil friend is an enemy of the good dharma. Therefore, bodhisattvas, you should at all times distance yourselves from evil friends."[13] For his part, Nichiren expressed the fervent hope that people would "not mistakenly trust in evil friends, adopt false teachings, and spend their present life in vain."[14] This was the impetus behind his assertive proselytizing.

CHAPTER TWENTY-EIGHT

Encouragement of the Bodhisattva Samantabhadra

The sūtra concludes with the arrival of the famous bodhisattva Samantabhadra, well known from other Mahāyāna sūtras, such as the *Avataṃsaka Sūtra,* but not previously mentioned in the *Lotus Sūtra,* a further indication of a late interpolation.

Samantabhadra arrives from the east, where he has been practicing in the realm of the buddha Ratnatejo'bhyudgatarāja ("King Surpassing the Awe-Inspiring Excellence of Jewels"); his arrival from afar would appear to be a narrative device intended to account for the later addition of this chapter, incorporating this popular bodhisattva into the *Lotus Sūtra.* Samantabhadra praises the Buddha and asks him what one should do to attain the *Lotus Sūtra* after the Buddha has passed into nirvāṇa. The Buddha replies that people will attain it if they achieve the "four necessary accomplishments" (331): they should be protected by buddhas, plant roots of merit, associate with those of right resolve, and arouse the aspiration to liberate all sentient beings. Samantabhadra then promises to protect the devotees of the *Lotus Sūtra* in the five centuries after the Buddha's passing, appearing on his famous six-tusked white elephant to console them and remind them if they forget a line of the sūtra. He provides a dhāraṇī for their protection and goes on to enumerate the many blessings awaiting those who preserve the *Lotus Sūtra*, including being reborn in the Tuṣita heaven in the company of Maitreya, the coming buddha.

Samantabhadra is often depicted seated on a six-tusked white elephant, as this final chapter mentions (332). The twenty-one-day period of single-minded perseverance referred to here became the basis of a repentance ritual for purifying the six senses, which takes the bodhisattva Samantabhadra as its object of worship and aims at visualizing him. The practice of this rite is described in the *Sūtra of the Practice of Visualizing the Bodhisattva Samantabhadra*, regarded as the concluding scripture to the *Lotus Sūtra*.[1] By means of this visualization ritual, one repents all one's prior misdeeds of body, speech, and mind. This sūtra emphasizes formless repentance, that is, not atonement for specific acts of wrongdoing but, rather, contemplation of the empty, nondual nature of all things, ignorance of which has prompted one to misguided action in the first place. It contains the famous passage, "Those who wish to repent should sit upright and contemplate the real aspect, and all their sins will vanish like frost and dew in the sunlight of wisdom."[2] "Real aspect" (J. *jissō*) here is the same term given in Chapter Two of the *Lotus Sūtra* to designate the insight that "no one but the buddhas can completely know" (24).

After Samantabhadra has spoken, the Buddha speaks, reiterating several themes that recur throughout the *Lotus*. One is the interchangeability of the Buddha and the sūtra. To encounter the *Lotus Sūtra* is to meet Śākyamuni and hear the sūtra from his own mouth. One who upholds the sūtra is to be respected as one would the Buddha. Thus, the Buddha declares that those who preserve the *Lotus Sūtra* will meet Śākyamuni, their head will be caressed by Śākyamuni, they will wear the robes of Śākyamuni, and they will hear the *Lotus Sūtra* directly from the mouth of Śākyamuni. They will be honest and will not be troubled by desire, hatred, ignorance, and the other afflictions. They are destined for buddhahood. Although they will have no greed for the possessions of this life, the Buddha declares, in a consequential phrase, "Their aspirations will not be unrewarded, and their happy reward will be attained in this world" (335). He goes on to say that those who speak maliciously about the devotees of the sūtra will suffer from leprosy, bad teeth, tuberculosis, and other maladies.

The chapter ends rather abruptly, with the standard praise of the Buddha's words by the members of the assembly. And so ends the *Lotus Sūtra*, at least in the most common sequence of its chapters.

In one passage, Nichiren gives a humorous account of Samantabhadra's late arrival at the *Lotus* assembly:

> Among all the many bodhisattvas, Samantabhadra and Manjuśrī were like ministers of the right and left to the Lord Śākyamuni. It was strange, therefore, that Samantabhadra, as one of those two ministers, should have failed to be in attendance during the eight or so years when the Buddha preached the *Lotus Sūtra*, which surpasses all the other teachings of his lifetime and which all buddhas and bodhisattvas of the ten directions, more numerous than the dust particles of the great earth, had assembled to hear. But when the Buddha had finished expounding the "King Śubhavyūha" chapter and was about to conclude his preaching of the *Lotus Sūtra*, Samantabhadra came hastily from the land of the buddha Ratnatejo'bhyudgatarāja in the eastern quarter, accompanied by the sounds of ten billion musical instruments and leading countless numbers of the eight kinds of nonhuman beings. Probably fearing the Buddha's displeasure at his tardy arrival,

> he assumed a serious expression and pledged in all earnestness to protect those who practice the *Lotus Sūtra* in the latter age. But the Buddha, no doubt pleased with his extraordinary sincerity in vowing to spread the *Lotus Sūtra* throughout the continent of Jambudvīpa, praised him even more highly than he had earlier praised other bodhisattvas of higher rank.[3]

In Nichiren's teaching, it is the bodhisattvas of the earth who play the lead roles in spreading the *Lotus Sūtra* in the Final Dharma age. But he recognized Samantabhadra as a protector and, in one letter written from exile to Sado Island, referred to him as manifesting through two of his most supportive lay followers, the samurai Shinjō Kingo and his wife, Nichigen-nyo: "You were both born of ordinary status, and you live in Kamakura [the seat of Bakufu authority], yet you trust in the *Lotus Sūtra* without fearing others' gaze and without begrudging your lives. This is no ordinary matter . . . Surely this is what the *Lotus Sūtra* means where it says that those living in Jambudvīpa who believe in this sūtra do so by the power of the bodhisattva Samantabhadra."[4]

As suggested in the long passage from Nichiren cited above, Samantabadhra is often depicted iconographically as Śākyamuni Buddha's attendant on the right, with Mañjuśrī attending him on the left. Where Mañjuśrī represents wisdom and realization, Samantabhadra represents teaching and practice. The *Lotus Sūtra* begins with Mañjuśrī playing a role in preparing the assembly to receive Śākyamuni's preaching of the sūtra just before his final nirvāṇa; it concludes with Samantabadhra vowing to protect those who uphold the sūtra after he has departed. On Nichiren's maṇḍala, the names of Mañjuśrī and Samantabhadra appear as representatives of bodhisattvas from other worlds and of the trace teaching.

Samantabhadra specifically promises to protect those who "preserve this sūtra in the troubled world of five hundred years after" (332). As explained above in connection with the "Bhaiṣajyarāja" chapter, the phrase "five hundred years after" was no doubt originally intended to designate the five hundred years following Śākyamuni's parinirvāṇa, when the sūtra's compilers believed they were living. However, East Asian commentators took the "five hundred years after" (which can also be read in Chinese as "the last five hundred years") to mean the last of five five-hundred-year periods in the gradual decline of Buddhist practice and understanding said to take place over the 2,500 years following the Buddha's passing. For Nichiren, it designated the beginning of the Final Dharma age, when he and his contemporaries believed they were living. This expression "five hundred years after" occurs twice in the "Bhaiṣajyarāja" chapter and three times in the present chapter. For Nichiren it predicted in the Buddha's very words both the task being shouldered by himself and his disciples and the surety of its fulfillment. It designated the time when the buddhahood of ordinary people could be realized. As he wrote: "Namu Myōhō-renge-kyō will spread for ten thousand years and beyond, far into the future. Its merit can open the blind eyes of all sentient beings in the country of Japan and block the road to the Hell without Respite [Avīci]. . . . A hundred years' practice in the Land of Bliss cannot equal the merit gained from one day's practice in this defiled world, and propagation [of the dharma] throughout the two thousand years of the True and Semblance Dharma ages is inferior to a single hour's propagation in the Final Dharma age. This is in no way because of Nichiren's wisdom, but solely because the time makes it so."[5]

Conclusion

Our first aim in this volume was to introduce readers to the rich content of the *Lotus Sūtra,* one of the most influential and yet enigmatic of Buddhist texts, and to provide a basic chapter-by-chapter guide to its often-bewildering narrative. Our secondary aims were related to hermeneutics. Through the example of the *Lotus Sūtra,* and its reading by Nichiren, one of its most influential devotees, we have sought to illuminate the dynamics by which Buddhists, at significant historical moments, have reinterpreted their tradition. Thus, this study has taken a very different perspective from that of commentaries intended primarily to elucidate the *Lotus Sūtra* as an expression of the Buddhist truth or as a guide to Buddhist practice. Our intent is not to deny the sūtra's claim to be the Buddha's constantly abiding dharma; rather, we have been guided by the conviction that the full genius of the *Lotus* as a literary and philosophical text comes to light only when the sūtra is examined in terms of what can be known or even surmised about the circumstances of its compilation. Adopting that perspective suggests how the compilers may have grappled with questions new to their received tradition and how they refigured that tradition in attempting to answer them.

The *Lotus Sūtra* belongs to what has been called the Mahāyāna movement, which extols the bodhisattva path. Its compilers undoubtedly understood it in some sense to be the Buddha's word and held that it superseded the model of the path embraced by the Buddhist mainstream. But Mahāyāna advocates faced a great challenge in asserting the legitimacy of their new vision. If the Buddha had intended that others should follow the bodhisattva path as he had done—and the *Lotus Sūtra* suggests that all Buddhists should be bodhisattvas—then why had he not said so? Why had he instead taught the two vehicles of the śrāvaka and the pratyekabuddha, culminating in final nirvāṇa? And how could they, proponents of the Great Vehicle, counter the charges of mainstream monastics that their teachings were not the Buddha's word but arrant falsehoods? Several Mahāyāna sūtras wrestle with these questions, but none more creatively than the *Lotus*. We have noted in this volume some of the seemingly inexhaustible devices by which the sūtra asserts its own legitimacy. It positions itself as older than any teachings spoken of in the earlier Buddhist tradition; as the final teaching of all buddhas throughout the universe; and as the perfect statement of Buddha's enlightenment, in whose service all his other teachings are to be regarded as temporary expedients, or "skillful means." It reinvents its buddha on the model of a heroic Mahāyāna bodhisattva, not as long since departed into final nirvāṇa, but as constantly active in the world to teach and benefit others. And most ingeniously, as seen in the parables of the burning house, the conjured city, and the excellent doctor, it thwarts mainstream accusations of being a false scripture by suggesting that it is not the *Lotus Sūtra,* but the Buddha of the earlier tradition who, in having preached the doctrine of final nirvāṇa, must defend himself against the charge of lying.

Just as the *Lotus Sūtra*'s compilers refigured the mainstream Buddhist tradition, later interpreters refigured the *Lotus Sūtra* to meet the needs of their time and place. There is a vast and not yet fully studied body of *Lotus* interpretation in East Asia that could not be adequately addressed in this short volume, although we have occasionally gestured in the direction of such important commentators as Zhiyi, Jizang, Zhanran, Saichō, Ennin, Enchin, Annen, and others. We chose instead to illustrate the dynamic interface of text and reader with the example of the medieval Japanese Buddhist teacher Nichiren, who was both the inheritor and the reinterpreter of these earlier commentators. For Nichiren, as for the sūtra's compilers, the *Lotus* was the Buddha's word—not just the word of the historical buddha, one among the many buddhas who are all "born" from the *Lotus Sūtra*—but the word of the primordial buddha, awakened since the inconceivably distant past and still carrying out his work in the world. But unlike the situation faced by the *Lotus Sūtra*'s compilers, Japan in Nichiren's day was a Mahāyāna country, and the *Lotus* was a mainstream, not a marginal, text; its teaching that all shall someday become buddhas was, at least in principle, widely accepted. Nichiren instead wrestled with different questions: What did it mean to uphold the dharma correctly in the degenerate Final Dharma age, in a peripheral country far from the Buddha's birthplace on the extreme eastern edge of the Buddhist world? How could the *Lotus Sūtra* be preserved and defended against critics who insisted it was too profound for deluded beings of the latter age and who sought to displace it with teachings long ago defined by the Tendai tradition as provisional and incomplete? We have seen how Nichiren advocated a mode of practice, chanting the sūtra's title in the formula Namu Myōhō-renge-kyō, that was simple enough for anyone to carry out, at the same time preserving the most profound Mahāyāna insights of nonduality in which self and cosmos interpenetrate, all merits are mutually contained, and buddhahood can be realized "with this very body." Troubled by the suffering he witnessed in the wake of famine, epidemics, and the Mongol threat, Nichiren also emphasized the *Lotus Sūtra*'s claim that the primordial buddha "constantly resides" in this Sahā world, and he argued that spreading faith in the *Lotus* would transform this world into a buddha land.

Significantly, Nichiren did not insist that his aggressive, *shakubuku* mode of proselytizing was universally relevant, but he held that it was demanded specifically by his own time and place—a historical moment when, in his eyes, attachment to provisional teachings threatened to eclipse the *Lotus Sūtra* with disastrous consequences for individuals and for the country. Other times, other places, might require other methods. Nor did Nichiren go into much detail about what the ideal buddha land to be realized in this world would look like. This open-endedness on his part has afforded considerable interpretive latitude to his later followers and others inspired by him, who down to this present day have developed widely differing readings of what the *Lotus Sūtra* teaches, how it should be spread, and what form an ideal society based on it should take. In this fluid interaction of text, individual readers, and interpretive communities, the *Lotus* has remained a living scripture.

As the authors of this volume, our own place in the history of *Lotus* reception is surely a modest one. Our hope has been to draw critical attention to the dynamics of interpretation by which this famous sūtra has repeatedly been appropriated over the course of centuries. We have by no means said all there is to say about the *Lotus Sūtra* or about Nichiren. We will be delighted if this volume inspires readers to ponder more deeply the potent challenges posed by the *White Lotus of the True Dharma*.

Notes

The following abbreviations are used here:

T *Taishō shinshū daizōkyō*, ed. TAKAKUSU Junjirō and WATANABE Kaigyoku. 100 vols. Tokyo: Taishō Issaikyō Kankōkai, 1924–1935.

Teihon *Shōwa teihon Nichiren shōnin ibun*, ed. Risshō Daigaku Nichiren Kyōgaku Kenkyūjo. 4 vols. Minobu-chō, Yamanashi prefecture: Minobusan Kuonji, 1952–1959. Rev. ed., 1988.

Authors' Introduction

1. On visual representations of the *Lotus*, see, for example, Eugene Y. Wang, *Shaping the Lotus Sutra: Buddhist Visual Culture in Medieval China* (Seattle: University of Washington Press, 2005); Willa Jane Tanabe, *Paintings of the Lotus Sutra* (New York: Weatherhill, 1988); and Bunsaku Kurata and Yoshirō Tamura, *Art of the Lotus Sutra: Japanese Masterpieces*, trans. Edna B. Crawford (Tokyo: Kōsei Publishing, 1987).

2. Philip B. Yampolsky, trans., *The Zen Master Hakuin: Selected Writings* (New York: Columbia University Press, 1971), pp. 116–17.

3. Ibid., pp. 121–22.

4. For a summary of recent scholarship on this issue, see John S. Strong, *Buddhism: An Introduction* (London: Oneworld, 2015), pp. 41–42.

5. On the origins of the Mahāyāna sūtras, see, for example, Paul Harrison, "Mediums and Messages: Reflections on the Production of Mahāyāna Sūtras," *Eastern Buddhist* (New Series) 35, nos. 1–2 (2003): 115–51; Jonathan Silk, "What, If Anything, Is Mahāyāna Buddhism? Problems of Definitions and Classifications," *Numen* 49, no. 4 (2002): 355–405; and Donald S. Lopez, Jr., "Authority and Orality in the Mahāyāna," *Numen* 42, no. 1 (1995): 21–47. On the possible role of visualization meditation, see Paul M. Harrison, "*Buddhānusmṛti* in the *Pratyutpanna-buddha-saṃmukhāvasthita-samādhi-sūtra*," *Journal of Indian Philosophy* 6 (1978): 35–57.

6. On the "Devadatta" chapter and its presence or absence in various versions of the sūtra, see Keisho Tsukamoto, *Source Elements of the Lotus Sūtra: Buddhist Integration of Religion, Thought, and Culture* (Tokyo: Kōsei Publishing, 2007), pp. 411–18. See also Paul Groner, "The *Lotus Sutra* and Saichō's Interpretation of the Realization of Buddhahood with This Very Body," in George J. Tanabe Jr. and Willa Jane Tanabe, eds., *The Lotus Sutra in Japanese Culture* (Honolulu: University of Hawaii Press, 1989), pp. 59–61.

7. On the sūtra's compilation process, see "Lotus Sūtra," s.v., *Brill's Encyclopedia of Buddhism* 1: *Literature and Languages* (Leiden: Brill, 2015), p. 152; Shiori Ryōdo, "Formation and Structure of the *Lotus Sūtra*," in Tanabe and Tanabe, *The Lotus Sūtra in Japanese Culture*, pp. 23–33; and Keisho Tsukamoto, *Source Elements of the Lotus Sūtra*, pp. 426–34.

8. "Lotus Sūtra," in *Brill's Encyclopedia of Buddhism*, pp.144–47; Institute of Oriental Philosophy, http://www.iop.or.jp/Lotus-Sūtra.html.

9. Jonathan A. Silk, "The Place of the *Lotus Sūtra* in Indian Buddhism," *Journal of Oriental Studies* 11 (2001): 87–105; MOCHIZUKI Kaiei, "How Did the Indian Masters Read the Lotus Sūtra?," *Indogaku bukkyōgaku kenkyū* 59, no. 3 (2011): 1169–77.

10. See Jan Nattier, "A Greater Awakening," *Tricycle: The Buddhist Review* 15, no. 3 (2006): 65–69.

11. For an English translation of the commentary attributed to Vasubandhu, see "The Commentary on the *Lotus Sūtra*," trans. Terry Abbott, in *Tiantai Lotus Texts*, BDK English Tripiṭaka Series (Berkeley: Bukkyō Dendō Kyōkai America, 2013), pp. 93–149. See also Abbott's "Vasubandhu's Commentary to the *Saddharmapuṇḍarīka-Sūtra*" (Ph.D. diss, University of California, Berkeley, 1985).

12. Donald S. Lopez, Jr., *The Lotus Sūtra: A Biography* (Princeton, NJ: Princeton University Press, 2016), pp. 28–29. On the *Lotus Sūtra* in Tibet, see James Apple, "The *Lotus Sūtra* in Tibetan Buddhist History and Culture," Part 1, *Bulletin of the Institute of Oriental Philosophy* 32 (2017): 129–143.

13. *Gaoseng zhuan, T* no. 2059, 50: 333a5–6.

14. Daniel B. Stevenson, "Buddhist Practice and the *Lotus Sūtra* in China," in Stephen F. Teiser and Jacqueline I. Stone, eds., *Readings of the Lotus Sūtra* (New York: Columbia University Press, 2009), pp. 132–50.

15. For a useful overview of scholarship on Chinese *Lotus* commentaries, see Hiroshi Kanno, "A General Survey of Research Concerning Chinese Commentaries on the *Lotus Sūtra*," *Annual Report of the International Research Institute for Advanced Buddhology at Soka University for the Academic Year 2006, vol. 10* (2007): 417–44.

16. On the three truths in relation to Zhiyi's system of contemplative practice and doctrinal classification, see Paul Swanson, *Foundations of T'ien-t'ai Philosophy* (Berkeley: Asian Humanities Press, 1989), pp. 115–56; and Neal Donner and Daniel B.

Stevenson, *The Great Calming and Contemplation: A Study and Annotated Translation of the First Chapter of Chih-i's Mo-ho chih-kuan* (Honolulu: University of Hawaii Press, 1993), pp. 9–17. See also Paul Swanson, trans., *Clear Serenity, Quiet Insight: T'ien-t'ai Chih-i's Mo-ho chih-kuan*, 3 vols. (Honolulu: University of Hawaii Press, 2017).

17. *Wuliang yi jing, T* no. 276, 9: 386b1–2; Tsugunari Kubo and Joseph Logan, trans., *Tiantai Lotus Texts*, BDK English Tripiṭaka Series (Berkeley: Bukkyō Dendō Kyōkai America, 2013), p. 21. The Tiantai classification system was further developed by later scholars, notably the Korean monk Chegwan (d. 971), and became known as the "five periods and eight teachings." However, this schema does not necessarily reflect Zhiyi's thought in all aspects. See David Chappell, ed., *T'ien-t'ai Buddhism: An Outline of the Fourfold Teachings* (Tokyo: Daiichi Shobō, 1983), pp. 36–42.

18. On this point, see Hiroshi Kanno, "A Comparison of Zhiyi's and Jizang's Views of the *Lotus Sūtra*: Did Zhiyi, after All, Advocate a 'Lotus Absolutism'?," *Annual Report of the International Research Institute for Advanced Buddhology at Soka University for the Academic Year 1999*, vol. 3 (2000): 125–47.

19. See Linda L. Penkower, "T'ien-t'ai during the T'ang Dynasty: Chan-jan and the Sinification of Buddhism" (Ph.D. diss., Columbia University, 1993), pp. 225–80; and "Making and Remaking Tradition: Chan-Jan's Strategies toward a T'ang T'ien-t'ai Agenda," in Tendai Daishi Kenkyū Henshū Iinkai, ed., *Tendai Daishi kenkyū: Tendai Daishi sen yonhyakunen goonki kinen shuppan* (Kyoto: Soshi Sangyō Daihōe Jimukyoku Tendai Gakkai, 1997), pp. 1338–1289 (reverse pagination) .

20. *Fahua jing anlexing yi, T* no. 1926, 46: 697c; trans. Daniel B. Stevenson and Hiroshi Kanno, *The Meaning of the Lotus Sūtra's Course of Ease and Bliss: An Annotated Translation and Study of Nanyue Huisi's (515–77) "Fahua jing anlexing yi"* (Tokyo: International Research for Advanced Buddhology, Soka University, 2006), pp. 225–29; for discussion, see pp. 188–91.

21. See Paul Groner, *Saichō: The Establishment of the Japanese Tendai School* (1984; reprint, Honolulu: University of Hawaii Press, 2002), pp. 183–90; and "Shortening the Path: Early Tendai Interpretations of the Realization of Buddhahood with This Very Body (*Sokushin Jōbutsu*)," in Robert E. Buswell Jr. and Robert M. Gimello, eds., *Paths to Liberation: The Mārga and Its Transformations* (Honolulu: University of Hawaii Press, 1992), pp. 439–73.

22. On the pronunciation of the daimoku, please see the "Notes on Sources" section at the beginning of this volume.

23. "Zenmui Sanzō shō," *Teihon* 1: 473.

24. One of the "four reliances," given at *T* no. 374, 12: 401b27–402c9; trans. Mark Blum, The *Nirvana Sutra (Mahāparinirvāṇa Sūtra)*, BDK English Tripiṭaka Series (Berkeley: Bukkyō Dendō Kyōkai America, 2013), 1: 193–99.

25. "Omonsu-dono nyōbō gohenji," *Teihon* 2: 1856.

26. "Myōho-ama gozen gohenji," *Teihon* 2: 1528.

27. *Dengyō Daishi zenshū*, ed. Hieizan Senshūin Fuzoku Eizan Gakuin, 6 vols. (Tokyo: Sekai Seiten Kankō Kyōkai, 1989), 2: 349. See also Groner, *Saichō*, pp. 180–83.

28. For the three-stage model of decline, see Jan Nattier, *Once upon a Future Time: Studies in a Buddhist Prophecy of Decline* (Berkeley: Asian Humanities Press, 1991), pp. 65–118. The date of 1052 was based on a Chinese tradition that the Buddha had entered *parinirvāṇa* in 949 BCE. Modern scholarship places the Buddha's death roughly five and a half centuries later.

29. *Wuliang yi jing*, *T* 9: 386b1–2, trans. Kubo and Logan, *Tendai Lotus Texts*, p. 21; *Miaofa lianhua jing*, *T* no. 262, 9: 10a19.

30. The *Ongi kuden* and *Okō kikigaki*, traditionally said to record Nichiren's lectures on the *Lotus Sūtra* given to his closest disciples, are now regarded by scholars as the work of later followers. The *Ongi kuden* has been translated by Burton Watson as *The Record of the Orally Transmitted Teachings* (Tokyo: Soka Gakkai, 2004).

31. Paul Groner, "A Medieval Japanese Reading of the *Mo-ho chih-kuan*: Placing the *Kankō ruijū* in Historical Context," *Japanese Journal of Religious Studies* 22, nos. 1–2 (1995): 49–81 (56).

Chapter One: Introduction

1. Ajātaśatru's repentance and conversion to the dharma are related in the *Mahāparinirvāṇa Sūtra* (*Dabanniepan jing*, *T* no. 374).

2. *Wuliang yi jing*, *T* 9: 386b1–2; trans. Kubo and Logan, *Tiantai Lotus Texts*, p. 21.

3. See Seishi Karashima, "Who Composed the Lotus Sūtra? Antagonism between Wilderness and Village Monks," *Annual Report of the International Research Institute for Advanced Buddhology at Soka University for the Academic Year 2000*, vol. 4 (2001): 171. This view is contested in "Lotus Sūtra," s.v., *Brill's Encyclopedia of Buddhism* I, p. 152.

4. The *Lotus Sūtra* is filled with astronomical numbers, with such phrases as "six hundred myriads of *koṭis* of *nayutas*" appearing throughout the text. A *koṭi* is ten million. A *nayuta* is variously said to be one hundred thousand, one million, or one hundred billion. Rather than seeking to calculate these figures, we have generally rendered these phrases simply as "billions."

5. See Nattier, *Once upon a Future Time*, p. 21. Alternative accounts list twenty-eight buddhas of the past, of whom Dīpaṃkara is the fourth.

6. See Laura Saetveit Miles, "The Origins and Development of the Virgin Mary's Book at the Annunciation," *Speculum* 89, no. 3 (2014): 632–69.

7. "Soya Nyūdō-dono gohenji," *Teihon* 2: 1407.

8. For the daimoku before Nichiren, see Jacqueline Stone, "Chanting the August Title of the *Lotus Sūtra*," in Richard K. Payne, ed., *Re-Visioning "Kamakura" Buddhism* (Honolulu: University of Hawaii Press, 1998), pp. 116–66, and Lucia Dolce, "Esoteric

Patterns in Nichiren's Interpretation of the *Lotus Sūtra*" (Ph.D. diss., Leiden University, 2002), pp. 294–315.

9. "Daimoku Mida myōgō shōretsu ji," *Teihon* 1: 300–301.

10. "Hokke daimoku shō," *Teihon* 1: 397, 398, 402. For the tradition that the *Lotus Sūtra* contains 69,384 characters, see KITAGAWA Zenchō, "The Words of the *Lotus Sūtra* in Nichiren's Thought," *Japanese Journal of Religious Studies* 41, no. 1 (2014): 25–43 (37–38).

11. "Ueno-ama gozen gohenji," *Teihon* 2: 1890. Zhiyi's teacher Huisi discusses the symbolism of the lotus in the sūtra's title in his *Fahua jing anlexing yi*, *T* no. 1926, 698b22–c12; Stevenson and Kanno, *The Meaning of the Lotus Sūtra's Course of Ease and Bliss*, pp. 236–38. Zhiyi himself produced an extensive commentarial passage on this topic (*Fahua xuanyi*, *T* 33: 771c17–774c24).

12. "Hokke daimoku shō," *Teihon* 1: 395–396.

13. *Shishin gohon shō*, *Teihon* 2: 1298; "Sōya Nyūdō-dono gohenji," 2: 1410.

14. "Shijō Kingo-dono gohenji," *Teihon* 1: 635.

15. *T* no. 1718, 34: 2a11–16.

16. Nichiren's discussion appears in *Kanjin honzon shō*, *Teihon* 1: 713–14; see also "Shishu sandan," s.v., in Nichirenshū Jiten Kankō Iinkai, ed., *Nichirenshū jiten* (Tokyo: Nichirenshū Shūmuin, 1981), pp. 153–55; and Asai Endō, *Kanjin honzon shō*, *Butten kōza* 38 (Tokyo: Daizō Shuppan, 1981), pp. 199–203.

17. *Kenbutsu mirai ki*, *Teihon* 1:742.

Chapter Two: Skillful Means

1. See Michael Pye, *Skilful Means: A Concept in Mahāyāna Buddhism* (1978; 2nd ed., London: Routledge, 2003).

2. For the story of Śāriputra's conversion, see T. W. Rhys Davids and Hermann Oldenberg, trans., *Vinaya Texts, Part 1: The Pātimokkha, the Mahāvagga, I-IV*, Sacred Books of the East, Vol. XIII (Oxford: The Clarendon Press, 1881), p. 147.

3. See Leon Hurvitz, *Chih-i (538–597): An Introduction to the Life and Ideas of a Chinese Buddhist Monk*, *Mélanges chinois et bouddhiques* 12 (Brussels: l'Institute Belge des Hautes Études Chinoises, 1963), pp. 275–82, as well as Stevenson and Kanno, *The Meaning of the Lotus Sūtra's Course of Ease and Bliss*, p. 175, and the Japanese sources cited there in n144. Jean-Nöel Robert has suggested that the apparent discrepancy between extant Sanskrit versions and Kumārajīva's Chinese reflects Kumārajīva's efforts to reconcile elements from the earlier Chinese translation of the *Lotus* by Dharmarakṣa—which Kumārajīva admired and drew upon but brilliantly revised—with the original sūtra passage. See Jean-Nöel Robert, "On a Possible Origin of the 'Ten Suchnesses' List in Kumārajīva's Translation of the *Lotus Sutra*," *Kokusai Bukkyō Daigakuin Daigaku kenkyū kiyō* 15 (2011): 142–61.

4. See Hurvitz, *Chih-i*, pp. 290–91.

5. *Mohe zhiguan*, *T* no. 1911, 46: 54a5–9.

6. Ibid., 54a13–18. "Realm of the inconceivable" could also be translated as "objects [of contemplation] as inconceivable." For discussion, see Swanson, *Clear Serenity, Quiet Insight*, 2: 816. Although our translation differs slightly, like Swanson, we take "realm" or "object" here to mean not objects as distinct from the mind, but the interdependent relationship of the mind and all phenomena.

7. *Zhiguan fuxingzhuan hongjue*, *T* no. 1912, 46: 295c23–24.

8. "Shōmitsu-bō gosho," *Teihon* 1: 822.

9. *Shugo kokka ron*, *Teihon* 1: 124–25.

10. For the relevant passage, see *Kanjin honzon shō*, *Teihon* 1: 705–706; MURANO Senchū, trans., *Two Nichiren Texts* (Berkeley: Bukkyō Dendō Kyōkai America, 2003), pp. 73–76; Burton Watson, *Selected Writings of Nichiren* (New York: Columbia University Press, 1990), pp. 155–56.

11. *Shishin gohon shō*, *Teihon* 2: 1298.

12. "Shijō Kingo-dono gohenji," *Teihon* 1:635.

13. *Kaimoku shō*, *Teihon* 1: 566.

14. "Shoshū mondō shō," *Teihon* 1: 25.

Chapter Three: A Parable

1. See Carl Bielefeldt, "Expedient Devices, the One Vehicle, and the Life Span of the Buddha," in Teiser and Stone, *Readings of the Lotus Sūtra*, esp. pp. 62–73. The question of whether the parable of the burning house entails three vehicles or four was raised early on by Kumārajīva's disciple Daosheng (355–434) and others. See Young-ho Kim, *Tao-sheng's Commentary on the Lotus Sūtra* (Albany: State University of New York Press, 1990), pp. 123–24. For a summary of different positions on this issue, see Mochizuki Shinkō, *Mochizuki Bukkyō daijiten* (1932–1936; rev. ed. by Tsukamoto Zenryū, Tokyo: Sekai Seiten Kankō Kyōkai, 1960–1963), 2: 1537–39. For a detailed discussion in light of the *Lotus Sūtra* text and a modern attempt to reconcile the two positions, see Fujita Kōtatsu, "One Vehicle or Three?" trans. Leon Hurvitz, *Journal of Indian Philosophy* 3 (1975): 79–166.

2. "Ōta Saemon-no-jō gohenji," *Teihon* 2: 1497.

3. "Daibyakugosha sho," *Teihon* 2: 1411–12; "Daibyakugosha goshōsoku," 2: 1900–1901; "Nyosetsu shugyō shō," 1: 733. See also Burton Watson and others, trans., *Letters of Nichiren* (New York: Columbia University Press, 1996), p. 65.

4. *Da banniepan jing su*, *T* no. 1767, 38 :55c9–11.

5. "Shu shi shin gosho," *Teihon* 1: 45.

6. "Yasaburō-dono gohenji," *Teihon* 2: 1367.

7. "Kyōdai shō," *Teihon* 1: 920–21.

8. *Kaitai sokushin jōbutsu gi, Teihon* 1: 12.

9. *Ken hōbō shō Teihon* 1: 260–61. See also "Hokke shoshin jōbutsu shō," *Teihon* 2: 1424–26.

Chapter Four: Willing Acceptance

1. Zhiyi himself taught a schema of "five flavors," which stresses differences in practitioners' level of development. In contrast, the "five periods," formulated in a time of greater sectarian rivalry, establishes a fixed hierarchy of sūtras. See Chappell, *T'ien-t'ai Buddhism*, pp. 36–40.

2. Ibid., pp. 55–69.

3. For more on the controversy, see Groner, *Saichō*, pp. 97–106; Robert Rhodes "Genshin and the *Ichijō yōketsu*" (PhD diss., Harvard University 1992), pp. 288–309 and 318–20; Jacqueline I. Stone, *Original Enlightenment and the Transformation of Medieval Japanese Buddhism* (Honolulu: University of Hawaii Press, 1999), pp. 12–14; and James L. Ford, *Jōkei and Buddhist Devotion in Early Medieval Japan* (New York: Oxford University Press, 2006), pp. 60–65.

4. *Kanjin honzon shō, Teihon* 1: 711.

Chapter Five: Herbs

1. See Leon Hurvitz, *Scripture of the Lotus Blossom of the Fine Dharma (The Lotus Sūtra)* (New York: Columbia University Press, 1976), pp. 111–19; rev. ed. 2009, pp. 104–10.

2. For a study of "this-worldly benefits" in Japanese Buddhism, see Ian Reader and George J. Tanabe Jr., *Practically Religious: Worldly Benefits and the Common Religion of Japan* (Honolulu: University of Hawaii Press, 1998).

3. "Yagenta-dono gohenji," *Teihon* 1:807.

4. *Foshuo da bannihuan jing, T* no. 376, 12: 877c21–22. See also Jaqueline Stone, "The Sin of Slandering the True Dharma in Nichiren's Thought," in Phyllis Granoff and Koichi Shinohara, eds., *Sins and Sinners: Perspectives from Asian Religions* (Leiden: Brill 2012), pp. 113–52 (137–39).

5. *Kaimoku shō, Teihon* 1: 601, 604.

6. *Kaimoku shō, Teihon* 1: 589.

7. "Nyosetsu shugyō shō," *Teihon* 1:733.

Chapter Six: Prediction

1. "Shijō Kingo-dono gosho," *Teihon* 1: 493.

2. Nichiren uses "ghee" to indicate the *Lotus Sūtra.*

3. *Kaimoku shō, Teihon* 1: 566.

4. *Kaimoku shō, Teihon* 1: 566.

5. Stephen F. Teiser, *The Ghost Festival in Medieval China* (Princeton University Press, 1996).

6. "Shijō Kingo-dono gosho," *Teihon* 1: 493–94.

Chapter Seven: The Apparitional City

1. Kumārajīva uses different words in this passage for the Buddha's parinirvāṇa (Ch. *meihou;* J. *metsugo*) and the nirvāṇa achieved by the future disciples (*niepan, nehan*), raising the possibility that their attainment may refer simply to the arhatship of a living person and not final nirvāṇa. Several English versions accordingly offer translations along the lines of "disciples of mine who . . . will by their own merits conceive the idea of extinction and enter [what they think is] nirvāṇa" (See *The Threefold Lotus Sutra,* trans. Bunnō Katō, Yoshirō Tamura, and Kōjirō Miyasaka [Tokyo: Kōsei Publishing Co., 1975], p. 161). However, this does not resolve the larger question of the postmortem status of arhats if the teaching of nirvāṇa is simply a skillful means.

2. *Wuliangshou jing, T* no. 360, 12: 268a27–28.

3. "Jōren-bō gosho," *Teihon* 2: 1076; "Soya-dono gohenji," *Teihon* 2: 1254.

4. The third, touched upon in the discussion of Chapter Sixteen, is that the *Lotus Sūtra* makes clear the original relationship of teacher and disciples.

5. "Kyōgyōshō gosho," *Teihon* 2: 1480.

6. *Senji shō, Teihon* 2: 1009.

7. *Dazhi du lun, T* no. 1509, 25: 145a18–29.

8. *Kaimoku shō, Teihon* 1: 601; "Kyōdai shō," *Teihon* 1: 919, 922, 923.

Chapters Eight and Nine: The Five Hundred Disciples Receive Their Predictions *and* The Predictions for Those Who Still Have More to Learn and for Those Who Do Not

1. Sōjō Jōen, *Kin'yōshū,* in Stephen D. Miller, translations with Patrick Donnelly, *The Wind from Vulture Peak: The Buddhification of Japanese Waka in the Heian Period* (Ithaca, NY: East Asia Program, Cornell University, 2012), p. 254. For more on *Lotus Sūtra* poems, see Yamada Shōzen, "Poetry and Meaning: Medieval Poets and

the *Lotus Sūtra*" in Tanabe and Tanabe, *The Lotus Sūtra in Japanese Culture*, pp. 95–117.

2. "Shu shi shin gosho," *Teihon* 1:47.

3. For Nichiren's idea of the buddha-seed, see Asai Endō, "Busshu," s.v., *Nichirenshū jiten*, 332c–333b.

Chapter Ten: Expounder of the Dharma

1. Hiroshi Kanno, "The Bodhisattva Way and Valuing the Real World in the *Lotus Sūtra*," *Journal of Oriental Studies* 17 (2007): 182–87.

2. "Nichinyo gozen gohenji," *Teihon* 2: 1377.

3. "Jakunichi-bō gosho," *Teihon* 2: 1669.

4. "Shijō Kingo-dono gohenji," *Teihon* 2: 1668.

5. *Hokke shūku*, *Dengyō Daishi zensho* (Seikai Seiten Kankō Kyōkai, 1989), 3:251.

6. *Kanjin honzon shō*, *Teihon* 1: 706.

7. Ibid.

8. "Shion shō," *Teihon* 1: 235.

9. "Shijō Kingo-dono gohenji," *Teihon* 1: 894.

Chapter Eleven: The Appearance of the Jeweled Stūpa

1. John Strong, "The Buddha's Funeral," in Bryan J. Cuevas and Jacqueline I. Stone, eds., *The Buddhist Dead: Practices, Discourses, Representations* (Honolulu: University of Hawaii Press, 2007), pp. 32–59.

2. See Gregory Schopen, "The Phrase *sa pṛthivīpradeśaś caityabhūto bhavet* in the *Vajracchedikā*: Notes on the Cult of the Book in Mahāyāna," 1975; reprinted in his *Figments and Fragments of Mahāyāna Buddhism in India: More Collected Papers*, *Studies in the Buddhist Traditions* (Honolulu: University of Hawaii Press, 2005) , pp. 25–62.

3. Adapted from Paul Harrison, trans., "The Diamond Sutra," in Donald S. Lopez, Jr., ed., *Buddhism* (New York, W. W. Norton, 2015), p. 334.

4. See I. B. Horner, trans., *Milinda's Questions*, vol. 2 (London: Luzac & Co., 1964), pp. 40–44.

5. For an English translation of Vasubandhu's discussion, see Louis de la Vallée Poussin, trans., *Abhidharmakośabhāṣyam*, vol. 2, English trans. by Leo M. Pruden (Berkeley: Asian Humanities Press, 1988), pp. 484–86. There is a certain irony in Vasubandhu's strong defense of the doctrine of one buddha per universe when one recalls that he later converted to the Mahāyāna and is said to have written his own commentary on the *Lotus Sūtra*. However, as noted above, the attribution

of this commentary to Vasubandhu is doubtful. See Abbott, "The Commentary on the *Lotus Sūtra*," and also Abbott's "Vasubandhu's Commentary to the *Saddharmapuṇḍarīka-Sūtra*. See Authors' Introduction, n11, p. 268.

6. "Abutsu-bō gosho," *Teihon* 2: 1144–45.

7. "Nichinyo gozen gohenji," *Teihon* 2: 1375.

8. Ibid.

9. "Myōhō-ama gozen gohenji," *Teihon* 2: 1526.

10. "Kyōgyōshō gosho," *Teihon* 2: 1488.

11. "Myōmitsu Shōnin goshōsoku," *Teihon* 2: 1166.

Chapter Twelve: Devadatta

1. See Bhikkhu Ñāṇamoli, *The Life of the Buddha According to the Pali Canon* (Seattle: BPS Pariyatti Editions, 1992), p. 258.

2. Reginald Ray reads the story of Devadatta in light of tensions between monks practicing austerities in the forest and those living in settled monasteries. Devadatta, he suggests, represents the forest monks, and his critics represent those living in or near villages and subsisting on lay donations; the positive treatment of Devadatta in the *Lotus Sūtra*, then, might point to a connection between the sūtra and forest monks. See his *Buddhist Saints in India: A Study in Buddhist Values and Orientations* (New York: Oxford University Press, 1994), pp. 162–73. Others, however, see the *Lotus* as having been compiled by village monks (e.g., Karashima, "Who Composed the *Lotus Sūtra*?" pp. 143–79). The issue has not been resolved conclusively. See also Max Deeg, "The Saṅgha of Devadatta: Fiction and History of a Heresy in the Buddhist Tradition," *Kokusai Bukkyōgaku Daigakuin Daigaku Kenkyū Kiyō* 2 (1999): 183–218, and Daniel Boucher, *Bodhisattvas of the Forest and the Formation of the Mahāyāna: A Study and Translation of the* Rāṣṭrapālaparipṛcchā-sūtra (Honolulu: University of Hawaii Press, 2008), pp. 46–49.

3. On the "Devadatta" chapter and its presence or absence in various versions of the sūtra, see Tsukamoto, *Source Elements of the Lotus Sūtra*, pp. 411–18. See also Paul Groner, "The *Lotus Sutra* and Saichō's Interpretation of the Realization of Buddhahood with This Very Body," in Tanabe and Tanabe, *The Lotus Sutra in Japanese Culture*, pp. 59–61.

4. For gender in the *Lotus Sūtra*, see Miriam Levering, "Is the Lotus Sūtra 'Good News' for Women?" in Gene Reeves, ed., *A Buddhist Kaleidoscope: Essays on the Lotus Sūtra* (Tokyo: Kosei Publishing, 2002), pp. 469–91, and Jan Nattier, "Gender and Hierarchy in the *Lotus Sūtra*," in Teiser and Stone, *Readings of the Lotus Sūtra*, pp. 83–106.

5. For a useful study of this issue, see Alan Sponberg, "Attitudes toward Women and the Feminine in Early Buddhism," in José Ignacio Cabezon, ed., *Buddhism,*

Sexuality, and Gender (Albany: State University of New York Press, 1992), pp. 3–36.

6. "Hakii Saburō-dono gohenji," *Teihon* 1: 749.

7. *Kaimoku shō Teihon* 1: 599; trans. Burton Watson and others, *Selected Writings of Nichiren* (New York: Columbia University Press, 1990), p. 134.

8. *Shuju onfurumai gosho, Teihon* 2: 972–73.

9. For the "five obstructions" in Japan, see YOSHIDA Kazuhiko, "The Enlightenment of the Dragon King's Daughter in *The Lotus Sūtra*" in Barbara Ruch, ed., *Engendering Faith: Women and Buddhism in Premodern Japan* (Ann Arbor: Center for Japanese Studies, University of Michigan, 2002), pp. 308–11.

10. *Kaimoku shō, Teihon* 1: 589–90.

11. "Gassui gosho," *Teihon* 1:291–93; Watson, *Letters of Nichiren*, pp. 255–57.

12. "Shijō Kingo-dono no nyōbō gohenji," *Teihon* 1: 857.

13. See Paul Groner, "Shortening the Path: Early Tendai Interpretations of the Realization of Buddhahood with This Very Body (Sokushin Jōbutsu)," in Robert E. Buswell, Jr. and Robert M. Gimello, eds., *Paths to Liberation: The Mārga and Its Transformations in Buddhist Thought* (Honolulu: University of Hawaii Press, 1992), pp. 439–73, and Ōkubo Ryōshun, "Tendai kyōgaku ni okeru ryūnyo jōbutsu," *Nihon bukkyō sōgō kenkyū* 4 (2005): 27–40.

14. "Niiike-dono goshōsoku," *Teihon* 2: 1642.

Chapter Thirteen: Perserverance

1. "Myōhō-ama gozen gohenji," *Teihon* 2: 1904–5.

2. "Teradomari gosho," *Teihon* 1: 515.

3. *Kaimoku shō, Teihon* 1: 559.

4. Rubin Habito, "Bodily Reading of the *Lotus Sūtra*," in Teiser and Stone, *Readings of the Lotus Sūtra*, pp. 198–99.

5. "Tsuchirō gosho," *Teihon* 1: 509–10.

6. "Nanjō Hyōe Shichirō-dono gohenji," *Teihon* 1: 327.

7. "Nyosetsu shugyō shō," *Teihon* 1: 737–38; Watson, *Letters of Nichiren*, p. 70, modified. The "land of Tranquil Light" is a metaphor for the realm of the Buddha's enlightenment.

Chapter Fourteen: Ease in Practice

1. "Nyosetsu shugyō shō," *Teihon* 1: 735–36; Watson, *Letters of Nichiren*, p. 68, modified.

Chapter Fifteen: Bodhisattvas Emerging from the Earth

1. See Chapter 12, note 2 above.

2. Yoshirō Tamura, *Introduction to the Lotus Sūtra* (Boston: Wisdom Publications, 2014), p. 80.

3. *Kanjin honzon shō, Teihon* 1: 712.

4. "Soya Nyūdō-dono gari gosho," *Teihon* 1: 902.

5. *Kanjin honzon shō, Teihon* 1: 719. Nichiren refers here to the parable of the excellent doctor in Chapter Sixteen; in his reading, "the children" are the people of the Final Dharma age.

6. *Kanjin honzon shō, Teihon* 1: 720.

7. "Shohō jissō shō," *Teihon* 1: 726–27.

Chapter Sixteen: The Lifespan of the Tathāgata

1. See Lucia Dolce, "Between Duration and Eternity: Hermeneutics of the 'Ancient Buddha' of the *Lotus Sutra* in Chih-i and Nichiren," in Reeves, *A Buddhist Kaleidoscope*, pp. 223–39.

2. *Kaimoku shō, Teihon* 1: 552.

3. "Myōichi-nyo gohenji," *Teihon* 2: 1798–99.

4. *Kaimoku shō, Teihon* 1: 539.

5. *Shugo kokka ron, Teihon* 1: 111.

6. *Kanjin honzon shō, Teihon* 1: 712.

7. *Shugo kokka ron, Teihon* 1: 129.

8. *Zhiguan fuxing zhuan hongjue, T* no. 1912, 46: 295c23–24.

9. See pp. 103–4.

10. Jacqueline Stone, "Japanese *Lotus* Millenialism: From Militant Nationalism to Contemporary Peace Movements," in Catherine Wessinger, ed. *Millenialism, Persecution and Violence: Historical Cases* (Syracuse: Syracuse University Press, 2000), pp. 261–80.

Chapters Seventeen and Eighteen: Description of Merits *and* The Merits of Joyful Acceptance

1. *Shishin gohon shō, Teihon* 2: 1295. The first stage is that of those who have yet to hear the dharma. Even though such people have not yet begun to practice, they are nonetheless, in principle, identical with the buddha. The second stage, verbal identity, where one encounters a teacher or sūtra text and embraces faith in its teaching, thus corresponds to the beginning stage of practice. The division into six stages

describes successive levels of practice and attainment, while the word "identity" (*soku*) affixed to the name of each stage indicates that, ontologically, no distinction between the buddha and the practitioner is made. See Groner, "The *Lotus Sutra* and Saichō's Interpretation of the Realization of Buddhahood with This Very Body," pp. 64–65; and Stone, *Original Enlightenment and the Transformation of Medieval Japanese Buddhism*, pp. 197–98.

2. *Shishin gohon shō, Teihon* 2: 1296.

3. *Kanjin honzon shō, Teihon* 1: 711.

4. "Jimyō Hokke mondō shō," *Teihon* 1: 283.

5. *Shishin gohon shō, Teihon* 2: 1295.

6. Ibid., 1298.

7. "Kyōgyōshō gosho," *Teihon* 2: 1484.

8. *Zhiguan fuxing zhuan hongjue, T* 46: 353b5–6.

9. *Shishin gohon shō, Teihon* 2: 1298–99.

Chapter Nineteen: The Benefits Obtained by an Expounder of the Dharma

1. "Jiri kuyō gosho," *Teihon* 2: 1263.

2. *Mohe zhiguan, T* 46: 54a12–18. See chap. 2, n. 6 above.

3. "Jiri kuyō gosho," *Teihon* 2: 1263.

Chapter Twenty: Bodhisattva Sadāparibhūta

1. "Matsuno-dono gohenji," *Teihon* 2: 1266.

2. Hiroshi Kanno, "The Practice of Bodhisattva Never Disparaging in the *Lotus Sūtra* and Its Reception in China and Japan," *Journal of Oriental Studies* 12 (2002): 104–122 (esp. see 110–15).

3. *Fahua jing anlexing yi, T* 46: 6987c22–24; Kanno, "The Practice of Bodhisattva Never Disparaging," p. 109.

4. Kanno, "The Practice of Bodhisattva Never Disparaging," p. 110; Jamie Hubbard, *Absolute Delusion, Perfect Buddhahood: The Rise and Fall of a Chinese Heresy* (Honolulu: University of Hawaii Press, 2001), pp. 117–18.

5. Miyoshi no Tameyasu, *Goshūi ōjōden* 1: 17, *Nihon shisō taikei* (Tokyo: Iwanami Shoten, 1974), 7: 650.

6. For these and other examples, see Kanno, "The Practice of Bodhisattva Never Disparaging," pp. 116–17, n14–18.

7. "Kyōgyōshō gosho," *Teihon* 2: 1480.

8. "Sushun Tennō gosho," *Teihon* 2: 1397.

9. "Tenju kyōju hōmon," *Teihon* 1: 507.

10. *Kaimoku shō, Teihon* 1: 602.

11. "Sado gosho," *Teihon* 1: 614.

12. "Teradomari gosho," *Teihon* 1: 515.

Chapters Twenty-One and Twenty-Two: The Transcendent Powers of the Tathāgata *and* Entrustment

1. *Fahua wenju ji, T* no. 1719, 34: 349c24–25.

2. "Zuisō gosho," *Teihon* 1: 874.

3. "Kashaku hōbō metsuzai shō," *Teihon* 1: 783.

4. *Kanjin honzon shō, Teihon* 1: 717. See Murano, *Two Nichiren Texts*, p. 104, or Watson, *Selected Writings of Nichiren*, p. 174. On the Buddha's long tongue and its significance, see Peter Skilling, "The *Tathāgata* and the Long Tongue of Truth: The Authority of the Buddha in *Sūtra* and Narrrative Literature," in Vincent Eltschinger and Helmut Krasser, eds., *Scriptural Authority, Reason, and Action*: Proceedings of a Panel at the 14th World Sanskrit Conference, Kyoto, September 1–5, 2009 (Vienna: Austrian Academy of Sciences Press, 2013), pp. 1–47.

5. "Jakunichi-bō gosho," *Teihon* 2: 1669–70. The second character, *ren*, or "lotus," in Nichiren's name is said to derive from the passage from Chapter Fifteen describing the bodhisattvas who emerged from beneath the earth as being as "undefiled by worldly affairs as the lotus blossom in the [muddy] water" (228), although Nichiren's writings make no specific statement to this effect.

6. For a detailed discussion of Nichiren's reading and its Tiantai precedents, see Asai Endō, "Fuzoku," *s.v.*, in *Nichirenshū jiten*, 328d–330c.

7. *Fahua wenju, T* no. 1718, 34: 114b21–23.

8. "Kashaku hōbō metsuzai shō," *Teihon* 1: 781–82.

9. "Kenbutsu mirai ki," *Teihon* 1: 743.

10. "Nanjō Hyōe Shichirō-dono gohenji," *Teihon* 2: 1884.

11. "Shōji ichidaiji kechimyaku shō," *Teihon* 1: 522.

Chapter Twenty-Three: Ancient Accounts of Bodhisattva Bhaiṣajyarāja

1. Extensive scholarly literature on the subject of self-immolation can now be found. See for example "Human Torches of Enlightenment: Autocremation and Spontaneous Combustion as Marks of Sanctity in South Asian Buddhism," in Liz Wilson, ed., *The Living and the Dead: Social Dimensions of Death in South Asian Religions* (Albany: State University of New York Press, 2003), pp. 29–50; and James A.

Benn, *Burning for the Buddha: Self-Immolation in Chinese Buddhism* (Honolulu: University of Hawaii Press, 2007).

2. See Daniel B. Stevenson, "Tales of the Lotus Sūtra," in Donald S. Lopez, Jr., ed., *Buddhism in Practice* (Princeton: Princeton University Press, 1995) p. 433.

3. See I-Tsing, *A Record of the Buddhist Religion as Practised in India and the Malay Archipelago A.D. 671–685*, trans. J. Takakusu (Oxford: Clarendon Press, 1896), pp. 195–98. Accounts of self-immolation by bodhisattvas also occur in the Pāli scriptures. The *Nidānakathā* contains the story of the former buddha Maṅgala,who as a bodhisattva set himself on fire and placed a burning butter lamp on his head. He spent an entire night circumambulating a shrine, but his body was not burned. See N. A. Jayawickrama, trans., *The Story of Gotama Buddha (Jātaka-nidāna)* (Oxford: Pali Text Soceity, 1990), p. 40.

4. "Myōichi-ama gozen goshōsoku," *Teihon* 2: 1001.

5. *Senji shō, Teihon*, 2: 1060. Bhadraruci, a monk of western India, was said to have debated with a highly influential brahman in Mālava who slandered the Mahāyāna and to have exposed the brahman's errors. For more on Nichiren's view of ascetic self-sacrifice, see Jacqueline Stone, "Giving One's Life for the *Lotus Sūtra* in Nichiren's Thought," *Hokke bunka kenkyū* 33 (2007): 51–70.

6. "Shiiji Shirō-dono gosho," *Teihon* 1:228; Watson, *Letters of Nichiren*, p. 405, modified.

7. On this 2,500-year chronology, see Nattier, *Once upon a Future Time*, pp. 54–56.

8. "Yakuō-bon tokui shō," *Teihon* 1: 340.

9. See Paul Harrison, "Women in the Pure Land: Some Reflections on the Textual Sources," *Journal of Indian Philosophy* 26 (1998): 553–72.

10. "Hokke daimoku shō," *Teihon* 1: 404.

11. "Hokke shoshin jōbutsu shō," *Teihon* 2: 1421.

12. Ibid., 1429.

13. *Kanke bunsō* 4, no. 250, *Nihon koten bungaku taikei* 72 (Tokyo: Iwanami Shoten, 1966), p. 301. For the history of notions of Vulture Peak as a pure land, see Tsumori Kiichi, "Ryōzen jōdo shinkō no keifu," *Nichiren kyōgaku kenkyūjo kiyō* 15 (1988): 23–51.

14. "Ueno-dono gohenji," *Teihon* 1: 836.

15. "Ueno-dono goke-ama gozen gosho," *Teihon* 2: 1794.

16. "Kashaku hōbō metsuzai shō," *Teihon* 1: 862–64.

Chapters Twenty-Four and Twenty-Five: Bodhisattva Gadgadasvara *and* The Gateway to Every Direction

1. The famous verse section extolling Avalokiteśvara's compassion and protection did not originally appear in the Chinese translations by Dharmarakṣa or Kumārajīva. It was included, however, in the 601 translation by Jñānagupta and Dharmagupta and added to Kumārajīva's version. Some Sanskrit and Tibetan versions contain passages not found in the Chinese versions that refer to a connection between Avalokiteśvara and Amitābha Buddha. See Tsukamoto, *Source Elements of the Lotus Sūtra*, pp. 380–81. In China, this chapter (or sūtra, in its independent form) was a major stimulus for burgeoning devotion to Avalokiteśvara, or Guanyin, inspiring miracle tales, visual depictions, and the production of indigenous scriptures about this bodhisattva. See Chün-fang Yü, *Kuan-yin: The Chinese Transformation of Avalokiteśvara* (New York: Columbia University Press, 2001); and Miyeko Murase, "Kuan-Yin as Savior of Men: Illustration of the Twenty-Fifth Chapter of the *Lotus Sūtra* in Chinese Painting," *Artibus Asiae* 33 (1971): 39–74.

2. Former Major Counsellor Kintō, *Goshūishū*, in Miller, *Wind from Vulture Peak*, p. 183.

3. "Nichinyo gozen gohenji," *Teihon* 2: 1509.

4. Yü, *Kuan-yin*, esp. pp. 293–351, 407–48.

5. *Kanjin honzon shō, Teihon* 1: 717–19. The identification of Huisi with Avalokiteśvara or Kannon appears on p. 719.

6. *Shimoyama goshōsoku, Teihon* 2: 1336–38.

Chapter Twenty-Six: *Dhāraṇī*

1. For a discussion of each of the *dhāraṇi* and speculation on their possible meanings, see Tsukamoto, *Source Elements of the Lotus Sūtra*, pp. 391–406.

2. Ruben Habito, "Bodily Reading of the *Lotus Sūtra*," in Teiser and Stone, *Readings of the Lotus Sūtra*, pp. 188–89.

3. Ryūichi Abé, *The Weaving of Mantra: Kūkai and the Construction of Esoteric Buddhist Discourse* (New York: Columbia University Press, 1999), pp. 246, 263–64, 267.

4. "Nichinyo gozen gohenji," *Teihon* 2: 1510.

5. Miyazaki Eishū, *Nichirenshū no shugojin: Kishimojin to Daikokuten* (Kyoto: Heirakuji Shoten, 1977), pp. 1–151; Dolce, "Esoteric Patterns," pp. 345–48.

6. "Hokke shoshin jōbutsu shō," *Teihon* 2: 1432.

7. *Shōgu mondō shō, Teihon* 1: 388.

8. "Myōmitsu Shōnin goshōsoku," *Teihon* 2: 1169.

9. "Kyōō-dono gohenji," *Teihon* 1: 750; Watson, *Letters of Nichiren*, pp. 280–81, modified.

10. "Kyōdai shō," *Teihon* 1: 925.

11. *Fahua wenju ji, T* 34: 234a24–25.

Chapter Twenty-Seven: Ancient Accounts of King Śubhavyūha

1. *Fahua wenju, T* 34: 147a13–b8.

2. "Jōren-bō gosho," *Teihon* 2: 1077–78.

3. "Jōzō Jōgen goshōsoku," *Teihon* 2: 1769–70.

4. Ibid., 1770.

5. *Shōgu mondō shō, Teihon* 1: 379. The sūtra passage is from the no longer extant *Chu qingxin shi duren jing,* cited in *Sifen lu shanfan buque xingshi chao, T* no. 1804, 40: 150a20–21, and elsewhere.

6. "Hyōe no sakan-dono gohenji," *Teihon* 2:1403.

7. For a more detailed discussion of this episode, see Jacqueline Stone, "When Disobedience is Filial and Resistance is Loyal: The *Lotus Sūtra* and Social Obligations in the Medieval Nichiren Tradition," in Reeves, *A Buddhist Kaleidoscope,* pp. 261–81.

8. "Matsuno-dono goke-ama gozen gohenji," *Teihon* 2: 1628–29; Gosho Translation Committee, *Writings of Nichiren Daishonin* (Tokyo: Soka Gakkai, 1999), 1: 958, modified.

9. *Teihon* 2: 1629.

10. *Mohe zhiguan, T* 46: 43a21.

11. *Shugo kokka ron, Teihon* 1: 123; *Mohe zhiguan, T* 46: 10b22–23.

12. *Da banniepan jing, T* no. 374, 12: 401b28.

13. *Shugo kokka ron, Teihon* 1: 122; *Da banniepan jing, T* 12: 497c26–28.

14. *Shugo kokka ron, Teihon* 1: 123.

Chapter Twenty-Eight: Encouragement of the Bodhisattva Samantabhadra

1. *Guan Puxian pusa xingfa jing, T* no. 277. For translations see *Sutra of Meditation on the Bodhisattva Universal Virtue,* in Katō, Tamura, and Miyasaka, *The Threefold Lotus Sutra*; and *Sutra Expounded by the Buddha on Practice of the Way through Contemplation of the Bodhisattva All-Embracing Goodness,* in Kubō and Logan, *Tiantai Lotus Texts.*

2. *Guan Puxian pusa xingfa jing, T* 9: 393b11–12.

3. "Nichinyo gozen gohenji," *Teihon* 2:1515; Gosho Translation Committee, *Writings of Nichiren Daishonin,* 1: 915, modified.

4. "Dōshō dōmyō gosho," *Teihon* 1: 633. The relevant sūtra passge is on p. 333.

5. *Hōon shō, Teihon* 2: 1248–49; Watson, *Selected Writings,* p. 316, modified.

Index

families: the Buddha's relatives, 36–37, 160–61, 162; King Śubhavyūha's story, 249–51; Nichiren on filial piety and *Lotus* devotion, 251–54; saving members of, 109, 249–54
Faxian, 152
Fayun, 48
filial piety, 252–54
Final Dharma age (*mappō*): dating of, 26, 176; defined, 16; Hōnen on, 27; Japanese perceptions of, 8, 26–27; Nichiren on, 21–22, 27, 29, 86–88, 118–20, 169, 176–78, 262
five flavors, 106
five natures, 94
five periods of teaching, 18, 91–93, 106, 269n17
five practices, 131–32
Flower Garland Sūtra (*Avataṃsaka Sūtra*), 6, 18, 91–92, 93, 96
formless repentance, 259
Fujiwara no Teika, 208
funerary and memorial rites, 107–9, 157

Gadgadasvara, 237, 239–40
Gautama. *See* Buddha
gender hierarchy, 154, 232. *See also* women
Genshin, 95
ghee, 106, 230, 274n2 (chap. 6)
Ghost Festival (Skt. Ullambana; Ch. Yulanpen; J. Urabon), 108–9
gohonzon. *See* great maṇḍala
good friends (Skt. *kalyāṇamitra*; J. *zenchishiki*), 256
Greater Amitābha Sūtra (*Sūtra of Immeasurable Life*), 116
great maṇḍala (*daimandara*) of Nichiren, 145–46. *See also* maṇḍalas
Guanding, 16, 82–83
Guanyin. *See* Avalokiteśvara
gyōja (practitioner), 164–65

Hakii Saburō, 155–56
Hakuin, 3
Hārītī (Kishimojin), 146, 243, 244–45
Heart Sūtra, 1–2, 11, 13
hells, 25, 80–81, 83–86, 87–88, 102. *See also* Avīci hell
herbs, parable of, 97–98
Hīnayāna, 10, 17, 25, 74, 92, 106, 142
hōbō. *See* slander of the dharma
Hokke hō (Lotus rite), 47, 144
Hōnen, 27–28, 83–84, 148, 251, 257
Hongzan fahua zhuan (*Accounts in Dissemination and Praise of the Lotus*), 226
honmon. *See* trace and origin teachings
Hossō (Faxiang) school, 93–96
Huayan school. *See* Kegon school
Huisi, 20, 144, 166, 175, 208, 241
Huiyi, 226
Huiyuan, 208
hungry ghosts, 107–9

ichinen sanzen (three thousand realms in a single thought-moment): "in actuality" (*ji no ichinen sanzen*), 50, 72, 146, 187; Nichiren on, 24–25, 66, 69–72, 104, 187, 189; Zhanran on, 69, 190; Zhiyi on, 24, 25, 68–69, 189–90
Ikegami family, 253–54
Iliad, 46
India: commentaries in, 8; *Lotus Sūtra* in, 10–13; Mahāyāna in, 10–11, 13, 83
Islam, legal interpretation in, 5

Jason and Argonauts, 170–71
jeweled stūpa: appearance in *Lotus Sūtra*, 138–46, 171; Nichiren on,

nāga princess story, 152–55, 156–59
Nāgārjuna, 13, 257
Nāgasena, 141
Namu Myōhō-renge-kyō. *See* daimoku
nenbutsu, 27, 28, 29, 72, 73, 84, 232
Nepal, Newar Buddhist community in, 13
"Never Despising." *See* Sadāparibhūta
Nichiji, 251–52
Nichiren: context of thought and teachings of, 9, 21–23, 26–31, 34, 85–86, 95–96, 265–66; critique of Hōnen's teaching, 27–29, 84, 85, 251; exiles of, 30–31, 101, 135, 163–64, 210, 247, 253; followers of, 22, 101–3, 155–56, 157, 162, 164, 177–78, 200; influence of, 22, 266; life of, 8, 23–24, 101–3, 134–35, 163–65, 221, 247; lineage of, 220–21; as manifestation of Viśiṣṭacāritra, 176; name of, 216–17, 280n5; persecution of, 30, 31–32, 133, 176; personal copy of *Lotus Sūtra*, 32–33; proselytizing by, 30, 31–32, 86, 163, 165, 190, 257, 266; writings of, 32. *See also* daimoku; maṇḍalas
Nichiren, thought, writings and commentary: on "boat for a traveler" analogy, 229–30; on bodhisattvas emerging from earth, 174–78; on bodhisattvas of True and Semblance Dharma ages, 239–42; on bodily reading of *Lotus Sūtra*, 164–65; on buddha nature, 126–27; on Devadatta, 155–56; on Final Dharma age, 21–22, 27, 29, 119–20, 262; on first stages of faith and practice, 196–98; on "good friends," 256–57; on healing power of daimoku, 235–36; on *ichinen sanzen* (three thousand realms in a single thought-moment), 24–25, 66, 69–72, 104, 187, 189; on immanence of the buddha land, 188–91; on jeweled stūpa, 145–46; on joy of the dharma, 189; *Kaimoku shō* ("Opening the Eyes"), 101–3; *Kanjin honzon shō* ("On the Contemplation of the Mind and the Object of Worship"), 70–71; on King Śubhavyūha story, 251–54; on Kishimojin, 244–45; millennial teaching of, 191; on mind and phenomena, 202–3, 205; on moon and stars analogy, 231; on nine easy acts and six difficult acts, 146–47; on one vehicle, 65–66, 127–28; "On Protecting the Country," 256–57; on precepts, 148; Pure Land Buddhism critiques, 27–28, 84, 85, 233, 234, 251; on pure land of Vulture Peak, 82, 221, 234–35; on *rākṣasīs*, 245–48; on realizing buddhahood with this very body, 187; *Risshō ankoku ron* ("On Establishing the True Dharma and Bringing Peace to the Realm"), 29–30, 52, 190; on Sadāparibhūta, 208–12; on Samantabhadra, 260–62; on Śāriputra receiving prediction of buddhahood, 81; on seed of buddhahood, 50, 118, 119, 127, 133, 175, 177; on self-sacrifice, 228–29; on sole efficacy of *Lotus Sūtra*, 8–9, 21–22, 24–25, 28–29, 31–32; on ten powers displayed by the Buddha, 215, 216; on ten realms as mutually inclusive, 25–26, 66, 69–72, 96, 125, 146; on title of *Lotus Sūtra*, 47–50;

classification system of, 24, 66; esoteric teachings of, 20–21, 85; importance of *Lotus Sūtra* for, 19–20, 65, 66; *kanjin* (mind contemplation) in, 187; Lotus rite of, 47, 144; one vehicle concept in, 72–73; ordination platform of, 144; original enlightenment doctrine of, 21; realizing buddhahood with this very body doctrine of, 119, 158–59; ten realms doctrine of, 25, 49. *See also* Tiantai school
ten realms: mutual inclusion of, 25–26, 49, 66, 70, 81, 96, 186; Nichiren on, 25–26, 66, 69–72, 96, 125, 134; represented on Nichiren's maṇḍala, 146; Tendai doctrine of, 25, 49; and three thousand realms in a single thought-moment, 68–72, 128. *See also* nine realms
"ten suchnesses" or "such-likes" (*junyoze*), 66–69, 70, 71
thirsty man, parable of, 129
"three carts or four carts" controversy, 78–79
three disciplines, 194, 196, 198, 233
threefold truth, 16–18, 20, 67
three kinds of powerful enemies, 163
"Three Stages" movement, 208
three thousand realms in a single thought-moment. See *ichinen sanzen*
three vehicles: Hossō view of, 94–95; as integrated in one vehicle, 18, 51, 72–73; parable of burning house and, 77–79, 82–83; as provisional teaching, 7; as skillful means, 58, 59–61, 62–65; "three carts or four carts" controversy, 78–79. *See also* one vehicle
three virtues, 82–83
Tiantai school: classification of teachings, 17–19; on five periods of the Buddha's teachings, 18, 91–93, 106, 269n17; *Lotus* assembly and origin legend of, 144; realizing buddhahood with this very body doctrine of, 158; "three carts or four carts" controversy in, 79. *See also* Tendai school; Zhanran; Zhiyi
Tibetan Buddhism: Avalokiteśvara in, 238, 240; *chöten*, 137; importance of commentary, 7–8; sole Tibetan *Lotus* commentary, 13
trace and origin teachings, 50–51, 65, 81, 127, 173, 186–87
Treatise on the Great Perfection of Wisdom. See *Dazhi du lun*
true dharma (*saddharma*), 57–59, 66, 87
True Dharma age (*shōbō*), 26, 118, 119, 169, 175, 239, 241
Tuṣita heaven, 38, 40–41, 189, 234, 259
"two buddhas seated side by side" (*nibutsu byōza*), 4–5, 141–43, 144, 146, 171. *See also* Buddha; Prabhūtaratna
two vehicles. *See* three vehicles

untainted seeds, 94, 127
Utpalavarṇā, 151

Varaprabha, 43, 44–45
Vasubandhu: *Abhidharmakośa*, 142, 276n5; commentary on *Lotus Sūtra* attributed to, 13
Vimalakīrti Sūtra, 59, 92
Virgin Mary, paintings of, 45–46
Viśiṣṭacāritra (Jōgyō): in "boat for a traveler" analogy, 230; the Buddha's transmission to, 218, 220; medieval